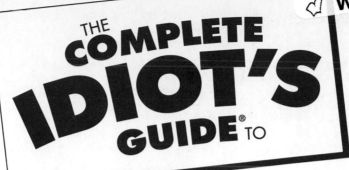

THE COMPLETE IDIOT'S GUIDE® TO

Wills and Estates

Third Edition

by Stephen Maple

ALPHA

A member of Penguin Group (USA) Inc.

I dedicate this third edition to my wife, Sarah.

ALPHA BOOKS

Published by the Penguin Group

Penguin Group (USA) Inc., 375 Hudson Street, New York, New York 10014, U.S.A.

Penguin Group (Canada), 10 Alcorn Avenue, Toronto, Ontario, Canada M4V 3B2 (a division of Pearson Penguin Canada Inc.)

Penguin Books Ltd, 80 Strand, London WC2R 0RL, England

Penguin Ireland, 25 St Stephen's Green, Dublin 2, Ireland (a division of Penguin Books Ltd)

Penguin Group (Australia), 250 Camberwell Road, Camberwell, Victoria 3124, Australia (a division of Pearson Australia Group Pty Ltd)

Penguin Books India Pvt Ltd, 11 Community Centre, Panchsheel Park, New Delhi—110 017, India

Penguin Group (NZ), cnr Airborne and Rosedale Roads, Albany, Auckland 1310, New Zealand (a division of Pearson New Zealand Ltd)

Penguin Books (South Africa) (Pty) Ltd, 24 Sturdee Avenue, Rosebank, Johannesburg 2196, South Africa

Penguin Books Ltd, Registered Offices: 80 Strand, London WC2R 0RL, England

International Standard Book Number: 1-59257-363-0
Library of Congress Catalog Card Number: 2005925417

07   06   05   8   7   6   5   4   3   2

Interpretation of the printing code: The rightmost number of the first series of numbers is the year of the book's printing; the rightmost number of the second series of numbers is the number of the book's printing. For example, a printing code of 05-1 shows that the first printing occurred in 2005.

Printed in the United States of America

Note: This publication contains the opinions and ideas of its author. It is intended to provide helpful and informative material on the subject matter covered. It is sold with the understanding that the author and publisher are not engaged in rendering professional services in the book. If the reader requires personal assistance or advice, a competent professional should be consulted.

The author and publisher specifically disclaim any responsibility for any liability, loss, or risk, personal or otherwise, which is incurred as a consequence, directly or indirectly, of the use and application of any of the contents of this book.

Most Alpha books are available at special quantity discounts for bulk purchases for sales promotions, premiums, fund-raising, or educational use. Special books, or book excerpts, can also be created to fit specific needs.

For details, write: Special Markets, Alpha Books, 375 Hudson Street, New York, NY 10014.

Publisher: *Marie Butler-Knight*
Product Manager: *Phil Kitchel*
Senior Managing Editor: *Jennifer Bowles*
Acquisitions Editor: *Tom Stevens*
Development Editor: *Jennifer Moore*
Production Editor: *Megan Douglass*
Copy Editor: *Emily Bell*
Cartoonist: *Richard King*
Cover/Book Designer: *Trina Wurst*
Indexer: *Angie Bess*
Layout: *Ayanna Lacey*
Proofreading: *Donna Martin*

Contents at a Glance

Contents

Foreword

There's one thing that we all can be sure of, and that's that one day we won't be here anymore. Unfortunately, we have no control over that certainty. But we do have control over what we leave behind for our families and loved ones.

In *The Complete Idiot's Guide to Wills and Estates, Third Edition*, Steve Maple gives us a good deal of valuable advice and information that makes estate planning understandable and doable for almost anyone. It's an enjoyable, readable, and instructive guide that's well-researched and thorough.

I compliment Steve Maple on this work and recommend it to anyone for interesting and informative reading on estate planning.

—Steven R. Nation, Judge Hamilton Superior Court No. 1, Indiana

Introduction

Welcome to the world of estate planning.

You'll notice I didn't say the "wonderful" world or the "fascinating" world. I don't want you rolling your eyes and muttering "Come *on*." But I *do* want you to continue reading this book.

Okay, making your way through a guide about putting together an estate plan will probably not be as lighthearted as reading about how to select wines or start a rock garden. Still, I honestly believe you will find this book not only informative but also engrossing.

Why? Because it's very relevant to *you* and your life, and perhaps there are some important parts of estate planning that you haven't given much thought to before. Learning something new, especially when it's about ourselves, is *always* interesting.

I think you'll soon be absorbed in exploring just how you want to lay out an estate plan, which includes a basic will and a few other documents. You'll set planning goals for yourself, now and at different stages of your life ahead. You'll learn about professionals who can help you along the way. You'll read stories about others and their experiences, too—tales that will be informative, puzzling, amusing, and sometimes even touching. You'll learn from the mistakes some of those folks made—and from reading about the right steps others took at particular times in their lives.

So this book is about people as well as legal documents and tax talk. It's about how we *use* those papers, those directives, and even those taxes, to put ourselves in control of our financial destiny.

If you have an estate plan—and you will when you finish this book, or will at least have started the ball rolling—then obviously you have an estate. Trust me. No matter how small you may think your assets are, you do have an estate. You'll want to protect it, watch it grow, and even see it spent in exactly the ways you choose.

Having an estate plan will make you feel like a million dollars—no matter that your net worth may be missing a few of those zeros.

How This Book Is Organized

The chapters that follow are laid out to guide you through the estate-planning process as it is likely to occur in your life, no matter what your age right now. Let me introduce you to the book's five parts.

Part 1, "Assets, Assets, Assets," introduces you to what an estate is and will acquaint you with the planning process. It will help you sort out your own assets, so that you know what you own and, in particular, *how* you own it.

Part 2, "About Wills, Trusts … and Probate," will take you into the heart of the book: preparing a will, and perhaps a trust if that can be useful to you. There are some cautions, too, about what happens when you *don't* have a will.

Part 3, "All in the Family—and Just a Little Beyond," talks about your nearest and dearest and how you will probably want to provide for them in some specific estate-planning situations. I'll tell you how to head off potential arguments and misunderstandings, too.

Part 4, "Taxes You Must Pay, and Those Maybe You Don't," will introduce you to the sometimes complex world of federal and state taxes and help you with terrific strategies for paying as little as possible on your estate, your income, and when making gifts.

Part 5, "Retirement, Elder Issues, and the Broad Planning Picture," eases you into planning for your retirement, no matter when that is coming up in your life. Along with other information, I'll tell you what you can expect from the government then—and what you'll have to put together on your own.

Extras

To help you even further, and just for fun, you'll find small boxes with special items of interest in every chapter. You'll immediately see a clue to the subject matter of each box by the little cartoon at the top. Here's what you'll find:

Words, Words, Words
Definitions of legal terms and other words that may be unfamiliar to you.

Quote, Unquote
The words of the famous, from early history to present day, speaking with humor or wisdom (and sometimes even both).

Briefs
Intriguing stories about people in specific estate-planning situations.

Tip	Watch Out
How to find more information or learn a different way of doing things.	Steps to avoid, products to skip, when to be careful, and when to seek help.

Acknowledgments

To Renee Wilmeth and Tom Stevens, my acquisitions editors; Keith Lyman, the technical editor; Debby McGary, my e-mail expert; Shirley Bigna, my research assistant; and my wife, Sarah. My special thanks to the editors of this edition, Megan Douglass, Emily Bell, and Jennifer Moore, who have made this a better book.

Special Thanks to the Technical Reviewer

The Complete Idiot's Guide to Wills and Estates, Third Edition, was reviewed by an expert who double-checked the accuracy of what you'll learn here, to help us ensure that this book gives you everything you need to know about wills and estates. Special thanks are extended to Keith Lyman, JD, CFP.

Keith R. Lyman has been practicing law for more than 20 years. He is a member of the American Bar Association; Indiana Bar Association; Probate, Trust and Real Property section of the Indiana Bar Association; National Association of Estate Planners; and the National Academy of Elder Law Attorneys. He is also a certified financial planner and frequent speaker on estate-planning issues.

Trademarks

Part 1

Assets, Assets, Assets

We're going to talk first about your estate and what it comprises. Makes you feel rather prosperous, doesn't it, to hear the words "your" and "estate" in the same sentence? You should feel that way. Your assets—all of your possessions acquired through the years—are valuable to you now for your own satisfaction and enjoyment, and will matter one day to your heirs.

What exactly are those assets? I'll help you sort them out. You might find you have more than you think you do—always a pleasant discovery.

You've Got to Have a Plan, Whether Simple or Deluxe

In This Chapter

- "Later," "Someday," "When I hit 40," and so on
- Understanding what comprises an estate
- The perils of having no plan
- Setting goals
- Creating your estate planning team

I don't believe in dying. It's been done. I'm working on a new exit. Besides, I can't die now. I'm booked.—George Burns, 1987

As you probably know, the much-loved comedian finally "exited" in 1996, at the age of 100. Burns even played God in two hit motion pictures, but that, of course, did not prevent him from eventually having to go on to meet his Maker and having to leave behind all of his earthly belongings for his heirs. Did George Burns have a proper estate plan? I was not one of his attorneys, but I'd bet the farm he left his estate in A-1 condition, spelling out his wishes clearly and taking advantage of every legitimate tax break.

Sure, George Burns had a larger estate—a lot larger—than you or I are likely to leave, and so he should have worked hard on its intricacies. However, whether we are young or old, employed or unemployed, wealthy or just getting by, single, married, or in a long-term relationship with a "significant other," we need to plan for when we are not here or, because of illness, unable to speak for ourselves. Why on earth would anyone want someone else—perhaps, Oh, God!, the state—to make important, and very personal, decisions for him or her and the family members left behind? If you do not have a will, state law determines who will inherit your estate.

What Is an Estate?

The area of wills and estates is likely to seem hazy if you have not given that subject area much thought. You certainly need to understand the terminology used in this book, so let's start with a few explanations right now.

Your Assets

The dictionary defines *estate* as the assets and liabilities left by a person at death. Well, that's true, but I'd expand that definition a little. If you are able to leave an estate at death, you carried its ingredients through much of your life, too.

Those ingredients are assets—everything you own by yourself or jointly with someone else. If you're 18 years old, you probably don't own very much. But as you grow older you begin to acquire possessions—a home, a car, a pension plan, perhaps some stocks, and the like. All of that is valuable, first, because all of it becomes your assets (which are good for anyone to have) and second, because you can will those assets to anyone you choose.

As you get older, your responsibilities increase, along with your assets. You will want to see that your spouse and children, especially young children, are taken care of if you die. You will want your debts to be paid, too. You might have elderly parents or an ailing sibling you're looking out for. Your wishes for after your death can be carried out with a proper estate plan. Which brings me to the next definition.

Your Estate Plan

An *estate plan* is an arrangement for the conservation and transfer of your wealth after your death. It's seeing that you keep the most money and other property at the least cost to you during your lifetime, and to your heirs when they inherit.

The minimum any estate plan should contain is a will. I'll touch on the contents of that document soon.

A good estate plan might also include a trust. A trust is a written agreement that allows you to hold property and manage it for your beneficiaries in accordance with whatever instructions are in that trust agreement. It's a little like a will, but without the necessity of probate. We'll get to a fuller explanation of a trust in Chapter 9, too.

Watch Out

Although your current will is usually valid if you move to another state, you will have to review your estate documents. Most states have their own requirements for those papers, and you might need to have some of them drawn up again.

Other documents you might want to add to an estate plan as you get older are a *durable power of attorney*, which legally gives someone you designate the right to make decisions for you should you become incapacitated and cannot act on your own. You might eventually want a *health care power of attorney*, which gives the person of your choice the right to make decisions for you about your health care if you cannot make them yourself.

There are some other papers you may elect for your estate plan that I'll mention later in the book, but the most important component of an estate plan—the cornerstone—is the will.

Your Will

A *will* is a legal document setting forth your wishes for the disposition of your estate after your death. Yes, it's that "I, William Jefferson, of Anytown, USA, being of sound and disposing mind and memory ..." document you've heard and read about over the years. It can be as long or as short as you like. You can briefly leave every last thing you own to your spouse or someone else, and that's that. Or—and there is more than one elderly lady who has done this—you can bequeath every piece of property, including individual jewelry items and various collections, to different persons. And you can revise that will periodically, as relatives and friends rise and fall in your favor.

Tip

You should review your estate plan every couple of years, certainly when there are major changes in your life: marriage, divorce, birth of a child, lottery win, and so on.

As you will see, you may leave anything and everything that is yours in your will, including your pets and requests for their future care.

A will might also include guardianship wishes for minor children. Keep in mind that what you are doing is essentially *nominating* the person or persons you choose. The appropriate court will ultimately make that guardianship decision.

What makes your will legal? Signing it in the presence of two or three—depending on what state you live in—witnesses who are not beneficiaries in the will makes it valid. But what makes it *effective* is its being filed in the appropriate state court after your death, and being recognized by the court as your valid will, revoking all previous wills and trusts.

Naturally we'll talk more about wills later in the book. A lot more.

Now that you know the basic terminology I'll be using throughout this book, let's move further into these topics.

Why Many of Us Don't Plan

Here's a statement that may ring a bell with you: "I think I'll see my lawyer next week, or certainly sometime this month, about drawing up a will. I'll *definitely* do it before the end of the summer (fall, winter, spring)."

Many of us who don't put off tasks in other important areas of our lives drag our feet when it comes to estate planning. Why is that?

Kim, a 26-year-old marketing executive says, "What do *I* have to make a will for? I share a rental apartment, I don't have a car, and I have $2,000 in the bank. Where's *my* estate?"

Ah, but who would she like to inherit that $2,000? Instead of having the money turned over to her parents, which would probably happen if she dies *intestate* (or without a will, versus *testate*, which is having a valid will), she might prefer that it go to her younger brother. Kim could also have funds invested in a retirement fund. Has she already designated a beneficiary for them?

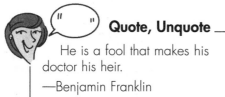

Quote, Unquote

He is a fool that makes his doctor his heir.

—Benjamin Franklin

And what about that brooch of her great Aunt Mary's, the one she clips onto her lucky suit when she's preparing to make a major presentation at the office? If you ask her right now, she would say she'd like her god-daughter, her best friend's child, to have that favorite piece of jewelry.

But no one is going to know, or carry out, Kim's wishes if those wishes are not set down in black and white in a will.

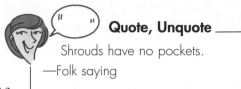

Quote, Unquote
Shrouds have no pockets.
—Folk saying

Then there is Frank, a 50-year-old telecommunications employee who shrugs off making a will, saying he wants his wife, Amy, to inherit everything of his and theirs. He says that's what will happen, even without such a document. It makes Frank uneasy to talk about a will, let alone take the first steps to having one drawn up for him. Why? Amy says she thinks it's because Frank's father died at the age of 47. Any mention of death or age or wills spooks Frank, since he himself has already passed that age.

Frank might not know that if he dies intestate the probate fees usually will be higher than if he had a valid will. Does Frank want Amy to pay that extra money? It's not likely. Besides a fee, property may go to children or Frank's parents, not just to Amy. With some advance planning, Frank could see to it that his estate is as large as it can be, with the least amount of taxes paid, through some clever investment and tax strategies.

Finally, there is Helen. She is 61 years old, manages a boutique, and, aside from a few minor ailments, is in good health. Helen and her friends talk a good deal about a living will and a health care power of attorney. Helen has been quite vocal about not wanting to be kept alive "by extraordinary means" if she should fall seriously ill, a directive that is a major component of a living will. But she has not taken care of that aspect of estate planning. She keeps putting off the paperwork. If some day it does come to those extraordinary measures, Helen might not be able to communicate her wishes about medical treatment.

Kim, Frank, and Helen are drifting along with what is usually called a head-in-the-sand approach, in this instance, to estate planning. They know what they should be doing, they read articles about wills and other components of a long-range plan, but each for their own reasons, they refuse to take action.

The Importance of Looking Ahead

If you see yourself in any of the above scenarios you are not alone. As many as 50 to 70 percent of the population die without having made a will. (We won't even get into the numbers who don't have other important estate documents.) For some, death is the only tragedy, but for others, the failure to plan an estate has catastrophic consequences for loved ones.

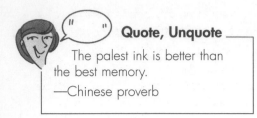

The state has made a will for you if you do not have one, and the heirs it decides upon might not be the ones you would have chosen.

Our trio above has rather simple estates, at least monetarily, but many other people have more complicated situations. There might be quite sizable sums of money involved. Or there could be second marriages where there are children from that union, as well as from a previous marriage, to be considered. Or guardianship issues for minor children must be decided. Or perhaps there is a business that is part of an estate, and one with a partner or two at that.

Lack of planning by the deceased can keep the disposition of an estate on hold, sometimes for years. Then it might still not be disbursed the way that individual would have liked.

And let's not forget how poor planning—or no planning at all—can result in heirs being hit with higher federal and state taxes and court costs for processing the will, that they would otherwise not need to pay.

The advice columns in newspapers and magazines are full of letters from frustrated readers whose parents didn't make a will or take the time to plan properly. As a result, the heirs were left with a financial mess, not to mention the stress of coping with sometimes incomprehensible paperwork and demands at a time of mourning and change in their lives.

Putting It All Together Can Be Enjoyable—Really

I can hear you saying, "Good grief, what do you mean enjoyable? We're talking about my death." No, we aren't. How and when you leave this vale is, of course, beyond the control of either of us. However, seeing the pieces of your estate plan fall into place and knowing how well organized you are now and that your wishes will be carried out later will bring you peace of mind and, yes, some pleasurable sense of accomplishment.

It might also give you the additional pleasure of knowing you're one up on many folks by being so farsighted.

(And, hey, come on, you are reading this book, so deep down, perhaps way down, you know you should be tackling at least some of these issues and are prepared to do so now, no matter how jolly or dreary the idea seems—am I right?)

As I said earlier in this chapter, planning ahead also means preparing for tomorrow, not just 10, 20, 30, or more years down the road. Judicious care of your current savings and plans for anticipated income can help your estate grow and bring you the comfort of knowing your money is working for you, working to make you even more comfortable in retirement. We're talking about a *life* plan here, with the opportunity to make wise choices and take advantage of perhaps unique opportunities from now on. Your aim should also be to build your assets and pay down your debts now so that you can retire to a pleasant, worry-free life later.

Look how many upbeat subjects we will touch on in this book that have to do with financial and lifestyle situations that could affect you in the years from now until … well, may you, too, live to be 100!

- An inheritance
- A salary increase and/or a special bonus
- A marriage or remarriage
- A new job, perhaps your own business
- Real estate purchases
- Your pension
- Social Security

So you see, an estate plan doesn't just focus on wills and other mechanisms that swing into effect when you are no longer here.

What Should Your Goals Be?

Everyone will have his or her own priorities, of course, based on age range and individual family and financial responsibilities and interests. You will learn more about the various topics that fall under estate planning and what you should strive for as you read on. However, generally speaking, after reading this book and implementing its suggestions, you will have achieved these specific goals:

- You will have a will (or a trust, or both).
- You will have important auxiliary documents, such as a power of attorney.
- You will know how to start saving money now.
- You will be able to protect the assets you now have.

Watch Out

Unmarried, same-sex or opposite-sex couples in a long-standing relationship especially need careful estate planning. That should include funeral preferences, because a family member can step in and perhaps carry out plans the deceased would not have wanted. Signed copies of funeral directions should be given to a friend or two, not locked in a bank's safe deposit box, which might be sealed immediately after death.

◆ You can reduce your taxes.

◆ You will be able to plan for retirement, securing the lifestyle you want in those years ahead.

You don't have to do everything covered in this book. No doubt some suggestions will not even apply to you, at least not at this point in your life. You may not be divorced, for example, or even married, so advice in those areas will not be relevant. You may not have your own business. Your parents might be in their early 50s, quite hale and hearty, with no need for you to concern yourself as a care-giver quite yet.

Still, whether you are 25 or 65, the information you need today to set up a solid estate plan can be found within these pages.

Starting Now

"What are your investments?" the broker asked.

I answered, "My sons, Ted, Josh, Ethan, and Zach."

That wasn't the reply the broker was looking for, of course, but he knew what I meant. You do, too. While the boys were growing up, as mentioned above, I had to tend to what is usually meant by the word "investments"—my home, my savings, a plan for retirement, and the like.

Are you as prepared as you think you are? Maybe yes, maybe no. To help you assess your particular situation right now I've created a planning quiz. After you've answered the questions, mark or fold over the corner of the page so that you can go back and refer to it again. By the time you finish reading this book, you'll know what you need to do to be able to answer yes to every question on that list.

Estate Planning Checklist

Yes	No		
❏	❏	1.	Do you and your spouse/significant other have current, signed wills?
❏	❏	2.	Have you discussed your estate plans with your family?
❏	❏	3.	Have you consulted an estate-planning professional?
❏	❏	4.	Have you reviewed the ownership of your assets to determine which are solely owned and which are co-owned?
❏	❏	5.	Have you reviewed your life insurance needs?
❏	❏	6.	Do you have a retirement plan?
❏	❏	7.	Will your estate have enough cash to pay the bills, and enough left over to provide adequately for your family?
❏	❏	8.	Do you know approximately how much you will receive in Social Security payments upon retirement?
❏	❏	9.	Have you designated anyone to handle your affairs if you are no longer capable of doing so?
❏	❏	10.	Have you made arrangements for your long-term care, or that of your elderly dependents?
❏	❏	11.	Have you taken any steps to reduce income taxes now, and death taxes on your estate?
❏	❏	12.	If you own a business, have you consulted a professional to plan for its future?

If you have checked a number of "No" answers, then this book is definitely for you.

Putting Together Your Estate Planning Team

Who can help define your needs, and then set you on the path toward setting up a valuable plan?

First, of course, *I* can. I won't hog the spotlight though. There are other professionals you may want to consult, either on a one-time or a fairly steady basis.

Your team will be made up of men and women with expertise in different aspects of estate planning. Their knowledge and guidance can be invaluable. However, do not forget for one moment that you are in charge. No one on your team should tell you what to do. He or she can offer options and discuss consequences, but only you can determine what your best estate plan is. So you will have to do some homework here, to be as competent as possible when taking charge.

You may not need every member of this team, or at least not all of them at the same time in your life. The more complex your estate, however, the more likely you will be to call on a range of professional services.

> **Tip**
>
> Try to attend a few free estate-planning seminars in your community, usually held in the evening and sponsored by brokerage offices and banks. You can learn about inheritance taxes and other estate matters as they apply specifically to your state, and you can probably ask questions of the speaker. Check your daily newspaper for news briefs or advertisements about upcoming seminars.

Here are some of the people you should consider:

♦ **Life insurance underwriter.** Most of us are underinsured. Life insurance should be an integral part of most estate plans. Young families need term insurance to provide support for the family if a parent dies. You may need life insurance to make an estate more liquid—to pay the taxes without being forced to sell assets.

The life insurance underwriter can determine your needs and the amount and type of insurance that best meets those needs.

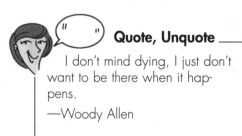

> **Quote, Unquote**
>
> I don't mind dying, I just don't want to be there when it happens.
> —Woody Allen

♦ **Trust officer.** You may need a retirement trust to help manage your assets. Your children could require a trust to avoid wasting their inherited assets because of their immaturity.

The trust officer at your bank or other financial institution can discuss his or her services and fees. It is time well spent.

♦ **Accountant.** No one is likely to be more familiar with your financial situation than your accountant. Few details in life are more intimate than one's tax returns. If you have a business, this is the individual who knows the balance sheet. Use your accountant to help gather the information necessary to focus on your financial picture, so that you can prepare a good estate plan.

◆ **Financial planner.** Your money can always be more productive. The financial planner's role is to advise you about appropriate investments that will meet your estate-planning goals.

◆ **Attorney.** The attorney drafts your will and prepares a trust, which you may also require. He or she also prepares all estate documents. You can try filling out your own documents from some form book or computer program, but you do so at your own risk.

Watch Out

Anyone can call themselves a financial planner. For some protection, try to engage a financial planner who belongs to a national professional group. For more information about these folks, contact the Financial Planning Association, at www.fpanet.org; the National Association of Personal Financial Advisors, at www.napfa.org; and the Society of Financial Service Professionals, at www.financialpro.org.

Where to Find Team Members

"Psst, know a good doctor?"

Most of us pick physicians, dentists—and estate-planning professionals—rather haphazardly. Consulting the telephone directory or asking your brother-in-law or next-door neighbor, both of whom seem to know everything, is not the best way to proceed here.

A much better strategy is to talk with a number of friends and relatives whose opinion you value. Find out whom they have worked with and whether they would engage the same professionals again. Interview prospective team members. Discuss fees. Do they seem more interested in your money than your estate-planning goals? Do they appear to be in a hurry, too busy to talk with you, or do they take the time to answer your questions thoughtfully and completely?

Check with the licensing or professional association for those you are considering engaging. That might be a state office regulating that professional or the group's statewide association, comprising members throughout the state. Ask whether there have been any

Tip

Call your state Insurance Department, and/or Office on Aging, to see if they offer free printed material on estate planning. Many have a number of brochures they can send you about various planning topics. And sometimes these include things to watch out for, like scams to avoid.

complaints lodged against that individual or firm. You might also ask that question of your local department of consumer affairs.

You are doing the hiring here, and it's certainly a buyer's market. Take the time to assemble the best team at an affordable price.

Okay. You have some idea what you will accomplish by reading this book and then taking steps to implement good suggestions. You know that planning is an ongoing process, to be revisited time and time again as situations change in your life. You have your planning team in place.

Let's proceed to succeed!

The Least You Need to Know

- ◆ Everyone needs a will, at the very least, in estate planning.
- ◆ If you do not have a will, the state will decide your heirs for you.
- ◆ Planning needs differ; determine your own personal goals.
- ◆ You should assemble a team of professionals to help you achieve your estate planning goals.

What You've Got and How You've Got It

In This Chapter

- ◆ A close-up look at your assets
- ◆ Common ownership forms
- ◆ How property is classified
- ◆ Where to keep all your "papers"

Just what *do* you own? You boast of having the patent for a gizmo that's going to revolutionize life as we know it? Good for you. That's certainly a rare asset. You have a tiny island in the Caribbean? Again, congratulations, especially in January and February. That, too, is not on everyone's list of "haves." Most of us count the standard possessions, such as a home, a car, some savings, perhaps some artwork and jewelry, maybe a few family heirlooms. Does that sound more like you?

Before we go on to consider your assets as part of your estate plan, you must know what those assets are. It's important to know, too, *how* you own them. Different ownership forms can be easier or more difficult to leave as part of an estate, as you will see throughout this book.

Taking Inventory

You might have—you *should* have—a household inventory you put together in case of fire or in the event you ever have a burglary at your place. That written list or collection of photographs of valuables describes items of value and lists their serial numbers or other identifying marks. Your written list or photographs should be kept in a fire-proof box at home, or perhaps with a relative or friend, or at your office. It will be helpful to the police and your insurance company in the unfortunate event your home is burglarized or catches fire. In the former instance, serial numbers can help the police reclaim your property.

> **Tip**
>
> Because household possessions are a part of your total assets picture, by all means put together an inventory like the one described here, if you haven't already done so. You can purchase inventory forms at a stationery or office supply store. Also, many police departments around the country lend residents etching tools for engraving names or numbers on bicycles and other possessions for identification.

It's reassuring to know you have such an inventory and, after you have put it together, perhaps surprising and nice to know, too, that you have so much. All those acquisitions over the years do add up, don't they?

In estate planning, a listing of your assets is also important. But in estate planning we are looking at a far broader picture than just household furnishings. Here, we examine items like your home, automobile, retirement plan, and the like. It's just as important to have all of that itemized. Even more so, actually, because those belongings have a higher monetary value.

What will be included in *your* estate? I've included a form that will help you determine your assets. Take a few minutes now to fill it in, and then keep it handy for easy reference as you read this book. (*Note:* Jot down everything. We'll be talking about insurance, pensions, and owning your business in the next few chapters, and about your other assets in this one.)

ESTATE PLANNING INFORMATION SHEET

Name _____ Birth _____ SS# _____

Name of Spouse _____ Birth _____ SS# _____

Residence Address _____

Names of Children _____

Age _____ Marital Status _____ Number of children _____

ASSETS

Real estate (residence and other land)

Description	Present value	Purchase price	Mortgage	How owned
_____	_____	_____	_____	_____
_____	_____	_____	_____	_____
_____	_____	_____	_____	_____

Business interests (sole proprietor, partnership, limited liability partnership, limited liability company, corporation)

Form of business	Value of interest	Who owns
_____	_____	_____
_____	_____	_____

Accounts (bank, brokerage, certificates of deposit)

Type of account	Account name	Value	Who owns
_____	_____	_____	_____
_____	_____	_____	_____
_____	_____	_____	_____

Stocks and bonds

Stocks/bond company	Market value	Cost	Who owns
_____	_____	_____	_____
_____	_____	_____	_____
_____	_____	_____	_____

Motor vehicles

Make	Model	Year	Value	Who owns
_____	_____	_____	_____	_____
_____	_____	_____	_____	_____
_____	_____	_____	_____	_____

continues

(*continued*)

Miscellaneous personal property (household goods, sporting equipment, jewelry, art, etc.)

Type of property	Value	Who owns
_____	_____	_____
_____	_____	_____
_____	_____	_____

Life insurance

Insurance company	Face value	Cash value	Insured	Owner	Beneficiary
_____	_____	_____	_____	_____	_____
_____	_____	_____	_____	_____	_____
_____	_____	_____	_____	_____	_____

Retirement benefits (401(k), pension/profit sharing, IRA, Keogh, etc.)

Type of plan	Owner	Beneficiary	Value to date
_____	_____	_____	_____
_____	_____	_____	_____
_____	_____	_____	_____

Other assets (including possible inheritances)

Type of asset	Owner	Value
_____	_____	_____
_____	_____	_____
_____	_____	_____

Total Assets $ _____

LIABILITIES

Type of liability	Amount	Who owes
_____	_____	_____
_____	_____	_____
_____	_____	_____

Total Liabilities $ _____

Total Assets minus Total Liabilities equals Net Worth $ _____

One Man's Story—Something Like Yours?

Okay, you have finished filling out your Information Sheet. Let's suppose that one John Fisher also filled out the form, and, in an abbreviated style, it looked something like this:

Property	Value	Ownership
Residence	$100,000	With wife, Ellen
Household goods	$20,000	With wife
Savings/checking account	$10,000	With wife
Automobile	$15,000	With wife
Corporate stock	$20,000	Solely
Family farm (inherited)	$125,000	With brother, George

I chose John because his estate shows the three most common ownership styles:

♦ **Solely**   John's corporate stock is in his name only. It's his to do with as he will. He can sell it or give it away. At his death it becomes part of his estate and passes to the beneficiary of his will, or to his heirs if he has no will.

Let's say at some point after filling out this form John decides to invest in U.S. savings bonds. If his name alone is on the bonds, they become part of his estate, too. But he may put a beneficiary designation on the bond. For example, they might read, "POD (pay on death) to Jenny Fisher (John's 22-year-old daughter)." Jenny would then inherit the bonds.

♦ **Joint *tenants* with right of survivorship**   If John dies tomorrow, his wife will own everything outright that was in both their names because they have those items as "joint tenants with right of survivorship." That's an ownership style that is … well, pretty much just what it says. The property, usually a home, is in both their names. When one party dies, the other automatically takes over that co-owner's share, without the need for any mention of it in a will.

Words, Words, Words

Tenants, as used in the ownership styles discussed in this chapter, means owning and not renting. Of course, "tenant" more commonly refers to an individual or company that is leasing real property.

You do not have to be married to be joint tenants. However, that is the most common ownership style among married couples. The next chapter talks more about joint ownership in the context of spousal property.

However, there is an important point to keep in mind here: Right of survivorship takes precedence over property bequeathed in a will. In other words, John can't leave his sister anything that is already jointly owned by him and Ellen, or him and anyone else, for that matter.

♦ **Tenants in common**   This is how the farm, which had belonged to John and George's parents, was deeded to the brothers. That means they equally co-own the property, but each can leave his share to anyone he chooses. Both chose their wives. They could, however, have owned as joint tenants with right of survivorship.

Unrelated homebuyers usually buy as tenants in common. For example, if the Fishers and their friends the Blacks bought a ski home together, that's how they would likely take ownership.

Your Life Estate Lasts as Long as You Do

Here is another ownership style, although one not nearly as common as the three previously discussed.

Sarah owned her home and everything in it. She lived on Social Security and the small amounts of money her two sons gave her. One son, Herb, was concerned that Mom's small estate would be tied up in *probate court*. That is a special state office that handles the management of wills and estates of those who have died with or without a will, and other similar estate situations, such as guardianships. Herb felt that once Mom's estate landed there, its monetary worth would go mostly to lawyers.

Herb read in a legal column of his daily newspaper that one could avoid probate by having an elderly homeowner deed over his or her property to a relative (or whomever else they wished to be the inheritor), but retain a *life estate* in it. That meant they could stay in it as long as they lived.

Words, Words, Words

A **life estate** can be created with any form of property, but usually it is in real estate. Ownership is divided into two parts: the **life estate**, which is the length of that homeowner's life, and the **remainder interest**, which is deeded to the heir and becomes his or her absolute ownership when the property owner dies.

The homeowner would continue paying expenses involved in maintaining that property, unless otherwise specified in writing.

Herb called his brother, Ed, and both suggested this to Mom. Sarah, trusting her boys, executed a deed that gave her the right to live on the property the rest of her days. At her death the title automatically would go to her sons as tenants in common.

The sons' goal of avoiding probate was accomplished. But was this best for Sarah?

Well, if Sarah needed, or wanted, to sell her home and use the proceeds to move into a retirement community, she would have to get her sons' consent, because they have an ownership interest in the property. Plus, there are gift tax consequences, because the future interest transferred to the sons is subject to gift tax. If a son dies, leaving his interest to his wife, Sarah would need to get her daughter-in-law to agree to her plan. Relatives, and particularly in-laws, sometimes do not act kindly when someone wants to spend their "inheritance."

To avoid that potential trap, but still avoid the time and expense of probate, Sarah should read Chapter 9 of this book, on trusts, and create a *revocable living trust*. Among other features, this document will allow her to control her own property, and use it as she needs it for the rest of her life.

Homeowners with no mortgage and no children, or perhaps children they have provided for in other ways, might want to leave their home to a favorite charity, retaining a life interest in it. You do not have to own a mansion for a charity to accept your place. There are some tax benefits to this gesture as well. The home's value is determined by a formula that includes your life expectancy and that of anyone else on the deed, using an approved mortality table and the appraised value of the residence. For example, let's say the value of your retained life interest, as determined by the actuarial tables, is $25,000 and the charity's future interest is $75,000, and then you have given an asset (the charity's right to a future interest in the property) worth $75,000 to charity.

> **Tip**
>
> You won't want to donate your home to charity when you are young—there are too many changes life can bring you, in finances and housing. This is usually a practice for those in their sixties, seventies, and beyond.

Talk with your tax adviser, and keep in mind that an agreement between you and the charity can contain whatever specific arrangements you choose—the possibility you might want to move to a retirement community, for example. You could also agree that the charity will maintain the property, or maintain it *and* pay the property taxes. In a few cases it may be possible to secure a small income from the charity.

Is It Tangible, Intangible, or Real Property?

Lawyers are experts at classifying things. Take property, for example: you might own *real property*, *tangible personal property*, and *intangible personal property*.

John and Ellen Fisher's home is *real property*, or, more commonly, real estate. Real property is land, buildings, and things permanently attached to the land, such as trees. In some states there are special inheritance and probate rights attached to real estate.

The couple's jointly owned household goods and automobile are examples of *tangible personal property*. Other items under this heading include machinery, jewelry, sporting goods, and art works. These are possessions we can see and touch.

Stock certificates owned by John, and the savings account jointly owned with his wife, are examples of *intangible personal property*. You can see it, but it's just paper, denoting ownership in something that also is represented by a piece of paper, like shares in a corporation. Other intangible personal property includes certificates of deposit, corporate bonds, patents, and copyrights. (The patent for that revolutionary gadget mentioned at the beginning of this chapter is intangible personal property, too.)

Tip

By all means get duplicates of missing documents you need for your estate file. Contact your local government office, perhaps the County Recorder, or a similarly named office, for help with a lost house deed. Insurance and brokerage houses can supply you with copies of those mislaid documents, too.

Inheritance laws, wills, and gifts distinguish among the three types of property. That's why you need to know *how* you own what comprises your estate, not just what's in it.

Okay, now it's time to attack those bureau drawers and rifle through cardboard files and anywhere else you keep valuable papers. Look to see how you own property. Check your deed(s), bank accounts, certificates of deposit, stock and bond certificates, title to your car—all should indicate which form of ownership you hold.

A Few Words About Condominiums, Cooperatives, and Timeshares

A home isn't always a single-family house on a half-acre lot, of course. Many millions of Americans live in condominiums and in cooperatives, or will be buying one in the years ahead. Does this apply to you? Then you might have special questions about estate issues and your home.

I've included timeshares in this section because owners of those vacation apartments also are frequently confused about just what they own, how they own it, and how they will pass it on to their heirs.

The Condo's Real

Condominiums were virtually unknown in the United States as recently as the early 1960s. My law professor told the class that this wasn't an important area for us to learn about in property law, so we'd skip it. So much for prognosticating profs.

A condominium is real property, or real estate. Your community might consist of one-story attached apartments, three-story townhouses, or even detached single-family houses. It's not the architectural style that determines a condo, but rather the joint ownership style. Each "unit" is owned separately. The rest of the property, known as the undivided common area, is owned jointly by all individual unit owners. That area consists of grounds, parking spaces, walkways, and the like.

How does condo ownership affect your estate? Well, because you own your condo outright, you are free to leave it to whomever you choose, depending on the individual ownership style you have selected (solely, joint tenants, and so on). You do not need anyone's "permission" to sell your condo, and prospective buyers do not have to be approved by the condo association.

Keep in mind, however, that if you bequeath your condo to your son, Fred, and his wife, Julie, knowing as you do that they would love to live there, the couple will have to join the condo association and abide by its rules. Those regulations might say, for instance, no children are allowed (that is legal in some adult complexes), and Fred and Julie have two preteens. Or the condo association could have a clause prohibiting pets, putting little Fluffy's future on the line. Or the rules and regulations might have other clauses that make it difficult, if not impossible, for Fred and Julie to live there. They might have to sell or rent the property instead.

Watch Out _____

Cooperatives often have important restrictions upon transfer, with the corporation retaining the right to veto a sale or, more accurately, veto the prospective buyer. You will want to check how your corporation handles inherited apartments. More of them these days are requiring heirs to qualify for entry as if they were new prospective buyers. That means conforming to the board's financial and other criteria.

The Co-op's a Different Story

If you own, or plan to buy, a cooperative apartment, or co-op, you will, as you probably know, purchase shares of stock in the corporation that owns your building or complex. In your monthly maintenance fee, you pay for your share of the cost of running the building—utilities, mortgages, taxes, and so on. Some states consider co-ops real estate, others say they are intangible property. (A co-op is intangible because ownership is your stock certificates, and not tangible property just because you can see the apartment.)

A cooperative may be co-owned or solely owned. If the latter, then the stock becomes part of a probate estate.

What Timeshares Are—and Are Not

Anyone who hasn't been living under a rock for the last decade or so knows what a timeshare is. It is, of course, a week (or two or more) that you buy and then own in a resort complex. You purchase the same week of the year for a specified period of time. That might be 25 or 40 years, or for as long as the complex is standing.

What you pay for your furnished timeshare apartment depends on its location, size, and most especially, the time of the year you choose to buy. "High season" in that resort will, naturally, cost you more than an off-season week.

The timeshare can be co-owned or solely owned, the same as all of the other assets mentioned in this chapter.

There are a couple of things to keep in mind about timeshare purchases as they apply to you and your heirs.

First, there are two styles of timeshares:

◆ **A Fee Simple Ownership.** If you bought under this type of ownership, you own your apartment as you would real estate. Your ownership is a percentage of that apartment's use. If you have one week, you own 1/50 of the year in Unit 240 (complexes usually keep two weeks open annually for cleaning and repairs). You also own an undivided share in the common areas.

You can leave your one-week real estate property in your will to anyone you choose, considering, of course, the ownership form you have adopted.

◆ **A Long-Term Lease.** Also known as *"right to use,"* this type of ownership means that you have personal property, not real estate. You can, however, leave this style of timeshare apartment to anyone you select, too, again depending on how you hold title to that unit.

Quote, Unquote

If all the year were playing holiday,
To sport would be as tedious as work.
—Shakespeare, *Henry IV*

It's important to keep in mind that timeshares can be difficult to sell, unless your week is in the most glamorous of resorts in the most exciting geographic community in the high season. The reason: There are always new resorts opening up, not to mention resales in existing complexes, causing a flood of timeshare units on the market. "Right to use" apartments can be particularly difficult because you are selling less than the top number of years on your lease; for example, if you bought it with a 25-year lease, and held the timeshare for 10 years, you now have only 15 years to sell.

Words, Words, Words

Illiquid refers to something not easily convertible to cash. A house, for example, is considered illiquid because even if you sold it the first day it was on the market, you would not have cash in hand from that sale for several weeks or more. Your timeshare apartment is likely to be illiquid, too.

Your heirs, should they want to sell your timeshare, no matter what its style, may have trouble doing so, or might have to wait a longer time than they would like for a buyer. They may also have to sell at a price lower, sometimes a good deal lower, than what you paid for it.

But you can certainly adjust your view of a timeshare and your expectations from it. You might want to tell your heirs not to expect a windfall profit here. But, hey, they may not *want* to sell their week in paradise, so the potential problem of unloading a timeshare may never come up.

Papers Galore: Where Do You Keep Them?

Where are you storing deeds, no matter what ownership style you have chosen for your properties, and other important papers in your life? Is there room for the additional documents you will add to that file when you have finished this book and implemented many of its suggestions?

Some folks purchase a fireproof box to keep valuable papers at home. Others turn to a bank's safe deposit box. I know someone who put all his treasures in a safe deposit box, including his baby's first tooth, which, as the tooth fairy, he purchased for 25 cents. His daughter's first report card is there, too.

A safe deposit box is honored by the Internal Revenue Service, which will allow a tax deduction for its rental fee if you store investments, like stock certificates, there.

CAUTION

Watch Out _____

Did you know that if a bank robber steals the contents of your safe deposit box, you might not be insured by the bank for that loss? True! The bank guarantees the box is fireproof, but not theft-proof. Theft of safe deposit boxes isn't a frequent, or even occasional, occurrence, so you're probably quite safe leaving your belongings there. But do keep that point in mind when storing some items in a bank. You might want to see if your homeowner's insurance can pick up that coverage.

Besides the deed to your home, you might want to keep investment certificates in the box, as well as papers like a power of attorney, birth certificates, and passports. Expensive, rarely worn jewelry could go into the box, rare coins and other valuable collectibles, and mementos like that baby tooth. One test of what to put there is gauging whether that item would be difficult, if not impossible, to replace, and if it has considerable value. If the answer is yes to those questions, put it in the safe deposit box.

Don't Put Your Will in the Box!

Your will goes elsewhere. Some states seal the deceased's safe deposit box immediately at death, so that the state can determine taxes to be paid by that estate. In other states, if the spouse survives and is co-owner of the box, it is not sealed. And still other states don't seal the box no matter who the co-owner is. In any event, it is more practical to keep your will, and funeral instructions if you have them, more accessible to your next of kin, or whoever will be handling your affairs. A home safe or fireproof box will do just fine for those papers. Or you might want to leave the original with the lawyer who drew up the will (making certain his or her name is in your estate file). Losing the original document will cause significant delay and increase costs of *probate*.

Here's a story that shows how well-meaning people can use a safe deposit box, which is good, but then put something in it that turns out to be, well, not exactly *bad*, but not a smart move either.

James died, leaving a will naming his wife, Mary, as beneficiary, so she received his probate estate. They had two daughters, Karen and Elaine. James had rented a safe deposit box in his own name at Trustworthy Bank. Among other items, he had placed two envelopes in the box, each containing $10,000, and each bearing a daughter's name. Mother and daughters were not on particularly good terms, and so they asked the estate lawyer to advise them about ownership of the cash.

The lawyer, after due deliberation and research, responded that because there was no actual delivery of the cash to the daughters, there could be no gift to them. Therefore, the cash became part of the probate estate.

This story does have a happy ending for the daughters, though. Mom gave them the cash anyway.

Words, Words, Words

Probate comes from the Latin *probatio*, which in Canon, or Church, law means "proof of a will." Throughout this book you'll read of "probate court," which administers the estate of a deceased resident of that area, whether he or she died with or without a will, and "probate estate," which consists of assets of the deceased that must go through the probate process.

Quote, Unquote

The rich have heirs, not children.

—Jewish saying

Dad had tried to leave his girls something special, but he almost failed. He should have given them the money outright, or established a joint bank account for each daughter, or left them the money in his will. Keep in mind that a gift of property requires (1) intent to make a gift; (2) delivery to the recipient; and (3) acceptance of the gift by the recipient.

The Least You Need to Know

◆ Get together an inventory of all your assets before you proceed with effective estate planning.

◆ You can select from among several forms of ownership. The form of ownership determines whether the property may be distributed through your will or go to the surviving co-owner.

◆ Your estate is divided into real, tangible personal, and intangible personal property.

◆ Be careful to store important papers where they are safe as well as reasonably accessible; don't put your will in a bank's safe deposit box.

Chapter 3

Yours, Mine, and Ours: Marrieds and Property

In This Chapter

◆ Forms of owning together

◆ Community property

◆ Switching from one form of spousal ownership to another

◆ The prenuptial agreement

Marriage is a partnership, and like many partnerships, the marital couple owns property together and jointly manages it. This can be done in several legal ownership forms. If you are married, you are certain to recognize yourself and your spouse in one of these examples.

As I've pointed out throughout these pages, you need to know how you hold title to property in order to plan properly for its management in your lifetime, and its disbursal in a manner you choose through your estate. Maybe you want it to go directly to your spouse … or maybe not.

Jointly Speaking

You read briefly about buying property as *joint owners with right of survivorship* in the previous chapter. I said that anyone, single or married, could use that ownership style. Now I'll tell you about it in more detail, as it applies specifically to married couples.

If you are married and live in a noncommunity property state (a listing of community property states follows in the next few pages when we talk about that shared form of ownership), and you own real estate, such as a principal and/or a vacation home, you probably own it as joint owners. That applies to your personal property as well—household goods, bank accounts, automobiles, and the like.

If one party dies, the other automatically inherits that co-owner's share, without it having to be mentioned in a will. It's quick, no questions asked. That's why it's so popular.

As an example, let's take Hal and Wendy. Like many couples across this broad land, they live in a noncommunity property state, have been married several years, have two careers and two children.

Early in their marriage the couple were thrilled to be able to purchase their first house. They still live there 15 years later. The deed reads " … Hal H. Higgins and Wendy L. Higgins, husband and wife, as joint tenants with right of survivorship."

For purposes of this illustration we'll have to interrupt this pleasant life, and have Hal go to his heavenly reward. Upon his death, Wendy becomes the sole owner of all of the property they owned jointly. She takes the house because of that language in the deed: " … right of survivorship." The same terminology is on the savings account card she and Hal signed when they set up that account. The household goods go to Wendy because they are also owned in that style.

Quote, Unquote

The truth is, I do indulge myself a little the more in pleasure, knowing that this is the proper age of my life to do it; and, out of my observation that most men that do thrive in the world do forget to take pleasure during the time that they are getting their estate, but reserve that till they have got one, and then it is too late for them to enjoy it.

—Samuel Pepys, Diary, March 10, 1666

Watch Out

With an estate of over $1,500,000, which is the beginning amount for having federal estate tax levied, joint ownership may have some tax disadvantages. Please turn to Chapters 16 and 20 for some suggestions here.

The benefits to this type of ownership are as follows:

- ◆ The ownership transfer is automatic.
- ◆ There is no probate (which means no delay, and no costly lawyers).
- ◆ There are no federal estate taxes if a spouse survives.
- ◆ There are no state death taxes for a surviving spouse.

Let's look at a different scenario. Even more unfortunately, Hal and Wendy die in an automobile accident. Wendy survives a few minutes longer than Hal. In this situation, Wendy's estate will include their jointly held property. If there is no evidence as to which one of the two survived the other, then the property is divided and one half is included in each person's probate estate. Using their house as an example, one half ownership of that residence would go into Hal's estate, the other into Wendy's.

"By the Entirety"

By the entirety is another marital ownership form. This applies to Sam and Ann, to take one example, a couple who also purchased a home a few years back. The deed *they* received read " … to Sam R. Black and Ann Decatur Black, as husband and wife …"

Some states recognize a form of spousal ownership in real estate that is known as *tenancy by the entirety*. Some recognize that form of spousal ownership in personal property as well.

If Ann dies before Sam, then Sam automatically becomes the sole owner of their home, because tenancy by the entirety transfers ownership to the surviving spouse. In other words, tenancy by the entirety has the same result as joint tenancy with right of survivorship, with the same advantages. This survivorship result applies no matter what the deceased's will provides because the house, due to the way it is owned, does not become part of the deceased's probate estate.

Although every state recognizes joint tenancy with right of survivorship, and it can be used by married couples or single persons, not all states recognize tenancy by the entirety, and in those states that do, it is confined to married couples. Some states recognize both forms of ownership.

Community Property: Not Just for Californians

Or should we say more specifically Hollywood? When we think of that form of marital property ownership called "community property," we almost always think of motion picture stars. Yet California doesn't have a lock on an ownership style that often makes headlines in front-page divorces. Besides the Golden State, other community property states are Arizona, Idaho, Louisiana, Nevada, New Mexico, Texas, and Washington. Wisconsin's law is similar to community property. Spouses whose legal residence is in any of these states are subject to community property laws.

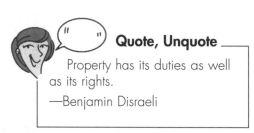

Quote, Unquote

Property has its duties as well as its rights.

—Benjamin Disraeli

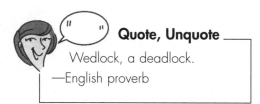

Quote, Unquote

Wedlock, a deadlock.

—English proverb

What exactly are we talking about here?

Community property assumes that the husband and wife are in a marital partnership in which both contribute to the material success of the marriage and so both should share equally in the material acquisitions of that union. Essentially, community property consists of earnings of either spouse during the marriage, and property acquired through such earnings.

Community property has these stipulations:

- One half of the assets are owned by each spouse. Upon the death of one, the survivor retains his or her half, and the deceased's half becomes part of that individual's probate estate.

- Income is considered community income, divided one half to each spouse.

- Pensions are treated as community property.

- Community property brings an income tax advantage not available with jointly held property.

- Upon divorce, courts usually divide the community property equally.

The following is a sample community property agreement:

COMMUNITY PROPERTY AGREEMENT

This Agreement is made and entered into between _____ and _____ , husband and wife, residing at _____

WHEREAS, husband and wife during the existence of their marriage have acquired and now own property of various kinds:

NOW, THEREFORE, it is hereby mutually understood and agreed between husband and wife, as follows:

1. The following is the separate property of the wife under (state) law.

    [list property]

2. The following is the separate property of the husband under (state) law.

    [list property]

3. That all other property of every kind, nature, and description now owned or held of record title by said husband and wife in their names as joint tenants, or in joint tenancy, or in the individual names of either, at all times herein mentioned has been, now is, and shall remain community property of said husband and wife without regard to the form and record of ownership under which the same was acquired or is now held.

4. All property that may hereafter be acquired by said husband and wife, during the continuance of their marriage, except that acquired by either of them by gift, bequest, devise, or descent, shall remain the community property of said husband and wife without regard to the form and record of ownership under which the same may be acquired or held.

5. This Agreement shall remain in full force and effect until modified or revoked in writing by said husband and wife, and shall be binding upon them, their respective heirs, executors, administrators, and assigns.

    IN WITNESS WHEREOF, the undersigned execute this Agreement this _____ day of _____ 20____, at _____.

_____   _____

Husband   Wife

Note to reader: This form applies to marital property acquired in a community property state. The couple is indicating what they agree is both their separate and community property.

Let's consider an example to help illustrate how community property works. Norman and Esther marry in California. Both are in the entertainment business. Esther is a huge star, but Norman is a struggling actor. Because this is only a story, we'll say they have no prenuptial agreement.

During the marriage Esther purchases a beach house in her name only, and then goes on to buy a condominium, with title in both her name and Norman's.

Norman, of course, is not earning anywhere near the major bucks Esther is bringing in. But "struggling" does not mean sacrifice for the young thespian. Thanks to Esther's income and generosity, his lifestyle is quite grand. He knows, too, that all of the property Esther purchases, no matter if titled in her name alone, is one half his under the state's community property laws. If it is sold, one half of the proceeds are his, too.

Of course, it should also be noted that one half of Norman's earnings come under the community property law and are Esther's.

While mulling his good fortune, and quite delighted with Esther and his present life, Norman gives the tiniest thought to all that he missed—monetarily—by not marrying the star sooner. He calls his attorney aside one day for an off-the-record chat. The lawyer informs him that whatever Esther acquired before the marriage is her separate property and Norman has no claim on it. But (always an important word in personal finance) if Esther were to use that separate property to purchase an asset in both their names, then Norman would have a one half interest in it.

What's This About "Separate Property"?

Well, *separate property* is whatever is owned by either spouse before marriage, as well as property acquired after marriage as a gift, or perhaps through an inheritance. What a spouse has or acquires as separate property belongs exclusively to him or her.

Separate property has these provisions:

◆ It becomes part of the deceased's estate.

◆ Income from the separate property—let's say rent from a small apartment building—can be treated either as separate or community ownership, depending on which community property state the couple claim as home. If there is any doubt as to whether property is separate or community, then there is a strong presumption that it is community property.

◆ If separate and community property are commingled in such a way that it is impossible to determine each source, then the commingled whole is presumed to be community property.

Does Community Property Last Forever?

It might not. The spouses may agree to convert it into separate property. That can be done with a written agreement signed by both parties.

On the other hand, husband and wife could agree to convert separate property into community property, tossing what they own by themselves into a communal pot. That would call for another written document, signed by the couple, of course.

Finally, you should know that community property, once it is in effect as that style of ownership, and is not changed, continues as community property no matter where the spousal parties move. So if you purchase a valuable painting under a community property law, then you move to a non–community property state, the painting is still considered community property. Think about the confusion for those who move often!

Watch Out _____

Never enter into a conversion agreement without consulting an attorney. That agreement, whether going from separate property to community property, or vice versa, will affect your inheritance rights and have income and death tax consequences.

About Those Prenuptial Agreements

If community property divorces make headlines, so, too, do prenuptial agreements between celebrities. However, it isn't only the famous who scribble their names to these documents. It can be any two people about to marry who are just a tad concerned about what will happen to what's theirs in the course of the marriage, and even in the event of a divorce one day. I say two people. Sometimes it is only one half of the couple that wants—demands—the "prenup." The other party goes along or there is no wedding.

Quote, Unquote _____

When poverty comes in at the door, love flies out the window.

—Anonymous, seventeenth century

A *prenuptial agreement*, signed by both parties, spells out any aspect of ownership in the marriage that the two can think of, and is a legally binding agreement. Unless a document is going to be recorded in a state office, most states do not require it to be notarized. And of course, to keep its contents confidential, neither half of a couple is likely to want to see a prenuptial agreement recorded. ("Recorded," by the way, means a document—a deed, for example—has been filed with a county recorder's office, putting everyone on notice of a legal agreement or relationship represented by those papers.)

A prenup can go into property ownership, salaries, pension plans, issues about existing children from prior marriages, specifically noting what belongs to whom going into the marriage, and perhaps for the duration of the marriage.

A prenup might take precedence over community property, and over joint ownership with right of survivorship, depending on the wording of the prenuptial agreement. However, prenups generally cover nonjointly owned property—that is the point of having one of these documents—so that does not often become an issue.

In case you have a prenuptial agreement in mind, or might some day, or are just plain curious about what is contained in such a document, a sample agreement for you to page through follows. This form is intended for a couple who have each been married before, and who both have children. That can make for a few extra pages. You will see there are even provisions, in the event of a divorce, for the distribution of the engagement and wedding gifts between the couple. A prenup can be quite thorough.

For more about prenuptial agreements, especially how they are treated in contested wills, see Chapter 13.

A cautionary note here: If you are considering adopting this form for your own purposes, better check with your financial planner, accountant, or attorney first. Different states have different requirements for legal documents to be effective within their borders. This warning holds true for most of the forms in this book you might want to use, but I'll remind you again when we come to those documents in upcoming chapters.

PRENUPTIAL AGREEMENT

THIS PRENUPTIAL AGREEMENT ("Agreement"), made in the City of _____, State of _____, this ___ day of ____, 20__, by and between _____, of (City, State)_____, (hereinafter referred to as "Wife"), and _____, of (City, State)_____, (hereinafter referred to as "Husband"), both of whom are also referred to herein individually as a "party" and together as the "Parties",

WITNESSETH THAT:

WHEREAS, the Parties intend to be married on _____; and,

WHEREAS, Husband has been previously married and has _____ children; Wife has been previously married and has _____ children. Each possesses or will possess wealth derived from their respective families or as a result of their respective employments.

WHEREAS, the Parties desire to clarify what their respective rights are to be in the property belonging to each other; to limit their respective rights in the property of the other during the marriage relationship and upon its termination by dissolution or death; and to accept the provisions of this Agreement in lieu and in satisfaction of all such rights; and,

WHEREAS, the Parties believe that this Agreement will enhance and encourage a harmonious marital relationship between them; and,

WHEREAS, the Parties have disclosed and discussed their mutual rights and obligations, in furtherance of which the Husband, through Exhibit A hereto, and the Wife, through Exhibit B hereto, have disclosed their respective assets, liabilities, and sources of income to each other, which disclosures each represent to the other to be substantially accurate and which include copies of their respective most-recently filed Federal Income Tax Returns; and,

NOW, THEREFORE, for the reasons stated in the Recitals hereof and in consideration of the promises and acts to be exchanged as set forth herein, the Parties agree as follows:

    1. Property Covered. The property of the Parties as listed in their respective exhibits, and property of business, tangible or intangible, real, and personal, which they have inadvertently omitted therefrom, and all interest, rents,

continues

(continued)

profits, and increased value which may in time accrue or may result in any manner, or any other property owned or to be owned by each party, shall be owned as separate property of each party during the marriage, except as elsewhere provided herein. Each party hereby waives, discharges, and releases all right, title, and interest in and to the property of the other party presently owned, or hereafter acquired, except as elsewhere provided herein. Each party shall have the absolute right to sell, transfer, convey, or otherwise dispose of his or her property as he or she sees fit. Each realizes that although the other now has property, there may be an increase or a decrease in the value thereof, or ultimately, there may be no property at all. From time to time, each party shall, if requested, join in the conveyance or other transfer of the other's property to third person, but shall not be required to assume personal liability in connection with any such transaction.

Joint use of separate property shall not give rise to joint ownership of that property, unless the Parties agree otherwise in a writing signed by each of them and executed in a manner which would entitle a deed to be recorded in _____. Notwithstanding the provisions of this Agreement that allow the Parties to maintain their separate income and assets, the Parties recognize that it is possible, through accident or intent, for their respective separate income or assets to become, or appear to be, commingled. It is the Parties' intention that such commingling or pooling of assets not be interpreted to imply abandonment of the terms and provisions of this Agreement and that the provisions contained herein addressing the Parties interest in separate property be applied so that each party be determined to be the owner of that proportion of the total fund or value of the assets in question which reflects the proportionate amount deposited or invested by him or her, respectively. Jointly owned property shall be deemed to be owned by the Parties as tenants in common, in proportion to the source of funds used to acquire and improve such property when determining the Parties' respective ownership interests in said property, except as elsewhere provided herein.

The fact that the Parties may file joint state or federal income, shall not be interpreted to imply an abandonment of the terms and provisions of this Agreement.

2. **Claims Covered.** Except as otherwise provided herein, each party with respect to the other party's property and estate now hereby waives,

renounces, relinquishes, and releases all rights as surviving spouse, heir, distributee, survivor, or next of kin, whether by common law or by statute, state or federal, now in effect or hereafter enacted to all claims, interest, estate, title, dower, curtesy, whether inchoate or otherwise, right to elect against the will, homestead, statutory widow's allowance, or statutory widow's family allowance nor to the property, real and personal or mixed, or distributive share of the other party. Each party shall, on the demand of the other party of his or her heirs, devisees, administrators, executors, or assigns, execute any and all acquittances, assurances, deeds, releases, instruments, receipts, and other documents that may be necessary to accomplish the foregoing. The rights of each party herein described as released and renounced are hereby assigned to the other party, his or her heirs, devisees, legatees, administrators, executors, successors in the interest, guardians, and assigns.

3. Provisions for Each Other. Except as elsewhere provided herein, each party shall make no provision for the other unless he or she voluntarily elects to do so. Each party may in his or her sole discretion, make additional provisions for the other, whether by lifetime gift, by future will or codicil, by joint or community property, by insurance, or otherwise.

4. Income Tax Refunds. Any federal or state income tax refunds or obligations with respect to a joint return, and any interest on any such refund or penalty on any tax obligation, shall be divided between the parties in proportion to their respective monetary contributions to the tax that is being refunded or that is owed.

5. Marital Residence. Husband owns the real estate located at _____, _____, _____, individually. Upon the death of either party, or divorce, Husband or his estate shall become the sole owner of the real estate. The household furnishings located therein shall be divided equally between the parties in the event of divorce. Upon the death of either party, the survivor shall become the sole owner of the household furnishings.

6. Adequate Provision. The Parties hereby agree that the provisions made herein by each party for the other are fair and equitable under the circumstances.

continues

(continued)

7. Gifts. Husband and Wife may make annual exclusion gifts to their respective children, and each party consents to make available to the other his or her annual exclusion gift exemption for gifts to each other's children.

   Either party may make a gift to the other party, which gift shall be the separate property of the other party.

8. Divorce and Dissolution. The Parties, in the event of marital discord resulting in the dissolution of this marriage, whether absolute or limited, renounce and release, except as elsewhere provided herein, all rights, present and future, each may have with respect to the other's assets now owned, including all business ventures and property owned by the Parties, as well as any inheritance they may acquire during the marriage. Each party renounces and releases all rights he or she may have with respect to the other party for spousal support, alimony, property settlement, attorney's fees, and court costs.

9. After Acquired Assets and Liabilities. The Parties agree that if either party should file for dissolution, all assets and liabilities acquired or incurred by either party in joint name during the marriage shall be shared equally between the parties, but not including: any inheritance; and increase in the value of the Parties' pension funds; or any other increase in the value of other property owned by either party prior to the marriage (including, but not limited to, increases in net value attributable to the retirement of any outstanding indebtedness with respect to such property during the marriage).

10. Wedding and Engagement Gifts.

    A. Death. If either party dies while the Parties are married, then all wedding and engagement gifts received by the Parties from third parties shall belong to the surviving party.

    B. Divorce. In the event of a divorce, said wedding and engagement gifts shall be distributed between the Parties so that each party receives wedding and engagement gifts which, in the aggregate, have a value which is as close as reasonable to being equal to the value of all the wedding and engagement gifts to be distributed to the other party.

11. Employee Plans and Employee Benefit Rights. Except as may be otherwise provided herein, each party (as "Releasee") hereby elects, and the other party (as "Releasor") hereby consents to a waiver and release of any and all benefits,

including without limitation, the qualified joint and survivor annuity benefit form of benefit and the qualified pre-retirement survivor annuity form of benefit under all pension, retirement, death benefit, stock bonus, or profit-sharing plans, systems, or trusts (hereinafter collectively called "Employee Plans") of which the Releasee is, or may become, a participant, beneficiary, or member. This waiver and release is meant, without limitation, as a waiver pursuant to Internal Revenue Code Section 417(a). If requested, the Releasor shall consent in writing, in any form requested by the Releasee, to any such election. The spousal consent of the Releasor set forth herein is irrevocable. Each party acknowledges that he or she has received an explanation of a qualified pre-retirement survivor annuity in accordance with the Internal Revenue Section 417(a)(3)(b) and the effect of this consent to the Releasee's election is to deny Releasor any right, interest, or annuity in or from the Releasee's benefits under any employee benefit plan, now or in the future.

Except as otherwise provided herein, the Releasor acknowledges and hereby consents to the Releasee's election that upon the Releasee's death benefits under any employee plan of the Releasee will be paid to such person as the Releasee may have designated at any time before the execution of the Agreement or may designate from time to time hereafter, in Releasee's sole and unfettered discretion.

If the Releasor shall receive any part of or benefits from the Releasee's account or accrued benefit in any employee plan, other than pursuant to a beneficiary designation executed after the date hereof by the Releasee which designated expressly names the Releasor as a beneficiary, the Releasor shall promptly turn same over to the Releasee (or if the releasee is not then living, to his or her designated beneficiaries under said employee plan, if any, or if there is no designated beneficiary, to the Releasee's estate).

The Parties intend that this Agreement be accepted as a spousal consent by each of them as Releasee to a waiver of a qualified pre-retirement survivor annuity pursuant to Internal Revenue Code Section 417(a). The Parties understand that certain laws and regulations [Internal Revenue Code Sec. 417(a)and Treasury Regulation Sec. 1.401(a)-20] require that, in order to be considered effective, the waivers and releases contained in Article must:

continues

(continued)

(1) Be consented to by a spouse;

(2) Designate a beneficiary other than the spouse; and,

(3) Acknowledge the effect of the waiver for the spouse.

In order to make the waivers and releases contained in this Article effective, the Parties agree that, within a reasonable period of time after their marriage ceremony (but no later than thirty (30) days after the date of their marriage, or with respect to any plan in which they commence to participate after their marriage, the date on which they commence to participate in such plan), they will sign a separate document which contains the waivers, releases, and acknowledgments set forth in this Article.

12. Spousal Support and Maintenance: Debts and Obligations. Each of the Parties acknowledges that, taking into consideration, among other things, each spouse's private estate, education, work experience, health, age, and ability to work and earn a living, each is fully capable of being self-supporting. Accordingly, if a Dissolution of Marriage occurs, each of the Parties waives, relinquishes, and releases any and all rights and claims as against the other and their respective successors to receive support, alimony, maintenance, or any other payment of a similar nature whether permanent or temporary.

13. Property Settlement. The amount of the property and support settlement Husband shall pay to Wife shall be based upon the length of the Parties' marriage and equal to _____ Dollars for the first year of the Parties' marriage, and _____ Dollars per year for every completed year thereafter of the Parties' marriage, with no maximum, and determined as follows:

Length of Marriage   Total Settlement Amount

_____   _____

The first installment payment of the property and support settlement shall be in the sum of $_____ and made on the 30th day after the dissolution occurs. The balance of the property and support settlement shall be paid yearly in $_____ increments. If, when Husband dies, there are remaining installments of the property and support settlement owed to Wife, then the remaining payments shall be accelerated and paid to Wife within a reasonable time after the settlement of Husband's estate. If Wife predeceases Husband, then any remaining installments of the property and support settlement shall be paid to Wife's estate as the installments come due. The property and support settlement will be made as and for a tax-free property transfer under Section 1041 of the Internal Revenue Code. Husband shall not deduct said payments or any part thereof on his income tax returns, and Wife shall not be obligated to include such payments or any part thereof in her taxable income on her income tax returns.

14. Vacating Residence. Wife acknowledge that Husband owns the residence located at _____, _____, _____, where she and Husband expect to reside immediately after their marriage. In the event one of the Parties files for separation or dissolution, within thirty (30) days after the filing for said separation or dissolution, Wife shall remove herself and her property from the _____ residence and give Husband all keys thereto, and consents that thereafter Husband shall have exclusive use and possession of all other rights pertaining to such residence. In the event of Husband's death, Wife shall be allowed to remain in the residence for her lifetime (a life estate) or until she remarries. Husband's Estate shall be the owner of the residence upon Husband's death.

15. Liability for Debts. The debts contracted by each party hereto prior to their marriage are to be paid by the party who shall have contracted the same, and the property of the other party shall not in any respect be liable for the payment thereof, except as elsewhere provided herein.

16. Representation of Parties by Counsel. The Parties hereto both stipulate that they, and each of them, were advised to be and have been represented by legal counsel of their choice in the preparation and execution of this Agreement; they were advised to and have read this Agreement and have had its contents explained to them, by such counsel. In addition, the Parties were advised not to and did not execute the document until they fully understood the terms, provisions and legal consequences of this Agreement.

17. Child Support. Nothing in this Agreement shall be construed to limit or in any way decrease any child support which might be awarded pursuant to a dissolution of the marriage, should a child or children be born to or adopted by the Parties together.

continues

(continued)

18. General provisions.

   (a) This Agreement shall become effective upon the date of the marriage.

   (b) This Agreement and the provisions hereof may be asserted as a bar and estoppel in any court of law or equity to the claims of the surviving party in the estate of the first to die.

   (c) The parties may amend, revoke, or rescind this Agreement only by written mutual agreement.

   (d) The Parties hereto and their respective heirs, devisees, delegatees, administrators, executors, guardians, successors in interest, and assigns, shall be bound by the provisions of this Agreement.

   (e) The domicile of the Parties at the time of the execution of this Agreement is the state of _____, and the law of such state shall govern. The Parties recognize that they may change their domicile to another jurisdiction by agreement. The Parties agree that all questions arising under or with respect to this Agreement and its interpretation or enforceability shall be governed by the substantive laws of the state of _____, state where Husband and Wife are presently residing and the state where the Parties expect to reside after their marriage.

   (f) At those places in this Agreement, including this sentence, except Exhibits A and B, where there appears a recitation of property, ownership rights, survivorship rights or interests, or otherwise which list shall be by way of illustration and not by way of limitation.

   (g) In the event a provision of this Agreement is held to be unenforceable for any reason, it shall be considered severable from all other provisions of this Agreement and the Agreement shall be binding upon the Parties in the same manner as it otherwise would have been, had the unenforceable provision not be inserted herein.

   (h) The Parties acknowledge and agree that it is difficult to value equity interest, agree to accept the valuation of such interest as set forth in this Agreement, and waive any right to secure an independent valuation thereof and to otherwise present any challenge to the values as set forth herein.

(i)   The Parties hereby agree, and state their intentions that, this Agreement shall be followed by, and considered binding upon, any judicial or quasi-judicial proceeding in any way concerning a dissolution of this marriage or death of one or both of the parties.

19. Complete Agreement. The Parties hereby agree, represent, and warrant that this Agreement comprises the entire understanding of the Parties regarding this matter and no promise or inducement not contained in this Agreement has been offered to either of them by anyone and that this Agreement is executed without reliance upon any statement or representation not contained in this Agreement by either the Wife, the Husband, their attorneys, or any other person or entity.

IN WITNESS WHEREOF, the Parties have executed this Prenuptial Agreement on the day and year first above written.

_____   _____
Witness   "Wife"

_____   _____
Witness   "Husband"

Briefs

It was said the document signed by Jacqueline Kennedy and Aristotle Onassis before their 1968 wedding was quite hefty, providing weeks of work for both parties' lawyers (and bringing in an okay to the agreement by Jackie's brother-in-law, Ted Kennedy). It was rumored there were even clauses about where each would maintain a permanent residence, and how often the two would spend time together. But then there was a good deal of property, real and personal, involved on both sides of this famous union. There was a business owned by Onassis, and children from previous unions to be considered.

The Least You Need to Know

- ◆ Most couples hold property as "joint tenants with right of survivorship."

- ◆ In community property states, what couples earn, buy, and so on, individually during the marriage becomes property that belongs to them equally.

- ◆ It is possible to switch from separate property to community property ownership forms, and vice versa.

- ◆ A prenuptial agreement can take precedence over some forms of property ownership.

Chapter 4

Life Insurance: You Need It!

In This Chapter

◆ How insurance can help your estate grow

◆ Choosing between term and whole life policies

◆ Determining how much insurance you need

◆ Naming your beneficiary(ies)

Do you have enough life insurance? No, no, come back, I'm not trying to sell you a policy. I ask because life insurance is an integral part of estate planning.

So force yourself to read this chapter and give the subject some thought. Then you will almost certainly want to take steps to make sure you (a) know what your own coverage entails and (b) beef it up in areas where it needs emphasis, or perhaps buy insurance in the event you have none.

What Life Insurance Can Do for You

You are probably underinsured. Remember, I am not an insurance broker, and have no stock in any insurance company, so I have no vested interest in making such a statement.

Sadly, many of us view life insurance like a bad lottery: if we win, we're dead. We often have little regard for life insurance salesmen as well (although I believe they still rank slightly higher than lawyers). Still, there are those folks who wisely look and plan ahead and do buy insurance. Life insurance industry statistics show that there was $9.3 trillion individual life insurance in force in 2002, and the average amount in force for each household was $119,310.

There are several reasons why coverage is a worthwhile expenditure.

Life insurance …

- Increases your estate, building wealth with a relatively small outlay of cash in the form of premiums.

- Provides ready cash for loved ones upon your death.

- Is received by its beneficiary free of income tax.

- May be owned by someone besides the insured and not be subject to death taxes.

- Can be used to fund a business buy-out plan.

- Could serve as a savings account, if it is whole life insurance.

Let's look at these statements in more detail.

Building Wealth

Most of us would like to have as substantial an estate as possible so our loved ones can live comfortably after our death. Unfortunately, most of us, me included, don't have a rich relative about to pass away and leave us her fortune—or rich relatives eager to share their wealth during their lifetime through generous gifts. We have to build up an estate the old fashioned way: by earning money and saving it, or by investing it very wisely.

Your estate can be substantial with the inclusion of life insurance. Take me, for example. I am 60 years old. My 401(k) pension and the house are my biggest assets. When I die, my wife will own both. But I am concerned that she and our children will not have enough to live comfortably, so several years ago I bought term life insurance (I'll talk about this in detail in the next page or so) with a face value of $450,000. That's in addition to the group term life insurance I have at work. I know that my family will be financially more secure because of that insurance.

I pay approximately $650 in quarterly premiums for my coverage. I hope my wife and I have many years together, and I'm certainly content with the insurance company keeping the premiums. That's a small investment for my family's financial future.

Quote, Unquote

Lack of money is the root of all evil.

—George Bernard Shaw

Ready Cash

Life insurance people like to emphasize that your estate may not be "liquid." That is a genuine concern, and one that some form of insurance protection can address.

Let's take Ed and Eve as an example here. The couple, in their mid-thirties, have two young children. They own their own home, have a small savings account, a little invested in stocks and mutual funds, and each has a small contributory retirement plan through their jobs. Ed earns considerably more than Eve, although it could be the reverse with other couples.

If Ed suddenly dies, his salary would end, but bills wouldn't stop coming in. The IRS in particular isn't all that patient if you owe them money. The cost of a funeral might be around $6,000, and funeral directors want to be paid, too.

Ed could solve those immediate problems with life insurance, at very little expense. Because he is young, the premium for coverage similar to my policy will be considerably less than what I am paying. Eve can deal with her grief and not have to worry about where the money is going to come from—it's in the mail from the insurance company.

Watch Out

Beware of skimping in this area. Two-income couples with children should each have an insurance policy. Look at it this way: if one party's death would result in a serious financial hardship for the family, then both husband and wife should carry insurance.

Not so incidentally, single people and couples without children can make use of an insurance policy, too, and for the same reasons: immediate cash for beneficiaries, money to pay funeral expenses and that individual's other bills—repayment of loans, credit card balances, and other debts that would have to be satisfied from the estate. Single persons often name children from a prior marriage or near relatives as beneficiaries in their life insurance policies. As with all estate planning, these beneficiary designations should be changed as personal situations alter.

Taxes

The beauty of life insurance is that the beneficiary receives the proceeds free of income tax. Eve, for example, does not have to pay a cent to the IRS. With proper planning—and I'll tell you how in Chapter 20—the proceeds may also escape federal estate tax.

Tip

Some folks purchase a life insurance policy as a gift, perhaps to a grandchild, making that individual the beneficiary. Others make a favorite charity a beneficiary. Money left in this manner goes directly where you want it to after your death, and is not held up as part of your estate.

Business Plans

If you are the owner, or part owner, of a business, you also need to consider life insurance. The business could purchase insurance on the life of the owner, and the proceeds could be paid to the business and/or the owner's next of kin. The business that has an owner or key employee who dies suddenly might experience a financial crunch for a short time, or perhaps even longer. That could be alleviated by the insurance proceeds. The owner's family may need cash, but can't sell his business interest to generate the necessary money. Life insurance can be an answer there, too. (Chapter 6 contains a good deal more about having your own business.)

Savings

If you choose whole life insurance—explained in detail in a couple of pages—your premiums are divided into two parts. One part pays for the insurance coverage, while the other becomes a savings account. If you have trouble saving money, this feature can help you build a small nest egg. Of course, the savings amount of the premium could be used to purchase more term insurance, which would increase that coverage.

Which Policy Is Best for You?

There is life insurance coverage to fit practically every reader of this book, and at a variety of costs, too. You just need to determine the type of policy best for your purposes.

We can divide most policies into two categories: term and cash value.

Term Policies

Term policies have one common feature: there is no cash value built up by your premiums. This is simple life insurance, offering the most coverage for the least cost. You can select whatever that amount will be, perhaps $50,000, maybe $500,000, or any other number. You pay an annual premium. If you die while you own the policy, your beneficiary receives the money.

You cannot borrow against a term life insurance policy because, of course, there is no cash value.

Briefs

Life insurance is one of the staples of the mystery novel (another is the will). When police investigate a murder, the first question they ask is "Who benefits from this crime?" Why, the murderer, of course, and that's rarely the butler. It's often the insurance beneficiary. Timing the purchase of life insurance may allay or enhance suspicion about that buyer.

There is the serial wife killer, who takes out an insurance policy on each new bride. Sadly, too, there is also the bomb exploding on an airline flight. Investigation leads to a relative of one of the passengers, who had purchased a large policy of flight life insurance before the departure—or straight life insurance back home. So much havoc and heartache caused by a few pieces of paper.

The premium you pay is based on the amount of insurance you purchase, your general health, and your age when you first buy the policy. The premium rises as you grow older. Also, insurance costs vary the way prices of other products do, so it pays to shop around to find the best, safest coverage with a company offering the lowest cost to you. As a gauge, keep in mind my age and the fact that I pay $650 a quarter for a $450,000 policy.

Here are some varieties of term policies:

♦ **Annual renewable.** This offers one year of insurance, usually renewable every year with an increased premium (because you are growing older). This has the advantage of giving you the greatest coverage at the

Tip

The American Council of Life Insurance, a trade association of some 600 life insurance companies, provides information about life insurance policies on its website, www.acli.com.

lowest cost to you. Read carefully any policy you are considering to see what your renewal rights are.

◆ **Level.**   Coverage here is for a guaranteed term, such as 3, 5, 10, or 20 years, with level premiums. That means they reach a certain plateau and stay "level" until the next change, or the premium remains the same but the coverage decreases from one level to another. Some insurance companies will allow cost-of-living increases at proportionally the same premium.

◆ **Decreasing.**   Coverage decreases over a set period of time, but the premiums remain the same. One plus of this program is it provides greater coverage when most of us need it, early in our family lives.

◆ **Mortgage or credit.**   With this style, coverage decreases as the debt you are insuring is paid down, but with a level premium. This is expensive, so you will want to consider purchasing another form of term insurance if you want that debt paid off at your death. Buy this only if you are otherwise uninsurable.

◆ **Group.**   Many employers carry group term life insurance policies for their employees. It's a great fringe benefit because the premiums for the first $50,000 of coverage are income tax free, and the employee pays a low rate of income tax on the policy beyond that coverage. My advice is to get as much group term life insurance as you possibly can.

Words, Words, Words

A **viatical settlement** is an insurance payout for those with terminal, or even chronic, illnesses. A company purchases your term life insurance policy for a percentage of the face value, usually around 70 percent. You get the money, and the company takes over premiums and collects on the policy when you die. Get bids from at least three viatical companies. The settlement may be subject to income taxes. For more information call the Viatical Association of America at 1-800-842-9811.

Cash Value Policies

Another option, *cash value life insurance*, is sometimes referred to as *whole life insurance*. Most of these policies have, as mentioned earlier, a savings account feature with variables in investment returns. Here are some cash value policy styles:

- **Whole (ordinary).** Coverage is guaranteed at a fixed amount, with level premiums. Part of each premium goes into a savings account at a predetermined amount and investment return. You can borrow against the cash value of the policy.

- **Universal.** The term and cash value portions are split into two accounts. Depending on the insured's allocation, the insurance can increase or decrease. It does have the flexibility of changing coverage as needs alter, but is more expensive than term if the insured uses most of the premium for insurance coverage.

> **Tip**
>
> If you have child support obligations under a divorce decree, you might want to consider a life insurance policy, payable to the children for their financial future should you pass away.

- **Vanishing premium.** Here, premiums are overpaid in the early years so that the cash value can accumulate more quickly. Then the later premiums are partially paid from the cash value, or the coverage could be reduced or lost.

- **Joint first-to-die or second-to-die.** This is life insurance coverage for two persons, usually spouses. It is less expensive than buying two separate policies. The proceeds are payable according to the first- or second-to-die provisions.

Discuss policies you are considering with your financial adviser. (Remember, you are going to call often on your estate planning team.) He or she might be more objective than a life insurance agent. Have your advisor read the fine print of policies. What the large print giveth, the small print often taketh away.

How Much Coverage You Need, and Where to Find It

First, you need to determine how much insurance coverage is sufficient for you. A life insurance company and your financial advisor can help you here. After your purchase, you will want to review your calculations periodically, perhaps once every year or two, to be sure your coverage matches current needs.

Coverage amounts are quite subjective, but usually the main purpose of life insurance is to provide a lump sum amount that will replace the deceased's income.

> **Tip**
>
> An excellent website to review life insurance coverage is www.moneycentral.msn.com.

If you want a quick calculation, here's a suggestion, keeping in mind your future income may vary considerably from these guesstimates.

Step 1. Calculate your annual income (reduced by personal expenses for you alone, such as clothing, lunches, and so on).

Example: You earn $45,000 after taxes and spend $5,000 on yourself = $40,000.

Step 2. Divide that amount by your expected rate of return from investing the life insurance proceeds.

Example: $40,000 divided by .05 = $800,000.

Step 3. Subtract your current total savings and investments.

Example: $800,000 minus $30,000 = $770,000, your life insurance needs.

The rough method I used for *my* life insurance was to add up all my debts—and don't think that's not a depressing experience—then determine how much money, when invested, would be needed once all those debts were paid.

Watch Out

Naturally, you'll want to choose a financially secure insurance company for your policy. Some are in better shape than others. Company financial strength ratings are published by A.M. Best, Standard & Poor, Moody's, Duff & Phelps, and Weiss Research. Your public library's reference department can help you access those reports, or you can check with your financial planner.

Example: Debts to be paid	$100,000 plus
Investment need (annual income of $30,000 divided by .05)	$600,000
Total needed	$700,000

With this kind of need, term life insurance is your best buy.

Yes, I know the $700,000 I list above as what I need is far from the $450,000 term life insurance policy I carry. I do have another policy, though—group life insurance through my place of business. However, I concede I'm still a little underinsured.

Don't forget if you have college expenses coming up for one or more children. Those costs could considerably alter the amount you will need.

Who Owns the Policy? Who Is the Beneficiary?

If the insurance is on *your* life, then probably you own the policy. It works that way for most of us. We can control premium payment and beneficiary designation because it is our policy.

However, someone else can own a policy on your life. For instance, your spouse might own your policy, or perhaps one of your children does. The proceeds are payable to them or anyone they designate. That way, the policy is not subject to federal estate taxes (see the following section for an explanation). If someone else owns your policy, they may look to you to pay the premium, but need not consider your wishes as to who will benefit from its proceeds after your death. Tax concerns may, or may not, override your choice to have another person own your policy (we cover this topic in more detail in Part 4). If you are married, you probably want to name your spouse as primary beneficiary of the policy and, if you have children, name them as alternate beneficiaries.

Quote, Unquote

I have enough money to last me the rest of my life, unless I buy something.

—Jackie Mason

Watch Out

Don't transfer a life insurance policy without consulting with your estate planning team. The potential tax savings may not be as important as the insurance coverage payable to the beneficiaries of your choice.

You ought to review your beneficiary designation at regular intervals, especially if your family needs and life situations change. Always make sure that you have an alternative beneficiary, because if the primary beneficiary dies before you do, without an alternative named, the proceeds become part of your probate estate. That is generally not desirable because it will delay distribution of the proceeds, and be subject to probate costs and, in some cases, state inheritance taxes. You can change your beneficiary designation by using the insurance company form provided for that purpose.

If you have minor children, then consider establishing a trust for them to receive the proceeds, and to manage the assets until they become more mature. Chapters 9 and 12 talk about trusts for minors.

Easy Go the Taxes

Keep in mind that life insurance proceeds paid to a beneficiary because of the death of the insured are exempt from income tax.

However, interest earned on the policy is not exempt from income tax. For instance, some policies allow beneficiaries to choose between a lump sum payment or a periodic payment over a number of years. If my wife chooses the periodic payment option, part of each check will include interest on the amount left with the insurance company. The interest portion is taxable.

If you own a policy at your death, or the proceeds are payable to your estate, then the insurance will be subject to federal estate tax, which begins with an estate valued at $1,500,000. You can avoid this by transferring ownership to another person, such as an adult child, even if he or she is also the beneficiary; however, transfers made within three years of death are subject to the estate tax. Then the proceeds will no longer be included in your estate. However, if the policy has a cash value, the transfer may be subject to a gift tax.

Is There Anyone Who Should Not Carry Insurance?

Empty nest couples, both of whom are reasonably healthy, *and* own their home free and clear *and* have sufficient investment income to survive fairly well financially if one or the other dies, *might* want to drop their life insurance coverage, or not take out a policy in the first place.

If you do some number crunching here and see that you can do without your term life policy, all you have to do is notify the company that you are canceling and not continuing payments. Dropping a cash value policy is more complicated, because while those policies are part death benefit, they are also part savings. Check with your financial planner or accountant to see if this is a wise step for you. If you are in poor health, for instance, it might be wise to keep the policy in effect. You could be considered uninsurable if you go to purchase another one some day.

If you want to stray outside your estate planning team, you can send your cash value policy to the Insurance Group of the Consumer Federation of America. They will analyze your rate of return and give you an idea of what you would have to earn investing to better it. The service costs $55. For more information, use the CFA website at www.consumerfed.org.

Think about it, though. You pay a reasonably small amount in premiums for insurance, and the return on investment can be very large. In my case, with term life insurance, for example, my policy will pay my wife more than $450,000 when I die; so far I have invested approximately $14,000 in premiums. Of course I prefer not to think about the downside for me personally should that happen, but at least I know the money will be there for her if I'm not.

The Least You Need to Know

- ◆ Life insurance can significantly increase your estate at very little expense.

- ◆ Work the numbers to determine what your specific coverage should be.

- ◆ Term insurance is straight insurance, payable at death, with a low cost compared to the coverage offered.

- ◆ Whole life insurance is a combination of term insurance and a savings account.

- ◆ Insurance proceeds paid to a beneficiary at the death of a policy holder are exempt from income tax.

Chapter 5

Will You Have a Pension?

In This Chapter

◆ Typical pension plans

◆ Other ways to save for retirement

◆ Deferring distribution—and taxes, too

◆ Borrowing from your pension

We're all certainly trying. A recent survey by the accounting firm of KPMG Peat Marwick LPP, found 89 percent of employers with 200 or more employees offer some kind of retirement plan. Many smaller employers have specific savings programs for workers, and some employees make contributions on their own for retirement.

We look to our future with some concern. No one wants to rely solely on Social Security after retirement, but many of us have trouble saving on our own. Pension and retirement accounts are an essential part of your estate plan. Fortunately, a variety of pension plans have been developed, with attractive tax incentives as well. This is a complex area, but after you've read this chapter you'll better understand your own choices, and have more confidence in building savings for your—let us hope—"golden years."

Qualified Pension Plans

A *pension plan* is simply an employee compensation program where the worker receives his or her benefits upon retirement.

What does *qualified* mean in the context of pensions? That's a pension plan in which the employer's contribution will not be taxed to the employee in the year it is contributed. The accumulated income and contribution will be taxed only upon distribution, which is usually a monthly payout to the employee after retirement. Those payments are *tax-deferred*, a term you'll read often in this chapter. In the context of pensions, that means taxes on that money are not due and payable until the employee has retired, when he or she is presumably in a lower tax bracket and will have to pay less than when employed.

I'll talk about three styles of qualified retirement plans in this chapter: defined benefit pensions, profit sharing, and stock bonus plans. Let's take them in that order.

Defined Benefit Pension Plan

The *defined benefit* pension is one in which the amount an employee will receive at retirement is specified. So if Joann walks into her company's Human Resources Department, or Plans Benefit Office, and asks how much she will be entitled to at retirement, the staff will do some calculations and perhaps tell her $2,000 a month for as long as she and her husband live.

Joann is enrolled in a defined benefit pension plan because it clearly states her retirement income. It might have some variables, such as a *cost-of-living adjustment (COLA)*, or a reduction equal to her Social Security benefit when that kicks in. But essentially Joann can count on that $2,000 coming to her each month at retirement.

Joann's husband will receive her pension benefits if she dies before him because she has a joint-with-survivor pension. If her husband had waived his right to that money, then her pension would be larger, but only for her life rather than paid over two persons' lives.

Generally, a husband or wife has a right to at least a 50 percent survivor benefit in the other spouse's qualified pension, unless that right is waived in writing in a prescribed form. (A prenuptial agreement won't ensure that a spouse has waived his or her pension rights.) If spouses agree to a waiver to those rights, then an employee can ask to fill out an employer waiver form, which can be given to him at his place of work.

Defined pension benefits are determined by years of employee service and average compensation during that work time, based upon a formula set into the plan. The employer is supposed to set aside enough money to fund your benefits, using actuarial calculations of how long you and your spouse are expected to live. There are limits to annual benefits $170,000 in 2005, with subsequent years adjusted for inflation, but you probably won't have to worry about that unless you are a retiring senior executive with a Fortune 500 company—or a pro athlete.

Tip

The Employee Retirement Income Security Act (ERISA) gives you the right to get information from your employer about your company's pension plan. Ask what type of plan it is, how it works, your options for collecting benefits, rules for participation, and so on. ERISA also gives you the right to your individual benefits statement. Request a statement at least annually.

Tip

Some companies offer employees no say at all in how they invest pension funds. But yours might allow you to select the type of investment you prefer. For growth you might want a selection of stocks, while bonds could be your choice for a fixed return. Discuss your options with your financial advisor. Your choice will depend on factors in your personal and financial life.

Defined Contribution Pension Plan

In a defined contribution plan what's fixed is not the amount of money you'll get out at retirement, but how much money—usually determined as a fixed percentage of your income—you put in before retirement. In a *defined contribution pension*, benefits are based solely on the amount contributed by the employee and employer, and the account's accumulated income. Each plan participant has his own account, which is much like a savings account. Usually the employer makes a contribution as determined by the plan. Upon retirement, it's easy to determine the amount available to the employee, and that amount usually will be reported on a quarterly basis.

For example, Ken works for Medium Company. He is enrolled in a defined contribution plan and contributes 4 percent of his salary, which is matched by his employer. Adjusted annually, the contribution limit for 2005 is $42,000. The quarterly statement on his retirement account shows his contribution, his employer's contribution, and the accumulated income. Neither his nor his employer's contributions are taxed when he earns the money, nor is the accumulated income. Ken only starts paying taxes on the money when he begins receiving retirement payments.

Profit Sharing Plan

A *profit sharing plan* is just what it sounds like: a program where employees share in any profits the company makes. It's set up by the employer, who contributes part of the company profits to separate employee accounts, as determined by the plan and those profits. The law generally treats a profit sharing plan like a defined contribution pension, although it could also be used to fund accident, health, or disability programs. When the profit sharing plan makes a distribution to the employee, then the employee is taxed on the money he or she receives.

CAUTION
Watch Out _____
Because the retirement account in a stock bonus plan consists of the employer's company stock, there is no diversification of portfolio. With this plan, market fluctuation in that stock will have an impact on your retirement benefits. In other words, your eggs are all in one basket, and that basket is your company.

Stock Bonus Plan

In a *stock bonus plan*, the employer establishes and maintains a program of contributing shares of its company stock to employees. The plan is subject to most of the same requirements as a profit sharing plan. When the employee receives the stock, he or she is taxed on its worth.

Quite similar to stock bonus is an *employee stock ownership plan* (also known by its initials, ESOP). In such a plan, the employer contributes its company stock to a qualified trust, which manages it for both employer and employee. The employee is taxed upon distribution.

Vesting Requirements

In pension language *vesting* means you have met the particular plan requirements for the legal right to receive pension benefits, based on your years of service. Your benefits start at retirement age, which is usually 65. In most plans, an employee is vested after contributing to the plan for a certain number of months. Once vested, the employer begins to contribute to the plan as well as the employee.

To use the jargon, you are 100 percent vested in, or own, what you contribute to that plan.

Your right to your employer's contribution is another matter. If, according to your plan, you are entitled to all of the employer's contribution upon completion of five years' service with that company, that's called *cliff vesting*. Or your plan might have *graded vesting*, which is a staggered ownership style likely to look like this:

What You Are Allowed to Keep of Employer's Contribution

Years of Service	Nonforfeitable Percentage
0–2	0%
3	20%
4	40%
5	60%
6	80%
7 or more	100%

As of 2002, a new vesting schedule has applied to most employer contributions, as follows: up to 2 years (20 percent), then a 20 percent increase each year for years 3 through 6.

Amy has worked for her employer for six years. Her retirement plan has five-year cliff vesting, so 100 percent of her accrued benefits are hers. Tommy has been employed by his company for the same six years, but his employer has graded vesting, structured as in the preceding table, so Tommy is 80 percent vested in employer contributions.

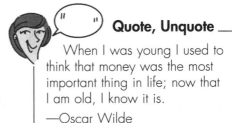

Quote, Unquote

When I was young I used to think that money was the most important thing in life; now that I am old, I know it is.

—Oscar Wilde

If you leave the company, the employer's contribution that is not vested remains in the pension plan. You take with you whatever you put into the plan.

Check your own retirement plan, and consult with the appropriate office at your place of employment, if you have any questions.

Distribution Requirements

Distribution, or payment, from any qualified retirement plan must begin no later than April 1 of the calendar year following the calendar year in which you reach age 70½. So if your birthday is January 1, then your half-birthday is July 1. If your 70½ birthday is July 1, 2002, then you must receive a distribution no later than April 1, 2003. Not only must you receive a distribution by a certain date, but that distribution must meet the IRAs minimum requirement guidelines. If you fail to follow this rule, you'll have to pay a penalty.

Use the following table to determine your minimum distribution requirement based on your age:

Uniform Actuarial Table

Age	Factor	Age	Factor	Age	Factor	Age	Factor
70	26.2	82	16	94	8.3	106	3.8
71	25.3	83	15.3	95	7.8	107	3.6
72	24.4	84	14.5	96	7.3	108	3.3
73	23.5	85	13.8	97	6.9	109	3.1
74	22.7	86	13.1	98	6.5	110	2.8
75	21.8	87	12.4	99	6.1	111	2.6
76	20.9	88	11.8	100	5.7	112	2.4
77	20.1	89	11.1	101	5.3	113	2.2
78	19.2	90	10.5	102	5	114	2.0
79	18.4	91	9.9	103	4.7	115+	1.8
80	17.6	92	9.4	104	4.4		
81	16.8	93	8.8	105	4.1		

Here's how to use the table:

>   **Step 1:** Find your age at distribution date on the table.

>   **Step 1:** Find out what your retirement account balance will be in the year prior to the current distribution. (Your Plans Benefit report tells this.)

>   **Step 3:** Divide the amount in Step 2 by the factor in the chart.

Let's use Bart as an example. Bart must receive his first distribution in 2004. According to the IRS table, his required distribution factor is 26.2 (for age 70). The amount in his retirement account is $500,000. Therefore, Bart must receive $19,084 ($500,000 divided by 26.2). Each year thereafter he recalculates his distribution requirement by the next age factor.

The IRS has other tables for joint lives IRAs (usually based on both husband and wife lives) and qualified plans, as well as for beneficiaries of such plans. Please contact your financial planner for advice. You may want to consult IRS Publication 590, or view the information on the IRS website (www.irs.ustreas.gov).

Generally, you can't take any distribution prior to reaching age 59½, but there are exceptions to this rule that I'll discuss later in this chapter.

401(k)s, IRAs, and Other Great Ways to Save

You've got several choices if you don't have a pension plan or you want to put away for retirement more than what your company is providing.

Watch Out

If you leave your company, you are entitled to all employee contributions to your pension and, depending on plan vesting requirements, the employer contributions. To avoid a tax upon distribution, you must invest the distribution within 60 days of receipt in another qualified plan or in an Individual Retirement Account (IRA). A direct rollover payment from your ex-employer's pension to your IRA also avoids the IRS requirement of a 20 percent withholding on the pension check if paid directly to you.

401(k) and SIMPLE

A 401(k) is a defined contribution plan for retirement. It is named after the section of the IRS Code numbered (you guessed it) 401(k). It has several attractive features that have made it popular with lots of folks:

- ◆ Contributions can be made by deducting money automatically from your pay (through a salary reduction plan). You're less likely to miss money you never see; even better, you don't pay taxes on the money deducted from your salary.

- ◆ Your employer might make a matching tax-deferred contribution.

- ◆ You're taxed upon distribution of the employee and employer tax-deferred contributions, plus the accumulated earnings, but that tax is when the retiree's income bracket is (probably) lower than it was when he or she was working.

- ◆ Plan distributions can be delayed until age 70½.

You can take your 401(k) plan with you if you leave your present employer. However, the employer contributions may have vesting requirements similar to a defined contribution plan.

Employers with 100 or fewer employees can establish a Savings Incentive Matching Plan (SIMPLE) as a 401(k) or IRA.

403(b)

A 403(b) plan is similar to a 401(k), except that it applies to not-for-profit companies. There are some slight differences in income limitations and investment opportunities.

Individual Retirement Accounts (IRAs) and Roth IRAs

An IRA allows you to contribute up to $3,000 to it annually. This contribution limit increases to $4,000 in 2005 through 2007, and $5,000 in 2008. The contribution of earned income may be tax deductible for lower income taxpayers and those who do not have a qualified pension. Each working spouse can establish his or her own IRA.

Roth IRAs permit the same contribution amount as the IRA, but the income earned in the account is exempt from income tax if the Roth IRA is held for at least five years. Contrast this with the IRA, which simply defers the income until withdrawn. Consult with your financial planner to determine which is more advantageous for you.

Expect to pay heavy financial penalties for early withdrawal from regular and Roth IRAs; both have age specific distribution limits. In addition, whether your contribution is tax deductible depends on your income and defined benefit or defined contribution plan limits previously discussed. There are some limitations on your choice of investment vehicles, but you still have plenty to choose from, including mutual funds.

Deductible contributions and the accumulated earnings of an IRA are taxable when distributed. That distribution may begin as early as age 59½ but no later than age 70½.

Keogh Plans

Self-employed individuals are eligible to receive qualified retirement benefits under a *Keogh* plan (pronounced *key-oh*). Keoghs cover partners and sole proprietors, and can include employees. The coverage requirements, contribution limitations, and taxability upon distribution are similar to defined benefit or defined contribution plans, depending upon which form is used in the Keogh plan.

If you are self-employed, consult with your financial planner for the Keogh plan that can be tailored to fit your needs.

Also, self-employed persons should consider adopting an Archer Medical Savings account to pay medical bills. Any balance in the account could be used for retirement.

> **Words, Words, Words**
>
> **Keogh** is a name, not a word. That pension plan was named after U.S. Representative Eugene James Keogh, who first suggested the benefits program in the U.S. House of Representatives.

Or Is There an Annuity in Your Future?

Whether through your place of employment or on your own, you can put as much money as you like each year into an annuity. An *annuity* is an investment vehicle that brings a fixed, periodic return for a specified number of years, or for a lifetime (or, if desired, the lifetime of a spouse). The annuity grows without taxation. But the amount you deposit is not deducted from your reported earnings.

Joe purchased an annuity from an insurance company for $20,000 in 2004. The company promised him that he will receive $3,000 a year for 10 years (a fixed term), beginning in the year 2014, when he is retired and in a lower tax bracket.

Each one of Joe's annual payments starting in 2014 will include income earned from his premium. His investment was $20,000, with an expected return of $30,000. His annual payment will be $3,000, but because $2,000 of that will be considered one-tenth of investment and not earnings on that investment, only $1,000 will be taxable to him each year.

The advantage of the annuity is, as you've read so often here, to defer payment of income earned until the future, when your tax rate is likely to be less. Contrast that with Joe putting his $20,000 into a Certificate of Deposit. Each year the interest earned from the CD will be taxed, while the income from the annuity will be tax deferred until payout begins.

Annuities are considered safe for future needs, but with limited returns. They appeal to people who don't like high-risk investment strategies.

Variable Annuity

You say you want something a bit more daring? Then you might want to consider what is known as the *variable annuity*, which puts your principal into the stock market. Now your annuity has become as responsive to the current economy as the performance of any stock or mutual fund. And any earnings are tax deferred.

Building Wealth at the IRS's Expense

You have been very patient in reading through this complex subject area. For that you are to be commended. But the bottom line, you are probably saying about now, is "Just tell me how much all of this will save me."

The answer is "Well, that will depend." For one thing, it depends upon how much you can afford to put into your retirement plan. Of course, there are limits. With an IRA, for example, you can contribute only $3,000 (or more after 2005) a year. A person age 50 and over can contribute an additional $500 annually ($1,000 in 2005 and thereafter). Here are the tax deductible limits for each year for some plans.

> **Quote, Unquote**
>
> April is a very trying month. I'm trying to keep my money and the IRS is trying to take it away.
> —Stephen M. Maple

- A defined contribution plan permits a contribution of up to $42,000 per year, with increases indexed to inflation after 2005.

◆ A 401(k) plan permits you to contribute up to $14,000 for 2005 and is increased $1,000 per year through 2006, thereafter any increase is indexed for inflation. If a taxpayer is at least age 50, a contribution may be increased by $3,000 in 2005, for a total of $17,000; thereafter annual additional contribution limits increase to $5,000 in 2006.

All of the above is income that is tax deferred. Here is an example of how one employee is working her pension to her advantage.

Hope has a 401(k) plan at work. She earns $50,000 annually, and has agreed to contribute 5 percent of her salary to her plan through a salary reduction plan. Her employer agrees to match her contribution. Hope's taxable salary for a year will then be $47,500 ($50,000 salary minus her $2,500 salary contribution, which is 5 percent of her income). Into her 401(k) goes her $2,500 contribution, which is tax deferred, and her employer's $2,500, which is also tax deferred. Thus Hope has $5,000 put away for retirement *and* has reduced her taxable income by the $2,500 she herself contributed. If she wanted to, she could make an additional contribution from her salary, which could also be tax deferred.

When Hope retires and starts receiving distributions from her 401(k), they will be taxable, but by then she will be making less money, so her tax rate will be less.

Compare the results in Hope's 401(k) account with her putting her contribution into a savings account. If she is taxed at a 20 percent rate, then she will have to earn $3,125 to save $2,500 (because the savings account is funded with after-tax dollars), and any interest earned each year would be taxed. She is, therefore, saving at the IRS's expense. And you would, too, if you had a 401(k). And as a bonus, her employer kicked in another $2,500! What you save in your retirement account is tax deferred, and the income earned by the account is tax deferred. I don't know about you, but I personally prefer paying taxes sometime in the future—when I retire, but certainly not now!

Other Deferred Compensation Plans

I like to get paid up front. The IRS prefers that I make money that way, too, and pay tax on it right away. However, most of us have some form of retirement plan that pays us later—after that magic 65 or 70 years of age, or whenever specified in the retirement plan. Our money is tax deferred until those payouts begin. A few folks have other deferred compensation plans I haven't talked about yet that deserve mention.

Note to readers: If you are not in the highest tax bracket, you can skip this section.

Tony "Tiger" Templeton is a running back for the Indianapolis Horses. Tony signed a four-year contract with the team for $500,000 per year. Actually he is only going to receive $250,000 each of the four years. The other $1 million will be paid beginning in the year 2010 in 10 annual installments of $100,000 each, quite a few years after Tony's knees will have started giving way. Tony's taxable compensation this year and for the next three years is $250,000. The rest will be taxed when he receives it, beginning in 2010 and each year after that, when he is in semi-retirement signing autographs and is in a lower tax bracket.

Quote, Unquote

Life does not begin at the moment of conception or the moment of birth. It begins when the kids leave home and the dog dies.

—Anonymous

If you are an employee in a high tax bracket, you may be able to contract with your employer for a deferred compensation arrangement, with part of your salary to be paid when you begin retirement. It would likely be taxed at a lower rate than it would be now, because your income then will have dropped. Besides deferred compensation plans, you may also want to investigate stock options with your employer. They also receive favorable tax treatment, with taxes often hitting when you're retired and in a lower tax bracket.

Early Withdrawals from Your Pension Plan

Most of us look at our assets and see that a big chunk of money is sitting right there in a retirement plan, doing absolutely nothing. What a crime! If we are short of cash, there is the temptation to withdraw some money to pay off debts.

You just might be able to borrow from your retirement plan. There are a number of restrictions in this area, and you need to consult your Plans Benefits administrator to do it correctly. Keep in mind, though, that the amount you borrow, if not paid back, may seriously deplete your retirement fund.

Early withdrawals (that usually means before age 59½) from qualified pension plans are subject to a 10 percent penalty tax. In addition, you must report the tax-deferred amount you withdrew to the IRS as income in the year withdrawn.

There are several exceptions to this withdrawal penalty:

◆ Employee separation from employment after age 55.

◆ Distribution to a beneficiary after the employee's death.

- ◆ Distribution to the employee due to a disability.

- ◆ Distribution to pay medical expenses.

- ◆ Distribution to a divorcing spouse.

- ◆ Distributions for higher education expenses.

- ◆ Distributions for first time home buyers.

Uh-Oh Department: Will Your Company Pension Be There When You Need It?

Well, we certainly hope so. During the coming few decades the baby boomers (those born between 1946 and 1964) will earn larger and larger incomes, rack up more years with their company and, as all of us must, approach retirement. Employers will have to make larger and larger contributions to their pension funds. Some experts fear that some companies will cancel that benefit when faced with the increased amount they must spend.

"Gee," you say, "Can they do that?" Yes, I'm afraid they can. A company does not have to file for bankruptcy, or even be in financial trouble, to justify terminating its pension plan. Actually, more than 30,000 American companies have done just that since 1980. However, most have replaced it with some form of employee contribution plan.

Quote, Unquote

There are two times in a man's life when he should not speculate: when he can't afford it, and when he can.
—Mark Twain

Whatever the future holds for you—and your company—your pension is probably safe, although its benefits might be frozen at the date the plan was terminated. You can thank an act of Congress, which in 1974 set up the Employee Retirement Income Security Act (ERISA) that now governs pension plans. It in turn established the Pension Benefit Guaranty Corporation (PBGC), which acts sort of like the FDIC does for banking.

For example, if Acme General Company wants to terminate its pension program, PBGC requires it to prove that it has enough money to pay all the scheduled benefits for retired and vested employees. If PBGC is satisfied, the company in question usually purchases an annuity from an insurance company to pay pensions.

If a company declares bankruptcy and has an underfunded pension plan, PBGC will take on the responsibility for paying its pensions. Broadly speaking—and there are a lot of "whereases" in this operation—as a retired Acme employee, you would likely be paid some, if not all, of your money.

Note: What we are talking about here is private company pensions. PBGC's role does not include government employees, not-for-profit groups, and professional associations, such as doctors or lawyers.

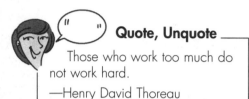

Quote, Unquote

Those who work too much do not work hard.
—Henry David Thoreau

So the answer to the question "Will my pension be there for me when I'm ready?" is "Very likely it will." But not knowing absolutely for certain, coupled with nailbiting about Social Security and whether *that* system will be around for us when we retire, should get all of us busy putting away as much as we can in savings and investments—just in case.

The Least You Need to Know

- ◆ A company retirement plan can sometimes be tailored to fit your own particular needs.

- ◆ If your company does not provide a pension, you can set up your own.

- ◆ Money you put into your pension doesn't get taxed until it's distributed to you at retirement, when you're probably in a lower tax bracket.

- ◆ Your company pension will probably be alive and well when you hit retirement age, but it still makes lots of sense to save as much as you can for retirement.

Chapter 6

Got Your Own Business? Then This One's for You

In This Chapter

- ◆ Sole proprietors
- ◆ When others are involved
- ◆ Tax savings
- ◆ The importance of a buy-sell agreement

This chapter is for you if you own a business, or perhaps are considering starting one. Your choice of entity—how you set yourself up to conduct that business—is important. It can impact the success of your enterprise tax-wise. And it can affect your estate as well, as you will see in explanations and tips woven throughout the next several pages.

What we'll talk about first is how you might choose to set up shop (or office, plant, shopping mall kiosk, and so on). You have several choices.

Sole Proprietor

If you are the only owner, with no partners or anyone else in the picture, that makes you what is known as the *sole proprietor*. That means you are personally responsible for your business's debts and all its income (or losses).

A sole proprietorship is easy to set up because most states don't require you to file any papers with a government agency. Well, all right, there are a few exceptions. For example, if you are opening a store, you will need a retail merchant license, and some other professions might call for a local license. Someone like Harry, who is doing business as (abbreviated as d/b/a) Harry's House of Wicker, may have to file a certificate stating his d/b/a name so that his municipality knows who is the owner behind that store.

Watch Out

Better check the name you want to give your business with your Secretary of State's office. Duplicates are not allowed within the state, so if the name you want is taken, it's back to the drawing board to come up with something else.

However, as a lawyer I don't have to secure anything from city or town hall to start my business, and many other enterprises don't, either.

Of course if you have anyone on your payroll, then you must follow IRS and state Department of Revenue reporting requirements.

It's as simple to exit this kind of business as it is to set it up. Just take down your sign. You don't have to file anything with any state agency.

If you die while owning your business, that asset is treated like any other. It goes into your will, passed on to whomever you choose. (That individual won't personally be obligated for any business debt, but the estate will be. That means that debt will have to be satisfied before any distribution of assets is made to heirs.)

The Buddy System: A Partnership

Let's say you and two or more associates co-own your business. If you haven't incorporated, you probably are a partnership, whether or not you have a formal partnership agreement. A *partnership* is a recognized form of business ownership in which who owns what and how much is set out in the partnership pact. That agreement controls each partner's share of the profits/losses, assets, and management. If there is no agreement, then each partner has an equal interest in those profits and losses and in management decisions. Many states have created a variant of the partnership, the limited liability partnership (LLP), which permits the partners to avoid personal liability for business debts. Your partnership should elect to become an LLP if available in your state.

Violet, Rip, and Mark have joined forces to become partners in a detective agency. They have no specific partnership agreement. Each contributed $5,000 to set up the agency. Therefore, each partner, according to the law, has an equal share in the profits and losses, and an equal voice in management decisions. Each has his or her $5,000 capital contribution on the partnership books.

This trio should have a specific written agreement, particularly if they want to divide profits/losses or management *unequally*. For example, let's say that Rip runs the partnership into $15,000 of debt by buying expensive disguises. Unless they have an agreement saying that each partner is responsible for the debt that he or she incurs, Violet, Rip, and Mark will have to contribute $5,000 to the partnership so that Rip's $15,000 debt can be paid. It is not just Rip's bill.

Let's say the partnership's net income for 2005 was $21,000. Because each partner has an equal share in the profits, each will report $7,000 income on his or her individual 1040 tax form.

> **Tip**
>
> The U.S. Small Business Administration can help you with your myriad questions, either in setting up a business or running one. They might have an office in your city. The website address is www.sba.gov.

Breaking Up: Hard to Do?

Our detectives might dissolve the partnership for several reasons: death or retirement of a partner, consensus termination, or involuntary termination by a court. Usually the latter involves bankruptcy.

In this case, Mark, while on a stake-out, chokes while eating a donut and dies. Because the partnership has no agreement, it has to terminate business, pay its creditors, then distribute any balance left to Violet, to Rip, and to Mark's estate. If they had a partnership agreement, then it could have provided that the company would continue on the death or retirement of a partner. It could also contain clauses for the selection of Mark's successor.

> **Watch Out**
>
> If your business requires a building, you probably should get a mortgage rather than take money from your retirement savings. Have that loan written so that business failure and foreclosure cannot affect your personal assets (your estate).

If you die while in a partnership, your partners are likely to buy out your share in the business, sometimes with periodic payments to whomever inherits from you. That comes from their having a buy-sell agreement, which I'll describe in detail later in this chapter.

Another Style

Also under the partnership umbrella is a *limited partnership*. This type of partnership involves two types of owners: general partners, who are personally liable for the business debts, and limited partners, who are not. The general partner runs the entity.

General and limited partners are taxed upon the business income, or may deduct its losses, subject to some tax restrictions.

Are You the Corporate Type?

Many small businesses incorporate. Most do so because incorporating makes the business, rather than the owners, liable for its debts.

A *corporation* is a separate legal entity, owned by its shareholders, with policy set by a board of directors and managed by the officers. You can elect to be the only shareholder, or you can sell shares to as many people as you want. The corporation is liable for its debts unless the shareholders personally guarantee a corporate obligation.

Tip

Always have a lawyer prepare corporate papers when there are two or more persons involved. Disputes can arise later, so you need to ensure proper documentation.

In most states, forming a corporation is pretty simple. You prepare a form called Articles of Incorporation, which you can get from your Secretary of State, and then file the document with that office. If you are setting up a one-shareholder corporation, you yourself can probably fill out the form and obtain and prepare any other corporate documents needed. However, I advise at least having an attorney review your work to determine if it is properly prepared.

Mike and Sharon have decided to form a corporation as consultants for TV and radio stations. The Articles of Incorporation are filed, by-laws drawn up, and the shareholder and board of directors' minutes recorded. The stock is issued: 49 shares to

Mike and 51 shares to Sharon. Because Sharon has control of this business, Mike will probably want a contract detailing his employment and other rights in the corporation.

If you are terminating a corporation, most states require you to file an Articles of Dissolution form with your Secretary of State.

If you die while part of a corporation, what happens? Well, your fellow owners will consult *their* buy-sell agreement, which I mentioned in an earlier section on partnerships and will describe in more detail shortly. Your share of the corporation is in stock, which is now considered part of your estate.

The buy-sell agreement may require the corporation to buy a deceased's share, perhaps with funding from a life insurance policy. Proceeds, of course, go to your heir(s).

The Limited Liability Company

Hey, everybody, there's a new kid on the block. It's the limited liability company, which is a sort of combination corporation and partnership.

This company is owned and managed by its members (co-owners). It is established by Articles of Organization (which are similar to Articles of Incorporation) and run according to an Operating Agreement, somewhat like a partnership agreement.

There are two attractive features to a limited liability company:

- Members (owners) are not personally liable for business debts; the company is.

- Members are taxed like partners or S corporation shareholders, rather than twice-tagged (paying income tax at the corporate level, and tax on dividends to shareholders) on the profits, as the C corporation is (S and C corporations are discussed in the following section).

> **Quote, Unquote**
>
> How happy the life unembarrassed by the cares of business!
> —Publilius Syrus (circa 42 B.C.E.)

> **Tip**
>
> State tax laws on business entities vary. Some states follow the federal tax law, while others do not. Always consider state laws when selecting a business entity.

The members can manage the limited liability company like a partnership, with all owners involved in decisions. Or they can have an arrangement similar to a corporation, with a board of directors.

The limited liability company usually requires filing organization and dissolution documents with the Secretary of State.

Ownership Styles at a Glance

The upcoming chart can help you differentiate among these various ownership styles at a glance.

Even More Tax Talk

You have seen some tax consequences in selecting a business entity. Naturally, you will want to consider all the tax ramifications of setting up your organization.

S or C?

Tax law allows small corporations (75 or fewer shareholders) to elect to be taxed as an S corporation (that's a tax code designation). S corporation shareholders report business income (or loss) on their 1040 Schedule E, similar to partners'. If there is no S election, then the corporation is designated a C corporation, and its income taxed at the corporate level (dividends paid are reported by the shareholders).

Your accountant or attorney can determine whether the tax status of S or C corporation is best for you.

Tax-Free Formation

Sole proprietorships, partnerships, and limited liability companies are formed without incurring a tax when established. Generally both S and C corporations may be formed tax free, but to do that at least 80 percent of their shareholders must make capital contributions of property (not personal services).

Comparison of Business Entities

FACTOR	PARTNERSHIP*	C CORPORATION	S CORPORATION	LIMITED LIABILITY CO.
Owner	Partners	——— Shareholders ———		Members
Formation (setting up)	Agreement	——— Articles of Incorporation & By-laws ———		Articles of Organization & Operating Agreement
Owner liability for business debts	Partners liable	——— Shareholders not liable ———		Members not liable
Income and deductions for tax	Partners	Corporation	Shareholders	Members
Division of profits	Agreement	——— Dividends based on stock ownership ———		Operating Agreement
Tax loss deduction	Partner, with limitations	None	Shareholder, with limitations	Member, with limitations
Limits on ownership	Agreement	None	75 shareholders & other limits	Articles of Organization or Operating Agreement
Transfer of interest	Partner approval	——— Usually freely transferable except if stock restriction agreement ———		Members approval
Continuity of life of business	See agreement	Perpetual	Perpetual but S election may be terminated	See Operating Agreement
Gain on sale	Capital & ordinary	Capital	Capital & ordinary	Capital & ordinary
Fringe benefits to owner/employee	None	Available	If own less than 2%	Available
Management	Partners	——— Board of directors ———		Members
Tax year	Partners' year	Any	Calendar	Members' year
Liquidation	Partners agree	——— Shareholder approval ———		Members agree
Dissolution filing required	None	——— Articles of Dissolution filed ———		Dissolution filing required

*Limited partnership not included in chart; LLP election avoids a partner's personal liability for partnership debts.

Reporting to Uncle Sam

The sole proprietor reports income (or loss) on his or her 1040, Schedule C. Partners and limited liability companies report theirs on federal form 1065, and then each owner's share of income (or loss) is reported on the 1040, Schedule E. Likewise, the S corporation reports *its* income on the 1120S, and the shareholder reports his or her share of the income on 1040, Schedule E.

The C corporation reports its income (or loss) on form 1120, and pays a tax on income. The corporation shareholder only reports dividends received, on Schedule B, 1040.

Partnership, limited liability companies, and S corporation shareholders report passed-through income as the same "character"—in other words, ordinary income or capital gain—as its source. For example, capital gain created by a partnership will be passed through to the partners as capital gain.

To sum up this mass of tax forms, only the C corporation—not its shareholders—pays its tax (except on dividends received). All the other owners report and pay income taxes on their share of the entity's income.

Briefs
A little boy looks up at his father and asks "Papa, what does it mean, business ethics?" "Well," explained the merchant, "It's like this. A man comes into the store and makes a purchase. He gives me a clean, new five-dollar bill, which is just the right amount. He starts to leave the store. I'm turning to the cash register when I discover that it's not one, it's *two* five-dollar bills stuck together. Now comes in the business ethics—should I tell my partner?"

Why a Buy-Sell Agreement Is Vital

Ah, now we come to that buy-sell pact.

Whether you are nearing retirement or just starting out, you ought to have a plan for succession upon your death, disability, or that longed-for retirement. Your work is a valuable asset, probably more so as a going business than just the sum of its assets.

Every partnership, limited liability company, and multi-shareholder corporation should have a *buy-sell agreement*. This is a contract among the business owners that usually (1) restricts transfer of each owner's interest and (2) provides a procedure to purchase an owner's interest upon death, disability, or other departure.

The agreement keeps ownership among the original owners, unless they want to allow in new people. The old group may be relatively compatible; a newcomer is an unknown quantity.

The agreement also provides a means of "cashing out" or paying those who no longer want to own the company, or who have become disabled. A buyout—perhaps through a life insurance policy—can also step in to pay the estate of a deceased owner for his or her share of the business, or pay a disabled owner.

Usually the buy-sell agreement provides for annual payments to a retiring owner over several years.

> **Tip**
>
> Don't transfer a majority business interest to your potential successor until you are ready to leave, so you don't lose leverage within the company. Also, you might want to stipulate in the agreement that you can buy back the transferred interest should that person not be a worthy successor, with profits, or perhaps company growth, as a standard for that determination.

If you and your co-owners do not have a buy-sell agreement, you are courting disaster, particularly if the death of an owner is involved. The deceased's heirs may need money right away, which may not be available if he or she has not planned for that possibility.

Remember: Time Marches On

Many owners select one form of ownership style, go on to do business, and forget about that set-up. That's not a good idea. Their choice might still be the best one for them, but then again, maybe now it isn't. Decisions made initially in a business do not have to last forever. Indeed, some of them should be scrapped somewhere along the way.

A business is a living, evolving entity. Tax and business laws are constantly changing, too. When it's your business, consult your accountant and attorney every few years to be certain the ownership style you have chosen is still the most beneficial for you.

April, for example, set up her umbrella sales corporation several years ago. At that time her accountant and lawyer suggested that she elect to be taxed as an S corporation, which was appropriate for her early years. Now the business has grown, and profits have increased dramatically. She must pay taxes on those profits, most of which she leaves in the corporation.

April may want to consider switching to a C corporation tax status. The corporation pays the tax on its income. In addition, the C corporation allows more flexibility in employee nontaxable fringe benefits, such as group term life insurance and medical insurance.

Quote, Unquote

Work spares us from three great evils: boredom, vice and need.

—Voltaire, *Candide* (1759)

Will, Evan, Jeff, and Carl have gone the partnership route with their marina. They are concerned about personal liability for business debts, but they like the pass-through tax aspect of partnership. They might want to consider changing to a limited liability partnership, which eliminates personal liability while keeping the same partnership tax structure.

State business laws and tax laws, and federal tax laws, too, have become more flexible in allowing you to change from one entity to another. So always keep in the back of your mind the fact that there *could* be a better way of your doing business.

Treating Yourself Well as the Key Employee

If you aren't good to yourself, who will be? Here are some points to consider with a growing business.

The key employee is you, the owner. You can only improve your financial picture by either increasing your income or lowering your expenses. But you may be able to add more fringe benefits, many of which are tax free and all of which can make a weary businessperson feel a little prosperous and coddled. Some will make your employees feel better taken care of, too. Discuss the following "perks" with your accountant, who will be able to help you determine if you can afford them:

- Group term life insurance
- Education assistance
- Business travel
- Business meals

- Medical and dental insurance

- Health or other club membership for business purposes

- Business-related entertainment

- Help with dependent care—for employees' children or parents they're tending

- Tax-sheltered retirement plan

- Cafeteria plan of benefits (employees select what they want and can afford)

- Use of corporate vehicles

- Office in the home deduction

- Disability insurance

Watch Out

Want to operate your business from home? Many towns have zoning laws that prohibit home businesses in some neighborhoods. Often those laws are directed at the obvious: converting the front of a home to a shop, for example. Keep in mind any exterior alterations and parking spaces you will need. You might have to apply for a zoning variance—and you could be turned down.

When You Want to Sell

When the time comes to sell, your choice of entity will make a difference, tax and otherwise. Consider the following situations:

- As a *sole proprietor*, you're simply selling individual assets, and the classification of gain or loss depends on the nature of the assets. Capital assets, such as land, create capital gain, and ordinary income assets, such as inventory, create ordinary income.

   An aside here: For taxpayers in the highest bracket (35 percent), capital gain is attractive because for most assets it is taxed at 5 or 15 percent, depending upon the taxpayer's bracket. Ordinary income, however, may be taxed to the highest rate.

- *Partnerships* and *limited liability companies* usually have some ordinary income to report in the sale of the business, as well as capital gain.

Quote, Unquote

Some will rob you with a six gun / And some with a fountain pen.

—Woody Guthrie, "Pretty Boy Floyd"

Quote, Unquote

Perpetual devotion to what a man calls his business is only to be sustained by perpetual neglect of many other things.

—Robert Louis Stevenson (1850–94)

Drew and Elsa, for example, are partners in a business selling art works. The art is inventory, which results in ordinary income, while the building the partnership owns and sells at a gain is a capital asset. When the two sell their partnership, part of the sale will result in ordinary income, and part will be capital gain.

◆ *Corporate shareholders* own a capital asset—their stock—so when that is sold, they have a capital gain.

Taking a Broad View

For your information now, and your plans for a future that might be years down the road, sit back and do a little thinking about these aspects of your work, keeping in mind what you have just read as well as the following suggestions:

Tip

If you would like to ease into retirement and start letting your successor take over, it is likely he or she will want some ownership interest in your business. A corporation may issue shares to the successor. A partnership or limited liability company could increase its number of owners and rearrange profit sharing to accommodate him or her.

◆ *Analyze the current status of the business.* Most have a life cycle for their owner: beginning, turning the corner, and maturity. The business likely will be less valuable and have significant debt at the beginning. When it turns the corner and starts becoming profitable, then its value increases, although the debt may still be considerable if the business is expanding. The mature business is profitable and thus attractive to others.

Where is *your* business at this point? Ask yourself again when you are considering retiring or selling. And ask yourself when you are putting together an estate plan. What would happen to the business, and your heirs, if you were to die suddenly?

◆ *Consider the cash value of the business.* It could be at a stage where you may have few purchasers for it, and it also could be valuable only if *you* are able to run it. Again, you need life insurance and disability insurance to provide an adequate estate for your family. If there are purchasers willing to pay its fair market value, and you are ready to retire or sell, then less insurance may be needed.

> **Tip**
>
> Family corporations can restructure stock ownership to create a new class of stock for the retiring owner. Consult your attorney for the best means of doing this.

◆ *Review your buy-sell and other business arrangements, if you have co-owners.* Your heirs may not want to continue owning a share of the business after your death, so a plan to "cash out" your interest upon death should be an ingredient of your estate plan.

◆ *If you have a family business, plan for an orderly transfer of ownership when you want to retire.* Your retirement funds might come from your withdrawal from the business. You may be able to restructure the business ownership to provide for a gradual withdrawal, with the minimum of adverse tax consequences.

Talk over all of your prospective business moves with the appropriate members of your estate planning team, certainly your accountant and lawyer.

Keep in mind that your will, trust, and other estate planning documents may be virtually useless if you haven't considered how best to arrange your business to maximize your estate, while minimizing taxes. This is the "bottom line." I'm afraid it gives you plenty of work to do, but it's time and energy worth investing.

Finally, you'll find suggestions specifically for physicians, accountants, attorneys, and other professionals licensed by the state and in business for themselves, and for those engaged in farming, in Chapter 14.

The Least You Need to Know

◆ You have several choices of business entities from which to choose; study the legal ramifications of each carefully.

◆ Examine your pay and fringe benefits because you, the owner/employee, may be missing some tax-free benefits at little cost to you.

- If you and another person, or several other persons, co-own, then sign a buy-sell agreement to protect you and the business.

- Always keep in mind your business's current status, and how it figures in a typical business cycle.

Part 2

About Wills, Trusts ...
and Probate

Now we come—ta-da—to one of the most important parts of this book. In the pages that follow, you'll learn all about what should go into your will, and how to examine your family and financial situation so that you can prepare a solid document. You say you thought trusts were only for those whose incomes are somewhere up there in the stratosphere? You may be surprised to find that not only is that not true, but also that a trust might be just what you need right now, or something to consider down the road, when you've built up your assets a bit more.

Probate is an interesting, and to many a mysterious, process that transfers your assets from your estate to your heirs or beneficiaries. What exactly goes on here? I'll tell you. The mystery will be gone, but I'll replace it with a few interesting, sometimes quirky, probate stories.

No Will? No Good!

In This Chapter

- How your property is distributed if you don't have a will
- Understanding guardianship issues
- Deciding who administers your estate
- How spouses and children fare

If you're with me so far you're making good progress in your planning. You have just analyzed and recorded what you own and how you own it, giving you a clear idea of exactly what constitutes your estate. We're coming soon to one of the most important parts of this book—having a will prepared.

Are you at all reluctant about making your will, perhaps because you're put off by all the decisions and details that it entails, or maybe because you just don't like to even *think* about the inevitable? You're not alone; many people feel that way. But by the end of this chapter, I guarantee you'll feel differently.

When you don't have a will things can get pretty sticky, with a string of complications that could some day, if you'll excuse the expression, have you spinning in your grave.

Dying Intestate Is About as Bad as It Sounds

If you don't have a will when you die (that's what dying "intestate" means), you may have given your family another reason to mourn your loss. Without a will they must turn to state statutes to determine who your heirs are and how much of a share in your estate they are entitled to inherit. The state poking its nose into your family affairs? Yes indeed, that's exactly what they will do, down to your last penny.

When you don't get around to making a will, you give up the right to …

♦ Select the beneficiaries of your estate.

♦ Make gifts to close friends.

♦ Name the executor of your estate.

♦ Designate a guardian for your minor child.

> **Watch Out**
>
> Just as bad as having no will is having an outdated one. If there has been a marriage, death, birth, and maybe a divorce or two in your family since you wrote yours, then get thee to a lawyer for a new one. Otherwise, the old one will be honored (although the inheritance rights of children born since that document was made are protected).

Here are a few other complications you may leave behind if you die intestate. All will be covered in depth in upcoming chapters:

♦ Federal estate taxes could be higher without the full marital deduction you might be entitled to.

♦ State death taxes might take a larger share of your estate.

♦ Income savings may be lost.

♦ Probate expenses will be higher.

Ah, Probate

There's that word you often hear in the same breath with "wills" and "estates." It's usually said with a shudder. What does it mean, and can it really be that terrible?

Probate is commonly defined as a state court procedure administering the estate of a deceased resident, whether that individual died with a will or without one.

It is designed to apportion your estate according to your own wishes if you have a will, or according to how the state sees fit if you don't. Naturally, it is also created to see that your creditors are satisfied and that any legitimate taxes due on your estate are paid before assets are disbursed to your family and friends.

If an individual dies with a will, the presumed beneficiaries bring it to the probate court. If he or she dies intestate, again heirs come in, this time with a list of the deceased's (or decedent's, in legal parlance) assets that comprise an estate, in order to begin probate administration. They file a "petition for probate," a simple form that contains essential information needed by the court, such as name and address of the deceased, and names and addresses of relatives and likely heirs.

Most times the family member or other individual petitioning an intestate estate to be settled through probate must post a bond, to cover any loss to the estate caused by their negligence or malfeasance. That might be, oh, let's say a bond of $17,000, for which the executor might pay a fee, or a premium, of say $100 a year until the estate is settled (and most estates are settled in less than a year). That cost varies, however. The executor would go to a local insurance company that has bonding power to purchase the bond, and then would return with it to the court. The premium cost comes out of the estate, not the executor's pocket.

(You'll find out more about probate court in Chapter 10. I thought you needed to know a little about the process right now, in the context of dying intestate.)

Estate Exceptions

A *probate estate* is defined as property a probate court has to administer. But there is property that *doesn't* go through probate. Any property owned jointly with right of survivorship (see Chapter 3), distributions from any life insurance policies, a pension fund, and other investments with a named beneficiary skip probate and go directly to the person named.

As a matter of fact, with the above-named exclusions, sometimes there is little that *is* subject to probate. The deceased might have done this on purpose, to avoid having his or her heirs spend time and money in probate court. Sometimes, though, it's just a coincidence on the part of the deceased.

Also note that many states have a simplified procedure for small estates, such as those worth $25,000 or less, which permit transfer of the decedent's asset by an affidavit signed by an heir.

> **Quote, Unquote**
> When it comes time to divide an estate, the politest men quarrel.
> —Emerson, *Journals* (1863)

Speaking of heirs, I'll digress a little here for a brief explanation. Technically, the word "*heirs*" is used for those who inherit in an intestate estate, "*beneficiaries*" for those who inherit from a legitimate will. Sometimes the terms are used interchangeably. I'll try to keep them separate throughout these pages, but once in a while you'll probably find I've just used one word or the other.

How the State Determines Your Heirs

Once your assets—minus a will—land in probate court, the process of settling the estate begins. Here is an example of how that court's thinking might proceed, again noting there are slight differences among states.

Let's use a typical family as an example. Albert is married to Susan. They have three adult children: Ken, Betty, and Clark. Ken has one child, Alice; Betty has no children; Clark has two, Chloe and Charity. Albert's father is deceased, but his mother is alive.

Albert dies without a will. Who inherits his probate estate?

In many states, that estate would be divided as follows: one half to Albert's wife, and one half divided equally among each of his children.

Some states give everything to the spouse, while others would give the spouse a specified amount of money from the estate, plus one half of the rest of it.

Albert's mother and his grandchildren would receive nothing.

Let's vary Albert's situation a little. Here are some other relationship possibilities for him:

 ◆ Let's say Susan is his second wife, and the children are all from his first marriage.

> **Quote, Unquote**
>
> Once in every half-century, at longest, a family should be merged into the great, obscure mass of humanity, and forget all about its ancestors.
>
> —Nathaniel Hawthorne, *The House of the Seven Gables*

Susan may receive only one third of the probate estate and Albert's children share the balance. Some states give the subsequent spouse, who had no children with the deceased, less than half the estate.

Once again, Albert's mother and his grandchildren receive nothing.

If there is no surviving spouse, but there are children, then the children receive the entire probate estate.

Grandchildren inherit their deceased parent's share. So if Clark were deceased at the time of Albert's death, his two girls Chloe and Charity would inherit Clark's share of his father's estate.

◆ If Albert were single—there is no surviving spouse and no surviving children— then most state intestate laws divide the probate estate among the parents and siblings. If the parents are deceased, then it is just among the siblings.

If Albert had no brothers or sisters, the estate could be divided among his grandparents, if they are living, and aunts, uncles, and cousins.

◆ If Albert were single but had been in a 10-year, live-in relationship with Lee, then since Albert died without a will Lee would come in for no portion at all of Albert's estate. (There is more about "living together" outside of marriage in Chapter 14.)

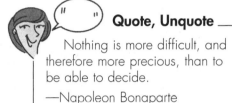

Quote, Unquote

Nothing is more difficult, and therefore more precious, than to be able to decide.

—Napoleon Bonaparte

If you're preparing a will, you can apply all of the above family situations to your own position, and discuss with your attorney just who you want your beneficiaries to be.

The following table helps you see at a glance how states typically divide the estate of a resident who dies without a valid will.

Dying Without a Will: How the State* Is Likely to Divide Your Estate

If You Are:	Your Property Will Go:
unmarried with no children, parents alive	to your parents and possibly brothers and sisters as well
unmarried with no children, parents dead	to your brothers and sisters; if an only child, to other next of kin: grandparents, aunts, etc.
unmarried with children	to your children, but not stepchildren; the court also appoints a guardian for minors
unmarried with no relatives	to the state
married with children	often divided between spouse and children
married with no children	usually to the surviving spouse, or part to the spouse and part to your parents, perhaps even siblings

State laws vary slightly regarding intestate property distribution.

The State Specifies the Guardian, Too

If you have minor children (under the age of 18), and your spouse survives you, then you won't need a guardian. However, if the other parent is not alive, or is not capable of caring for the minor children, or you have a child of any age with special needs, then a guardian is necessary for them if you die.

Naturally, parents of young children should appoint a guardian for them in the event they both die at the same time. Naming a guardian is especially important in a one-parent situation.

Let's consider Jane's situation. It is a potential guardianship nightmare because there is no will. Her husband passed away several years ago. Jane has two minor children, Jason and Joan, both in their early teens. Because Jane doesn't have a will designating who will be guardian, then state law takes over.

Whom would the state appoint? Well, grandparents and siblings are usually in line for that appointment. If they agree on who will care for the child, fine. But if they cannot, then a court battle may ensue.

It's bad enough to have relatives fighting over child custody. Worse yet is when *no* family member wants the child or children. Perhaps both sets of grandparents in Jane's situation define their golden years as not including child rearing. And Jane's siblings might have children of their own and say quite frankly they don't want to be responsible right now for a couple of teenagers.

Watch Out

It's trendy, but is it legal? If you'd like to try "shooting" a video will, which is a videocassette of you reading your will out loud—and probably with comments from you throughout—you ought to consult a lawyer to see whether your state law permits a video will to substitute for a proper written one. The video might only be considered a supplement to a written will.

What happens then?

Jane might have a close friend who would be competent, and quite capable and willing, to serve as guardian. But the friend might not be able to take on that role without being nominated in Jane's will. Can Jane's kids recommend that friend? Sure, and because they are older children, the judge is likely to listen to their recommendation and seriously consider that nominee.

But if there is absolutely no one to take Jane's kids, the kids become a ward of the state and are then placed in a foster home. They are, after all, orphans.

If you have a will, name a primary and alternate guardian to be sure that one will serve. Always get that family member's or friend's permission before naming him or her as guardian. A guardian is not required to serve just because you name that individual.

You can see that a will matters with property, but that it is absolutely vital when it comes to the welfare of your children. (For more about guardianship, see Chapter 12.)

The Administrator: It Could Be a Stranger

The *executor* of an estate is a person nominated to handle the disposition of that property according to the wishes of the deceased. We'll get into that role in more detail in Chapter 10.

The *administrator* of an estate is an individual, typically the spouse or child, appointed by the probate court to handle that function for the deceased who dies intestate. The administrator handles the paperwork of an estate, such as composing a list of the deceased's assets, hearing from likely heirs, processing claims from creditors, and the like.

Here's yet another reason why you should have a will: although you are apt to ask a relative or friend to be your executor, if you die without a will the state might appoint a stranger to handle your estate and deal with your family on estate-related, certainly personal, matters. The judge has quite a bit of leeway in appointing an administrator, and could even name a friend of his to that position.

The administrator usually is paid for his or her services. Fees run quite a wide range. I hesitate to offer even a ballpark figure because so much depends on the size of the estate and the amount of work facing the administrator. But I'd say perhaps that fee could be as much as 5 percent of the estate's worth. It is paid from the estate before any part of it is disbursed to heirs.

> **Tip**
>
> Here's another good news/bad news reason for having a will. The good news: if you die in an accident of some kind, a court could bring in a sizable judgment, payable to your estate. You'd certainly want that money to go to specific loved ones. (The bad news? You're not around, of course, to enjoy the windfall.)

Divorce, Remarriage—and No Will

There are complications here, too, as you might imagine.

Consider Hank and Wanda. The couple both work outside the home. Wanda had been previously married and has one child from that union, Willie, who is under 18. Hank likewise had had an earlier marriage, and he has two minor children: Hank Jr. and Karen. Hank and Wanda have one minor child, Holly.

Wanda has custody of Willie; Hank does not have custody of his children from the prior marriage.

Wanda dies suddenly. She does not have a will. Let's look at possible consequences:

♦ **Inheritance.** Wanda owned the house where she and Hank lived, and she had a substantial investment in stocks and bonds in her own name, all of which is in her probate estate. What happens to that property?

In most states the surviving spouse, Hank, will have to divide ownership of the house and investments with Wanda's child of her previous marriage, Willie, and his and Wanda's daughter, Holly, as follows: half to the spouse, and one quarter to each child.

Whether Hank can continue living in the house is a question; he may have to pay rent to the children for their share, or the estate may have to sell the house. Is this what Wanda would have wanted?

♦ **Probate administration.** The surviving spouse is usually, but not always, appointed administrator. If Hank is named to that position, very likely his administration will be closely scrutinized by the child from the prior marriage (Willie) and/or his supporters (his biological father, for example, or a maternal aunt). Because of a potential conflict there, a simplified probate provided for by many states might not be available (because all the heirs would have to consent to use such a procedure), so estate expenses could be considerably higher, due to added attorney time, than they would have been if Wanda had had that will.

♦ **Guardianship.** Hank and Wanda's child will have Hank around to serve as her guardian. Wanda's son from her prior marriage may have his father appointed as guardian. If the father has been out of Willie's life for years, that may not be a viable option. Hank could be the seemingly likely choice, but he might not be chosen by the court, which could favor the biological father. This could be quite a lengthy, even messy, issue.

An additional worry: The guardian manages the minor's money until he or she is 18 years old. What if Wanda's previous spouse had made a career of maxing out credit cards?

◆ **Death taxes.**   The tax situation will be worse for Wanda's estate because she has no will. We'll get into tax unpleasantries in detail in Part 4 of this book.

◆ **Simultaneous death of spouses.**   Finally, with this couple, we must consider what could happen if both Hank and Wanda died at the same time, in a boating accident, say, or a car or plane crash. Of course neither has a will. All of the problems we just discussed remain, or are magnified. Now we also have an orphan—their child, Holly.

The state would likely split the house and investments that Wanda owned solely as follows: one half to Willie and one half to Holly.

Any property that Hank owned solely at his death (which in this example is simultaneous with Wanda's, remember) would likely be shared by Hank Jr., Karen, and Holly. However, those children may or may not have a claim for child support from the estate during the rest of their minority, so they may be in financial distress. Children in some states can make a claim for child support from an estate, sometimes until they are 17 or 18, sometimes up to age 21, which can include college expenses. Naturally, Wanda's son Willie could make the same claim against Wanda's estate.

Any property the two owned jointly as spousal property would be equally divided and put into each estate. For example, Hank's estate would be distributed this way: one third each to Hank Jr. and Karen (children of a previous marriage) and one third to Holly (child of a current marriage). Wanda's share would be divided equally between Willie and Holly.

You'll learn more about simultaneous death of spouses, both with and without a will, in Chapter 11.

> **Tip**
>
> A written (typed or computer-printed) will is best. However, some states will recognize an *oral* will or a *holographic* will—one that's handwritten and unwitnessed. A few states have will forms where blanks can be filled in, which is not likely to be useful if you have a large or complicated estate. Check with your state's probate court to be sure what you have in mind is acceptable.

Adoption

Adopted children inherit from their adopting parents. In most states the adopted child will not automatically inherit through the biological parent, unless that parent is married to the adopting parent.

So let's look at Al, who adopted Ally, the daughter of his wife, Tracy, from a prior marriage. He and Tracy have a child of their own from their marriage, a son, Cory. Al has no will. If he dies, his probate estate will be divided like this: one half to his wife and one half divided equally between the adopted child (Ally) and the biological child (Cory). If he had not adopted Ally, she would have received nothing from his estate.

And Children Born Out of Wedlock

Social Security, child support, survivor's rights, and inheritance are but a few heavy legal issues swirling around children born out of wedlock.

Clearly, a child born out of wedlock can inherit automatically from his or her mother. What is less certain is the child's inheritance (not to mention support) rights from the father.

Most state laws provide that the child may inherit from the father if paternity is established in court or the father marries the mother and acknowledges the child born out of wedlock as his child.

A *paternity suit* is a court action to have it acknowledged that a man is the father of a specified child and, usually, to secure financial support for that child by that father.

Paternity actions require the assistance of the mother, who is often reluctant to bring the lawsuit. If a paternity action is initiated, blood tests will disclose whether that man is the biological father.

If no paternity action is taken and the biological parents don't marry, then the child will not be able to inherit automatically from the father or the father's parents without a will.

Have I motivated—or perhaps scared—you into writing a will yet? Good. Now you're ready for the next chapter, in which I'll explain to you just how to go about it.

The Least You Need to Know

- ◆ If you die without a will, state law specifies who inherits your probate estate.

- ◆ If you are married when you die and there's no will, your spouse will usually receive half of your probate estate and your children divide the other half.

- ◆ The court appoints a probate administrator and a guardian for your children if you have no will.

- ◆ Adopted children inherit automatically from the adopting parent, but step-children do not when there is no will.

Chapter 8

The Basic Will, and a Few Extras

In This Chapter

- Identifying yourself in your will
- Arranging for your taxes and bills to get paid first
- Determining who gets what
- Avoiding snags

Now we come to the most important element of your estate plan: your will. Here you decide (a) who will inherit your property (beneficiaries); (b) who will administer your estate (executor); and (c) who will take care of your minor children (guardian).

For the person with an average estate (certainly under $1,500,000, sometimes several hundred thousand dollars under) and a rather uncomplicated business and family life, preparing a will is not difficult work, and the document needn't be long, as you'll see. Short, but important. Let's start.

First, Do You Know Where You Live?

That's certainly a silly question. Or is it? Some of you might have a home here and another one there, perhaps a vacation home—or two.

For purposes of your will, you must clearly designate your legal residence. That is likely to be your voting address, where you have your driver's license, and where you file tax returns. It is important to use that address—and have evidence backing it up in the form of those documents—to determine the county and state where your will is submitted to probate court administration.

If there is no clear evidence of your legal residence, each state where you have a home could claim death taxes against your estate. (For more about which state to make your legal residence, as that decision applies to tax matters, see Chapter 19.)

Words, Words, Words

Lawyers use the word **domicile** a lot. In legal documents it means your permanent residence.

Tip

You can pay anywhere from around $100 to $250 for a will. The fee depends on how complicated the will is and price ranges of individual law firms.

Another complication might be that one state in which you own property is a community property state and the other is a common law property state (any state that is not a community property state), so that some property may be considered community property (husband and wife) even in a common law state.

Incidentally, if you own real estate in a second state, probate proceedings may be required in that second state to transfer title to your beneficiary. This means that if, for instance, you are a legal resident of New Jersey, and have a second home, say, in Florida, probate will occur in New Jersey for all of your estate except your Florida house. There will be a limited probate, or *ancillary administration*, for the Florida property.

You should look to a Florida financial institution, or a trusted relative living in Florida, to be your ancillary executor for the property located there. A Florida bank or Florida attorney can help you.

The Simple Will

It helps to see what's being described in text, so I've reproduced a sample will on the following pages for you to follow along with me. It's a basic, very brief document that

I call "bare bones." It's for a woman who is rather typical in that she leaves everything to her next of kin, which in this case are her spouse and children. She made no other bequests.

You will see from time to time in this chapter and in a few others, that I suggest clauses that should be added to any will. Heed my advice. They are not in the will reproduced here because, as I said, this is a bare bones document just to show you what absolutely must go into a will, not necessarily what also should or could.

I'll explain this will practically line byline so that it's crystal clear to you. Im-mediately following the will you'll see another document called "Self-Proving Provision." It is attached to a finished will, and I'll explain its purpose after discussing the bare bones will.

First, though, I'll issue the caution you're expecting when you come across a legal form in this book: because state laws vary with regard to an enforceable will, do not adopt this as a will form for yourself without being certain it is valid where you live.

> **Tip**
>
> Did you pay for tax advice in connection with writing your will? If so, you're entitled to a federal tax deduction. Ask your lawyer to itemize your bill. I know what you're probably thinking now, but no, you can't deduct an attorney's bill for preparing a will document.

Introduction

The introduction introduces the name and residence of the person making the will, and—very important—revokes any prior wills and codicils by that individual. A *codicil* is an amendment to a previous will. (*A warning here:* If you begin rearranging assets and beneficiaries in a codicil, you're running the risk of having your will challenged, or contested, by a beneficiary or heir. If you need to make a codicil, keep it short and simple, such as changing your executor from one person to another. If it's much more complicated, then write a new will.)

Use your legal name on your will, of course. That is the name that should appear on all your official papers, such as deeds to real estate, stock certificates, insurance policies, and the like. Problems for your estate *could* arise if, for example, you were to refer to yourself on a legal document as Biff Hanover instead of Barton T. Hanover.

LAST WILL AND TESTAMENT OF

_____

I, _____, of _____, being of sound and disposing mind and memory, do make, publish, and declare this to be my Last Will and Testament, and I hereby revoke all Wills and Codicils heretofore made by me.

I. Identification, Definitions, Comments

   A. I am married to _____. I have _____ children:

      _____

   B. A beneficiary must survive me by thirty (30) days to be entitled to receive a devise.

   C. "Issue" is to be construed as lawful lineal descendants, and include adopted persons.

Issue shall receive any devise by representation.

II. Debts, Expenses, Encumbrances, Taxes

   A. I direct that my enforceable debts, expenses of my last illness, and funeral and administrative expenses of my estate shall be paid by my personal representative from my residuary estate. In his or her discretion, my personal representative may continue to pay any installment obligations incurred by me during my lifetime on an installment basis or may prepay any or all of such obligations in whole or in part, and my personal representative may, in his or her discretion, distribute any asset encumbered by such an obligation subject to the obligation.

   B. I direct that all inheritance, estate, and succession taxes (including interest and penalties thereon) payable by reason of my death shall be paid out of and be charged generally against my residuary estate without reimbursement from any person.

III. Specific Devises

I devise all my personal effects and household goods, such as jewelry, clothing, furniture, furnishings, silver, books, pictures, motor and recreation vehicles to _____. If he does not survive me, I devise said property, in equal shares, to _____. If a child does not survive me, then his or her share devolves to the deceased child's issue, or if none survive me, then the share devolves, equally, to the surviving children.

IV. Residuary Estate

I devise my residuary estate to _____. If he does not survive me, I devise my residuary estate, in equal shares, to _____. If a child does not survive me, then his or her share devolves to the deceased child's issue, or if none survive me, then the share devolves, equally, to the surviving children.

V. Personal Representative

I hereby appoint _____ as personal representative. If he cannot serve, I appoint _____ as personal representative. I authorize unsupervised administration of my estate. I request that the personal representative serve without bond, or if a bond is required, that a minimum bond be required. My personal representative shall have all powers enumerated and granted to personal representatives under the Probate Code, and any other power that may be granted by law, to be exercised without the necessity of Court approval, as my personal representative determines to be in the best interest of the estate.

VI. Miscellaneous

If my spouse and I executed Wills at approximately the same time, this Last Will and Testament is not made pursuant to any contract or agreement with my spouse.

I have signed this Last Will and Testament in the presence of the undersigned witnesses on this day of _____, 20__ .

_____

testatrix

The foregoing instrument, consisting of two typewritten pages, this included, was at _____ (city, state), this _____ day of, 20__, signed, sealed, published, and declared by the testatrix to be her Last Will and Testament, in our presence, and we, at her request and in her presence and in the presence of each other, have hereunto subscribed our names as attesting witnesses.

_____ residing at _____.
_____ residing at _____.

Self-Proving Provision

UNDER PENALTIES FOR PERJURY, we, _____, and _____ , the testatrix and the witnesses, respectively, whose names are signed to the foregoing instrument, declare:

(1) that the testatrix executed the instrument and signified to the witnesses that the instrument is her will;

(2) that, in the presence of both witnesses, the testatrix signed this will;

(3) that the testatrix executed this will as her free and voluntary act for the purposes expressed in it;

(4) that each of the witnesses, in the presence of the testatrix and of each other, signed the will as witness;

(5) that the testatrix was of sound mind when the will was executed; and

(6) that to the best knowledge of each of the witnesses, the testatrix was, at the time the will was executed, eighteen (18) or more years of age.

Date: _____, 20____

_____, testatrix

_____
Witness

_____
Witness

I. Identification, Definitions, Comments

The document in Paragraph A. asks for your spouse's name, if you are married, and the number and names of your children, if you have them.

Careful identification of your beneficiaries by name avoids possible confusion. Fathers and sons often have the same name as cousins, so stating your relationship with the person is essential for identifying them.

Paragraph I.B. seems self-explanatory, until you get to the word *devise*. In legal terminology, that means gift. The first sentence in Paragraph I.C. is understandable. But what is that legalese in the second sentence? (Could it, by chance, have been written by a lawyer?) Essentially it means that *issue* (or grandchildren) shall receive any gifts by taking their deceased parent's share that happens to pass on to them through the grandparent's will.

Words, Words, Words

The word **testament** means a disposition, or distribution, of personal property to take place after the owner's death, according to his desire and direction. It is used, of course, in the expression "last will and testament."

Words, Words, Words

Issue is just another name for descendant. Thus you are the descendant or issue of your father and mother, and your children are descendants, or issue, of you and their grandparents.

II. Debts, Expenses, Encumbrances, Taxes

In Paragraph II.A. that first sentence seems clear. *Residuary estate* means what is left in an estate after debts, taxes, and other expenses are deducted and other gifts or bequests made. You'll see that term often in the next chapter. *My personal representative* is the executor. Here you are asking your executor to keep paying installment bills, such as a mortgage, perhaps until the estate is settled.

Tip

You can forget about awarding a family member $1 in your will so that he or she cannot contest that document and claim the right to more. That $1 business is the legal equivalent of an old wives' tale.

Let's say you own a cabin by the water, or a cabin cruiser in the water. You leave it to your son. It has a mortgage or other lien, or financial obligation/debt, perhaps a bank loan, against it. In many states your son inherits that property subject to that mortgage or lien. If you want him to have the property free of debt, then you need to specify in your will that the estate pay off that debt.

Paragraph B. directs that all due taxes be paid from the estate. I'll get into what those taxes are likely to be in subsequent chapters.

III. Specific Devises

Here we talk about particular gifts you want to make. This can be almost the fun part of a will, where you look at your possessions and, like royalty, proclaim "I bequeath my stamp collection to …" and so on. You will read more about some different kinds of specific devises later in this chapter.

Listing their current home address after the names of your beneficiaries is not necessary with family members. Believe me, if someone is in your will they will hear about it and will be there to come forward for their bequest. Besides, people do move frequently and addresses become outdated. Friends might be another matter. If you are leaving your sterling silver tea set to a good friend, you might include her address. It will give an executor a place to start with a search, because the family might not know your friend, or have kept up with her moves over the years.

IV. Residuary Estate

Section IV seems pretty clear. In the third line, the word *devolves* means *goes to*.

Remember, no one can be awarded anything from your will until your debts and taxes have been paid.

> **Watch Out**
>
> It's best not to make a separate list for special gifts and then attach that list to your will. If you want specific items to go to certain individuals, then make those bequests in the will. Many courts do not consider the separate list as part of the will, and do not allow the executor to honor the list.

> **Words, Words, Words**
>
> Alas, legal terminology remains politically unfashionable in some ways. For example, **executor** is used for a male in that position, **executrix** for a female. A **testatrix** is a woman signing her will, a **testator** a man. For ease in reading, I'm using "executor" and, if the occasion arises, "testator" throughout this book.

V. Personal Representative

Here's another section that seems pretty obvious. I'll talk more about executors in Chapter 10.

VI. Miscellaneous

What does that first sentence in section VI mean? Briefly, it is there so that no one interprets the survivor's will as unchangeable, written with the spouse as a two-will package. Her spouse's will, if he has one, is a separate document. And this woman *can* write another version of her own will at any time she chooses.

Your lawyer will bring in two witnesses from his office. They must not stand to inherit from the will, and they must "witness" your signing that document in their presence. (If you worry about strangers seeing your will, there is no need. The lawyer can cover all but the signature lines for the witnesses.)

Finally we come to the document titled "Self-Proving Provision," which is filed along with this woman's will. It is a common for such a document to be attached to a will. It avoids the need for witnesses to come to court to identify the signature of the deceased on the will, which is otherwise usually mandatory.

How to Distribute Your Worldly Goods

In Part 1 you read how to list your assets, and how you own them. What you need to do now is figure out what property you can leave in a will, and exactly what you'd like to bequeath to family and friends before making out that document.

Take a look at the Estate Planning Information Sheet you prepared in Chapter 2. You know that property owned jointly with right of survivorship goes automatically to that other owner and need not be mentioned in a will. Property that names a beneficiary, like a life insurance policy, also avoids probate.

However, if you have any of the following assets, they are distributed in your will:

♦ Solely owned property

♦ Property held as tenants in common

♦ Your share of community property

♦ Life insurance, retirement plan, or employee death benefits, or any similar asset with no named beneficiary

Here's a worksheet to fill in that will help you sort out what you can bequeath, and whom you would like to receive that property. You might want to work this out in pencil—you could change your mind a few times before deciding on final dispositions.

Will Worksheet

Here's some homework. Doing it will help you see what assets you have to leave in a will and, if you bequeath them to anyone at all, whom you would choose. This is just a scratch sheet to help you in thinking about bequests, so mark it up as much as you like.

In column one, "Assets," you might, for example, list your condominium. In column two, you could jot down 'solely.' In the third column you might write 'no.' Then, under 'I'll leave it to:' in column four, you can name the person you'd like to inherit the property if you do not own it jointly, or if you have already named a beneficiary.

Asset	How I own it	Does anyone automatically inherit?	I'll leave it to:
_____	_____	_____	_____
_____	_____	_____	_____
_____	_____	_____	_____
_____	_____	_____	_____
_____	_____	_____	_____
_____	_____	_____	_____
_____	_____	_____	_____
_____	_____	_____	_____
_____	_____	_____	_____
_____	_____	_____	_____
_____	_____	_____	_____
_____	_____	_____	_____
_____	_____	_____	_____
_____	_____	_____	_____
_____	_____	_____	_____
_____	_____	_____	_____
_____	_____	_____	_____
_____	_____	_____	_____
_____	_____	_____	_____
_____	_____	_____	_____

Who Gets What

If you are single, you will probably leave assets owned by you alone to anyone you choose—parents, siblings, a significant other, friends. There is no usual "order" here.

If you are married, you probably want your spouse to inherit, and can so specify in your will. Your children are likely to be next in line. Who receives what and in what percentage is up to you—or almost. Please read Chapters 12 and 13 about spousal and family rights before finalizing your disbursements to see if the information there affects your decisions.

> **Tip**
>
> Can you present your will out loud, just by speaking it? An oral will, usually in the presence of witnesses, is recognized by a few states. Usually it is limited to those on their deathbed, and those in military service. It may dispose of personal property only, and is limited to no more than $1,000 of that property.

How They Get It: The Specific Devise

You usually provide for the distribution of tangible personal property, such as household goods, automobiles, antiques and collectibles, tools, jewelry, and sporting equipment in the specific devise section of your will.

> **Tip**
>
> If you have keepsakes or family heirlooms, consider asking your children now if they wish one day to inherit specific items that might have special meaning for them.

I once had a client who owned an extensive collection of Hummel figurines. She bequeathed each one to a different family member or friend, a list that ran two single-spaced legal size pages. That was her prerogative, of course, and many people do leave specific items that do not necessarily have monetary worth, but perhaps have heirloom or memento value to family and close friends. Specific devises may be for specific property, for a sum of money, or from a specific source. For example, you could say:

I devise my diamond wedding ring to …

I devise the sum of Five Hundred Dollars to …

I devise one half of my Trustworthy Bank savings account to …

Often you will have several beneficiaries named as co-beneficiaries in your specific devises. You should consider how amicably they will divide that property. If you believe amicable won't enter into it, then your will should carry a provision specifying a method of selection, such as rotation among the children, with specific dollar limits for each rotation. For instance, let's say that Sandy, Ginger, and Toni are each allowed to select $1,000 of personal property from your estate. They can make their selection in whatever order you like, perhaps with Sandy, the oldest, going first, then Ginger, and finally Toni, the youngest, choosing. The next $1,000 of property is rotated, with Toni now having first dibs on the remainder of the property, with Ginger next, and Sandy following her. That should keep everyone happy and not bickering over the tea towels.

When Beneficiaries Die Before You

You need to consider that the person given the specific devise might not survive you. The provision "I bequeath my Rolex watch to my cousin, Fay Summersby, if she survives me" is preferable to just bequeathing the watch to Fay. If you don't name an alternative to Fay, the watch will go to the residuary beneficiary, who receives the balance of the estate after the specific devises.

Many states—and you can ask your lawyer if yours is one—have an *anti-lapse law*, which provides that another of your descendants will receive the specific devise from your will if the descendant you named did not survive you.

Here's how that works. Suppose that the following list represents your family:

You and your spouse

Your daughter, Debbie

Your daughter's child, Geraldine Carole

Your daughter's grandchild, Georgia Gloria

In your will you left a specific devise of your grandmother's ruby ring to your daughter, Debbie. If your daughter predeceases you and you haven't made a new will, then the anti-lapse statute would automatically provide that her child, Geraldine Carole, your granddaughter, would receive the ring.

The anti-lapse statute only applies to descendants. For example, if in your will you leave me $1,000—for which I truly thank you—and if I die before you do, because my descendants aren't yours, they receive nothing. If no one is alive to receive that ring, it goes to the residuary beneficiaries in the will.

Or When You No Longer Own What You've Willed

Let's leave the anti-lapse statute, and consider another potential problem with wording in a will. Let's say you leave your collection of baseball cards to your friend, Mickey. But then your mother, in a cleaning frenzy, tosses them out at some point (an often-told tale of woe). Or you sell the collection to George Steinbrenner. And you die without changing your will.

Common sense (not always applicable in the law!) would dictate that Mickey gets nothing. Your will only distributes what you own at your death, and the cards are now long gone. But more than one court has held that the equivalent amount in cash should be distributed to that beneficiary.

You might want to put the following phrase in the will:

"… if I own the collection at my death."

CAUTION

Watch Out _____

> Be very careful to identify beneficiaries specifically. No one receives anything from your will unless he, she, or it (such as a pet, which we'll get into later in this chapter) is named: Joseph Carl Turner, Spot, or the American Heart Association. You can identify a person as "child" or "my aunt," if you have only one of each, but if there are more than one, use the specific name. You can also name a class of benefices, such as "my nephews and nieces living at my death."

Here's still another occasion for misunderstanding. Let's suppose you want to leave "100 shares of Brewski Co. to my friend, Ted Foster." In these days of mergers and business tremors, strange things sometimes happen to corporate stock. Perhaps the best solution is to word this as follows: "I devise to Ted Foster the amount of stock I own in Brewski Co., or its corporate successor, at my death." That's better.

Finally here, add up all your specific devises to determine if they significantly reduce what the residuary beneficiaries receive under your will. After all, they are the persons you want to receive the bulk of your estate. Don't shortchange your family by being too generous to others in specific gifts.

How They Get It: The Residuary Devise

You may have an extended family of the yours, mine, and ours variety. In other words, you and your spouse each have children from a prior marriage, as well as children from this union.

Let's consider the possibilities here. Remember that the residuary beneficiary receives the balance of the estate after your special devises, and, of course, after debts have been satisfied.

Perhaps you want everything to go to your spouse. Fine, just say that in the will. What about the children? Therein might lie some difference of opinion between spouses (but remember, your will can be different from your spouse's). If, for example, you name your spouse as residuary beneficiary, but don't specify further, you have a problem if your spouse dies before you do. Your estate could go intestate because you do not have a surviving beneficiary by name. It's best to name an alternate beneficiary to your residuary estate. Using an alternate beneficiary class, such as "my children" would provide for the children should the spouse not survive. An appropriate clause might read like this:

> … if my brother, Seth A. Baker, does not survive me, then his share devolves to his children who survive me.

Do you think you might have more kids one day? Then you should provide for them in your will, too. State laws vary here, but most allow a child born after you make your will to inherit through the will even if he or she is not named. The safe practice, though, is to specify that possibility with a phrase like this:

> "to my daughter, Rose, and to any afterborn or adopted children of mine …"

Here's a reminder in passing: Children *can* be cut out of a will (except perhaps in Louisiana). I tell my college students they had better be *very* nice to their parents.

Also, you may choose to divide the residuary estate into several shares going to different persons or institutions. For example:

> I devise my residuary estate as follows: 45 percent to my brother, Seth A. Baker; 45 percent to my sister, Charlene C. Dewey; 10 percent to the University of Indianapolis.

Briefs

Jack Kelly, self-made Philadelphia millionaire and father of the actress Grace Kelly, wrote his own will. "For years," it went, "I have been reading Last Wills and Testaments, and I have never been able to clearly understand any of them at one reading. Therefore, I will attempt to write my own will in the hope that it will be understandable and legal. Kids will be called "kids" and not "issue," and it will not be cluttered up with "parties of the first part," "per stirpes," "perpetuities," "quasi-judicial," "to wit," and a lot of other terms that I am sure are only used to confuse those for whose benefit it is written. This is my Last Will and Testament and I believe I am of sound mind. (Some lawyers will question this when they read my Will; however, I have my opinion of some of them, so that makes it even.)"

Hey, What About Rover?

Oh, yes, your pets. I wouldn't think of forgetting them. If you are married, your spouse will probably take over caring for Fluffy and Spot. But if you are single, you'd had better give some thought to who *will* care for those animals after you're gone.

Remember, if you die intestate, a judge will decide who gets the animals. If you have a will, you have more control over their fate.

Before naming a beneficiary for Fluffy and Spot, it's smart to ask the person you'd like to be responsible for them whether he or she would be willing to take care of the animals. Even smarter is to name an alternate in the event your first choice is unable to come through. You might want to include a small (or larger, if you can afford it) sum of money as a gift to that individual for taking over the care of your pet. If you have a quite sizable estate, you probably have a trust and can authorize payment to that person periodically for your pet's care. If you find no one willing to take your animal(s), you might look into humane societies in your area that accept household pets, giving them a home there for the remainder of their lives.

If there's any doubt about who will care for a beloved pet, resolving that concern can bring you as much peace of mind as having a will made. Perhaps more.

Tip

Twenty states allow you to create a trust for your pet's care during its life, with the remainder left to whomever you designate. Consult your attorney to see if a pet trust is appropriate. The Humane Society of the United States has an article, "Providing for Your Pet's Future Without You" on their website: www.hsus.org.

Now you know what a simple, and slightly more complex, will is. But before you run out to have one prepared—a quite commendable step—you will want to read the next chapter, about trusts. A trust could serve you better than a simple will. Also, there is more information in upcoming chapters that could have some bearing on the contents of your will. So continue reading and gathering information before having that document drawn.

The Least You Need to Know

♦ A will can be the simplest of documents, or as complex as your needs and wishes require.

♦ You have quite a bit of latitude in leaving what you solely own to anyone you choose.

♦ Wording is important in seeing that your gifts go to the beneficiary you select.

♦ Don't write your will just yet—continue reading.

Chapter 9

A Trust and a Will (The Best of Both Worlds?)

In This Chapter

- ◆ How a trust works
- ◆ Who a trust is for
- ◆ Living and testamentary trusts
- ◆ Selecting a trustee

Depending on the size of your estate, and what you would like it to accomplish for you, a trust can be an excellent financial tool.

A trust will see that your estate directives are carried out now, or that your assets are passed along to your beneficiaries. It can save you money, through your own funding of it and in tax strategies. In this chapter, you'll learn about these and other pluses to having a trust. Drawbacks? Well, of course there are a few. I'll talk about those as we go along, too.

Definition, Please

A *trust* is a legal instrument to hold and manage your real property, and your tangible and intangible personal property. Putting all of those assets into a trust transfers them from your ownership to the ownership of that entity known as the trust. That trust will hold the property for your benefit, or for the benefit of anyone you name.

> **Quote, Unquote**
>
> Money, big money (which is actually a relative concept), is always, under any circumstances, a seduction, a test of morals, a temptation to sin.
>
> —Boris Yeltsin, *The Struggle for Russia* (1994)

Trusts can be set up and run while you are alive, or you can prepare a *trust* as you would a will, to take effect upon your death. For example, in this chapter I'll talk about a *living* (or *inter vivos*) *trust* and a *testamentary trust*. Generally speaking, as you can pretty much determine from their names, the living trust is set up for use in your lifetime, and the testamentary trust comes into existence after your death, when your will is probated. Trusts used to be just for the very wealthy, or at least that's what most of us thought. But in the last decade or so, the use of trusts has grown significantly in popularity as more and more folks of less than millionaire means take advantage of their benefits. However, the workings of a trust are still not that well known by the average person. How a trust can help in estate planning is also a mystery to many.

What a Trust Offers that a Will Does Not

A trust has several advantages over a will. It …

◆ Manages property for you while you are alive.

◆ Can reduce your taxes, depending on how it is written and on laws in your state.

◆ Easily transfers your assets to beneficiaries after death.

◆ Could allow you more flexibility in how you dispose of your assets—for example, passing your money on to your children from a prior marriage while omitting your present spouse.

◆ Avoids probate, and its time and expense.

◆ Protects your privacy; it is not filed and open to public scrutiny the way a will is.

Who Would Want or Need a Trust?

People establish trusts for a number of reasons, but these are the main ones:

◆ **Minor children**   Parents might use a trust for minors after the parent's death, or for the special-needs child of any age throughout his or her life. You'll read about trusts for kids in Chapter 12.

◆ **Spendthrift children**   A trust can be set up for a child of any age thought to be unable to manage money prudently. I talk about a trust for the adult child (sounds like an oxymoron, doesn't it?) in this chapter.

◆ **Retirement management**   If you want a trust to manage your funds during your retirement, no problem. It can take care of you and your spouse when you can no longer look after your own affairs; read all about it in this chapter.

> **Tip**
>
> You can, if you like, skip generations in your trust, with income going to your children, and the principal secured for future grandkids.

◆ **Tax planning**   A trust can help you in a number of ways here, not the least of which is legitimate tax avoidance, always a welcome benefit of any estate plan. If your estate is more than $1,500,000, then you can certainly make use of a trust for tax savings.

◆ **The charitable trust**   You may be philanthropically inclined, and want to establish a trust, perhaps for worthy college students attending your alma mater. Or you might have a pet charity you'd like to contribute to in an ongoing way. Or you could participate in a trust already established by your favorite charity. The choice is yours. I explain charitable trusts in Chapter 18.

Who Does *Not* Need a Trust

Would a trust be right for you? That depends on the type of assets you own, the size of your estate, and your plans for it. If you have few assets right now—say you're young and single, or newly married and just starting out—you can skip a trust for a while. If none of the earlier-mentioned family or lifestyle situations quite fits your needs at the moment, you do not need a trust.

Keep in mind that a trust is likely to be more expensive to set up than having a will drawn. You might have to pay around $1,200 for a trust versus a couple of hundred dollars, or less, for a will. So a trust's cost alone might put off some people, which could be another good measuring device for deciding whether or not you need one.

Speaking of cost, by all means comparison-shop when looking for a lawyer to help you set up a trust. You should be able to do better than that high-end figure cited earlier.

Here's the Lingo

More words! Each area of the law has its own special terminology, of course. You've been introduced to many terms so far in this book. Here are a few more—words having to do with trusts that I'll be using in this chapter, with an explanation of each, to help you as you read on.

- **Creator**   This is the person who establishes, or sets up, the trust. That's you, in other words. The creator can also be called the *grantor, donor, settlor,* or *trustor.*

- **Beneficiary**   You probably have a handle on this term by now—it's the person who receives property, in this instance from the creator, according to the provisions of a trust.

- **Trustee**   This is the individual or institution entrusted to carry out the terms of the trust. So it's the person (or institution) who turns property owned by one person (you) over to another person, in accordance with your wishes as creator. A trustee also invests property for the beneficiary's benefit. A trustee can be a relative, friend, lawyer, or bank.

- **Successor trustee**   This is the second-string trustee, also known sometimes as the surviving trustee. He or she continues to manage assets in the trust should the primary trustee die or become incompetent.

- **Trust estate**   All the property legally transferred to the trust by the creator for the benefit of the beneficiary or beneficiaries.

- **Trust agreement**   This is the legal document itself, spelling out the terms of the trust and how it is to be administered.

> **Briefs**
>
> The Roman emperor Augustus (63 B.C.E.–14 C.E.) is said to have instituted trusts. They first appeared as a method of apportioning assets, for the most part to family members other than the oldest son, who otherwise was always the sole inheritor. Records credit Augustus with using a trust to try to make inheritance fairer for younger sons, who often suffered financially from inheritance customs.
>
> Thomas Jefferson set up a trust to avoid passing his estate to his bankrupt son-in-law, who otherwise would have controlled Jefferson's daughter's property (those were the days before women could own property in their own name).

One Choice: The Testamentary Trust

A *testamentary trust* is a directive established in a will and becomes effective when the will is probated. It isn't a separate document from a will; rather, it's incorporated into a will. Your assets are transferred to the trustee as if the trustee were the beneficiary of the will (which he is in a way because he's holding your property for the real beneficiary). For example, the wording might be "I devise my residuary estate to ABC Company as trustee for my sons, John and Jeffrey."

The trust survives probate and continues to exist for as long as you, the creator, have designated. A standard will, of course, is wrapped up and the assets distributed after probate proceedings.

Tip

Keep in mind a trust might not exist forever. It can last until a date you specify in the trust document, or upon a particular event—the date a young child reaches a particular age, for instance, or the amount in the trust is too small to administer, such as under $50,000. Many states limit a noncharitable trust to 90 years.

Downside to This Kind of Trust

With a testamentary trust your assets have to go through probate and are subject to creditor's claims. So if your goal is to avoid probate, you'd be better off setting up a living trust.

Another Choice: The Living Trust

A *living trust* is a legal instrument established during its creator's life. It might serve as a partial substitute for a will. At the death of the person creating the trust, his or her assets are distributed to beneficiaries according to the terms specified in the trust.

CAUTION

Watch Out

Don't confuse a living trust with a living will. The latter relates specifically to health matters. There's more about living wills in Chapter 23.

You designate a trustee, who can be your spouse, another person, or a financial institution, like a bank's trust department. If you have a living will, you can be your own trustee. It's your choice (you'll read about choosing a trustee later).

A living trust would also be a good choice for any "adult child" who perhaps spends too freely. Or you might have an older child who, at the moment, abuses drugs or alcohol. The umbrella term for a solution in those situations is known as the *spendthrift trust*, and is set up to prevent that child from spending a legacy foolishly. With this trust, specified amounts of money are released periodically to the beneficiary rather than a lump sum as in the case of most bequests. For a child who unwisely chooses a mate, you might want to restrict access for ex-spousal support.

A living trust can be established in either of two forms: revocable or irrevocable. You must determine which you want at the time the trust is set up. Let's first take a look at revocable living trusts.

Tip

If you act as your own trustee, you are likely to specify that the alternate trustee begin serving when you become incompetent. Who makes that decision? You might put into the trust agreement a clause stating that there must be medical evidence of incompetence from your own physician. A lawyer can help you with the wording, in accordance with your wishes.

Revocable Living Trust

This type of trust gives you the freedom to sell, spend, or give away your assets while you are still alive. You can also change any of the trust's conditions.

A revocable living trust may be an important part of your estate plan. It isn't for everyone, but it does have some features that warrant your attention:

◆ Assets in the trust pass to the trust beneficiaries outside of probate.

◆ Creator(s) can serve as trustees or select another to serve.

- ◆ The alternate trustee can serve when the creator/trustee is no longer capable.

- ◆ The trust can receive assets from the creator and the creator's estate.

The revocable living trust does not have any special tax advantages, because all income is taxed to the creator, and the assets are subject to federal estate taxes upon the creator's death.

On the following pages is a sample of such a trust, to give you an idea what such a document can contain.

Irrevocable Living Trust

Irrevocable trusts allow you to make a gift of property while you are still alive. That gift is then subject to federal gift tax, which must be paid by the donor (see Chapter 17 for a discussion of federal gift taxes), but is exempt from federal estate taxes. What's the downside? You forfeit all control of the trust in order to receive the federal estate tax exemption. So you'd better be careful: once this trust is established, it is impossible to revise.

When does it make sense to consider an irrevocable trust? If you're wealthy and want to minimize estate taxes, *and* you can afford to give away assets to others, such as children or grandchildren.

Let's look at the details.

Funding the Living Trust

You might want to *fund* the trust, which simply means putting some assets in it to begin with. Once a trust exists, you can add to it if the document allows you to do so. In some states you can set up a fund with just $1 to get it going. Trust language calls this the trust *res*, or *principal* (depending on whether you prefer the Latin or English version).

A living trust can have contingent funding, such as a life insurance policy payable to it, or be partially funded at the time it is established, with later additions. A trust can also be funded at the creator's death from his or her probate assets through the will, called a "pour over will" because the probate assets fund the trust.

CAUTION **Watch Out**

Putting your money in a trust *could* jeopardize a homestead exemption, which is a local or state government reduction in your property taxes, or cause your property to be reassessed for real estate tax purposes. You'll want to look into those possibilities before taking any actions.

The trust principal is invested and generates income, which the IRS likes to see because it can tax that money (the state might tax it, too). That principal may be distributed to you if you have established a revocable living trust and made yourself a beneficiary. Similarly, you have access to the income. Any trust income is taxed to the creator of the trust.

REVOCABLE TRUST AGREEMENT

This Trust Agreement is made this _____ day of _____, 20_____, at _____, between _____, the Creator and _____ also serving as the Original Trustee under this Agreement.

The Creator desires to establish a Trust for the purposes outlined in this Agreement, and has enumerated the terms and conditions that the Trustee shall follow in administrating the Trust corpus.

Article I

The Creator has delivered to the Trustee the property indicated in Exhibit A attached hereto, receipt of which is acknowledged by the Trustee of the Trust by signing and dating Exhibit A.

That property and any other property that may be received by the Trustee from the Creator as additions to this Trust, shall be held and disposed of by the Trustee in accord with the terms stated in this Agreement. Property other than cash may be added to the Trust and any property added to the trust shall be acknowledged by the Trustee by signing and dating additional exhibits, and any such property added to the trust shall be retitled in the name of the Trustee designating as holding the asset in his capacity as Trustee.

Article II

Creator may, by signed instrument delivered to the Trustee, revoke this Agreement in whole or in part or amend it, but no amendment changing the powers, duties, or compensation of the Trustee shall be effective unless approved in writing by the acting Trustee.

An individual Trustee may resign by giving the Creator written notice thirty (30) days in advance of the effective date of the Trustee's resignation. If there is no Successor Trustee designated, then the personal representative of the estate of _____ shall designate a Successor Trustee.

Article III

During the life of the Creator, the Trustee shall pay all the net income of the Trust estate to the income beneficiaries, and such portions of the principal as the Creator may from time to time direct in writing. However, during any period in the Creator's life in which he is deemed mentally and/or physically incapacitated pursuant to a medical statement obtained from the Creator's physician, wherein said physician is of the medical opinion that _____ is unable to handle his financial affairs or make financial decisions, then the Successor Trustee shall proceed with the administration of this trust and shall, in his sole discretion, use so much of the net income and any portions or all of the principal to maintain the lifestyle of the Creator. Disbursement of such amounts may be made by the Successor Trustee as he deems desirable, including to the Creator, to a qualified legal representative of the Creator, to some relative or friend who has care or custody of the Creator, or by the Successor Trustee using such payment directly for the benefit of the Creator. The receipt of any such party shall release the Trustee from any liability for its expenditure. After the death of the Creator, the Successor Trustee shall continue to administer the trust estate as set out in Article IV and V of this Trust Agreement.

Article IV

The Successor Trustee shall continue to hold title to all assets in the trust until appropriate distribution can be lawfully made.

A. In the event that the Creator's probate estate is insufficient to satisfy the deceased Creator's legal debts and obligations, then the Successor Trustee may collect the Creator's bills, debts, and expenses incurred as a part of the Creator's last illness and may proceed to pay all legitimate debts of the deceased Creator and may process all medical claims prior to the distribution of the residuary trust estate as provided in Article V.

B. The Successor Trustee may prepare or supervise the preparation of all tax returns that are due as a result of the Creator's death. These returns include the federal estate tax return, any state death tax return, the Creator's personal federal and state income tax returns and federal and state fiduciary tax returns that are required as a result of this Trust. After the appropriate tax returns are filed and the taxes paid, then the Successor Trustee shall proceed to distribute the residuary trust estate as outlined in Article V.

continues

(continued)

Article V

After satisfaction of the Creator's legal debts, obligations, death taxes, personal and fiduciary income taxes, then the Successor Trustee shall distribute the remaining balance held in the Trust as follows:

If the Creator's spouse, _____ ("spouse") survives the Creator, the Trustee is directed to pay the net income from the trust estate to her at least annually and to use any portion or all of the principal necessary to maintain her lifestyle. At the death of the spouse, the Trustee shall distribute the entire trust estate, in equal shares, to _____ and _____ ("child"); however, if one child is not then living, her share shall be distributed to her issue, and if the predeceased child has no issue then her share shall be distributed to the surviving child, or to her issue if she is not then living. If none of the foregoing survive the spouse, the then Trustee shall distribute the trust estate to the intestate heirs of the Creator who are surviving at the time of this distribution. After the distribution, the trust shall terminate. In no event shall the trust continue in violation of any ____(state)_____ law limiting the term of its existence.

Article VI

_____ as the Original Trustee and all Successors as Trustees under this Agreement shall have all powers enumerated under the ____(state)_____ Code and any other power that may be granted by law, to be exercised with the necessity of Court approval, as my Trustees, in their sole discretion, determine to be in the best interests of the beneficiaries. Said powers are to be construed in the broadest possible manner and shall include the following and shall pertain to both principal and income, but shall in no way be limited thereto:

A. To retain any property received from the Creator without liability for loss due to lack of diversification or nonproductivity.

B. To invest and reinvest the Trust estate in any kind of real or personal property without regard to any law restricting investment by Trustees and without regard to current income.

C. To sell any Trust property, for cash or on credit, at public or private sales; to exchange any Trust property for other property; and to determine the prices and terms of sales and exchanges.

D. To take any action with respect to conserving or realizing upon the value of any Trust property, and with respect to foreclosures, reorganizations, or other changes affecting the Trust property; to collect, pay, contest, compromise, or abandon demands of or against the Trust estate, wherever situated; and to execute contracts, notes, conveyances, and other instruments, including instruments containing covenants and warranties binding upon and creating a charge against the Trust estate.

Article VII

The following provisions govern the administration of this trust as established by the Creator.

A. Any named Trustee of this Trust is relieved from any requirement as to routine Court accountings that may now or may hereafter be required by the statutes in force in any jurisdiction, although it is not precluded from obtaining judicial approval of its accounts. The Trustee shall be required to account on at least an annual basis to the income beneficiary of the trust.

B. This instrument and the dispositions hereunder shall be construed and regulated and their validity and effect shall be determined by the laws of the State of _____.

C. Any Trustee shall be entitled to reasonable compensation for services rendered in administering and distributing the trust property which shall be paid in accordance with an hourly rate if the Trustee is an individual. If the Trustee is a corporate fiduciary, it shall be compensated in accordance with its current fee schedule. During the administration of this Trust, the Trustee shall be entitled to reimbursement for expenses.

D. No person paying money or delivering property to a given Trustee need see to its proper application by the Trustee.

E. In the event that _____ dies, resigns, or is unable to serve as Trustee of this Trust, then _____ is nominated to serve as Successor Trustee under this Trust Agreement. The Successor Trustee shall automatically assume his position as Successor Trustee upon the signing of an oath without the necessity of any Court order or approval of the same.

IN WITNESS WHEREOF, I, _____, have hereunto signed my name as Creator and as the Original Trustee of this Agreement on the ___ day of ___, 20___.

_____, Creator   _____, Trustee

WITNESSES: _____

_____

Retiring? How a Trust Can Simplify Your Life

Let's look at an example of a couple who could make good use of a living trust. Reed and Shirley are in their late sixties. They own their home, have household goods, cars, retirement plans, and significant investments in stocks and bonds. They have two adult children who are both married and have children.

The couple has assets worth more than $500,000, not counting their home. At some future time, when they are unable or are unwilling to manage their property, they may want someone else to act as trustee and handle their estate so they can enjoy retirement days in other pursuits. Their trust could have the following features:

◆ Reed and Shirley as joint trustees

◆ Trustworthy Bank as the alternative trustee if the two become incompetent or choose to resign as trustees

◆ Trust income paid to Reed and Shirley

◆ Trust principal possibly used by Reed and Shirley as they determine

◆ Assets added or withdrawn by Reed and Shirley

◆ Trust revoked by Reed and Shirley at any time, except after the survivor becomes incompetent or dies

Quote, Unquote

Cessation of work is not accompanied by cessation of expenses.

—Cato the Elder, "De Agri Cultura" (second century B.C.E.)

Watch Out

Watch out for telemarketers or door-to-door salespeople selling living trusts. You might end up paying a high fee here for a document that isn't valid where you live. It's wiser to pay a lawyer to answer your questions and draw up a trust document.

Reed and Shirley may choose to put some or all of their property in the trust. If one of their goals is to avoid probate upon the death of the last of them, they can put their assets, such as their home, household goods, cars, and investments into their trust. If they have retirement plans such as 401(k)s and Keogh accounts that they want to keep out of probate, they can add successor beneficiary designations, such as their children, to these plans. Only in exceptional cases would a trust be designated as a pension beneficiary; consult your attorney before considering a trust as beneficiary.

If the house is put into the trust, then a deed must be prepared to reflect the trust as holding legal title.

Household goods and the cars placed in trust have to be accounted for if sold, exchanged, or abandoned. Those complications should be considered before the couple contributes real or tangible personal property to a trust. Certainly putting their liquid investments—stocks, bonds, mutual funds, and the like—in the trust would be simple.

Downside to a Living Trust?

Well, one "down" is the foregoing paragraph—all that personal property in the trust could cause a lot of record keeping, too much for some. Some assets, like cars and household goods, could be kept outside the trust.

How to Select the Right Trustee

If you establish a trust, you name the trustee. His or her duties are specified in the trust and by state law. Naturally you will want to be sure the person you choose is willing to serve in that capacity.

A trustee's duties may include the following:

- Administering the trust according to its terms
- Managing trust property, which can include reinvesting assets
- Investing the trust principal
- Maintaining trust accounting records
- Making tax decisions and filing tax returns for the trust
- Distributing assets to various beneficiaries
- Terminating the trust at the time specified by the trust agreement

If you are creating a revocable living trust, then you and/or your spouse, if you are married, may be the logical choice for trustees.

Or you might consider appointing co-trustees where one of the trustees is someone who understands what you intend the trust to accomplish, and the other trustee is an institution. The institution is (hopefully) going to be around for a long time, while the individual may retire, become disabled, or die. Review the trustee duties. Do you have a relative or friend who would be capable of and willing to perform them?

Watch Out

It's smart to provide in the trust a way to replace the institutional trustee if the beneficiaries are not satisfied with the trustee's performance, whether because of poor investment return or other problems. The replacement should be another institutional trustee.

Most trusts are not supervised by a court, so there is always a danger of misappropriation. If you decide on an individual as trustee, at the minimum you should arrange for an annual accounting to the beneficiaries. You should also consider requiring the trustee to provide a bond to protect you from wrongdoing.

If you elect to name an institution as your trustee, investigate the various trust departments at area banks. Discuss their fees (usually a small percentage of the trust assets, probably no more than 5 percent). Inquire about their investment policy and who in the department is likely to invest your assets. Be wary of a trust department that assigns inexperienced employees to your trust or that has a high rate of employee turnover. You want continuity and sound investments.

"So I Need a Trust Instead of a Will?"

No, no, no. You almost certainly need a will, even if you have a trust. For one thing, as you have read in this chapter, you probably don't want all your assets placed in a trust. It can be a nuisance to do that with some personal property.

Many of your assets should remain outside the trust, even if one day they are subject to probate. You need a will to cover that residue. Probate, as you will see in the next chapter, is not the money gobbler it used to be (and there are legitimate ways around that expense).

Be wary of anyone who suggests that all your problems will be solved by establishing a trust. That just isn't so. On the other hand, a trust can be an excellent ingredient in a comprehensive estate plan.

Don't forget, though: you still need a good old reliable will. The will can be used with a trust. The beneficiary of the will could be a revocable or irrevocable trust. This is often referred to as a "pour-over" will, because the deceased's assets "pour" into the trust.

The Least You Need to Know

- ◆ You don't have to be wealthy to set up a trust.

- ◆ A testamentary trust is part of a will.

- ◆ A revocable living trust gives you the most freedom; it allows you to change your mind. An irrevocable living trust, on the other hand, is etched in stone, so to speak.

- ◆ Even with a trust you need a will.

Chapter 10

All About Probate

In This Chapter

- ◆ The probate process
- ◆ The executor and his or her duties
- ◆ What expenses you can expect to pay
- ◆ How to avoid probate altogether

I gave you a brief overview of probate and probate court in Chapter 7, pointing out what happens if you have no will (and you won't let that happen, will you?).

But by now you've probably guessed that there's more to probate than the concise explanation I've already provided. This chapter tackles the frequently puzzling and misunderstood judicial arena of probate.

Let's Bring This Court to Order

As you learned in Chapter 7, probate provides for an orderly transfer of property from the deceased to his or her beneficiaries.

Let's go on from there.

Laws governing probate procedures vary slightly from one state to another, and so can the court itself. Probate court is under a state's court system. Some states have a special court for adjudicating probate and guardianship issues only, whereas in other states and jurisdictions within a state, courts handle other legal issues along with probate.

A judge always presides at probate court, to oversee proceedings, review various documents—the will, inventory of assets, petitions from possible heirs (we'll get into that later), and so on—and make decisions where necessary. However, the judge basically plays a supervisory role, and only adjudicates—hands down a decision—when a will or claim is contested, or when a guardianship issue must be decided.

Is Probate Really That Formidable?

Of course not. You might have read or heard over the years that folks seem to run from probate or even the mention of it. And probate courts have had a reputation for being time consuming and expensive, because federal and state governments take a chunk of that estate in the form of taxes. The message you may have picked up in your general reading has been "avoid probate at all costs."

Well, let's see. If you die without a will, it's true that probate can be longer and more costly for your heirs than if you had had that document.

On the other hand, some folks easily avoid probate because all of their property consists of jointly held assets, life insurance, pensions, and other assets with named beneficiaries, which ordinarily are not subject to probate. Other people use a living trust, which also does not go through probate. So, you see, not everyone makes use of probate court.

Probate really isn't a problem for the average estate, and especially where practically all the decedent's worldly goods go to his or her spouse, with perhaps a few bequests to other family members and friends. In such situations, the estate is closed quickly—usually within three or four months after the time for creditors to file claims has elapsed. Consider that most states allow four or five months after probate opens for creditors to file claims, and that means most estates should be closed within eight or nine months of death. State laws do vary, and complications arise, particularly if there is no will, numerous heirs, complicated property holdings, business interests, will contests, or complex tax issues, all of which take more time to close an estate.

The Probate Process Step-by-Step

Now that I've (hopefully) convinced you that probate isn't always the nightmare it's often characterized as, let's take a closer look at the probate process. I'll walk you through the system step by step, but keep in mind that each state's system will vary somewhat.

When a person dies with solely owned property, or other property that will be in his or her probate estate, such as tenants in common, or an insurance policy with no named beneficiary, someone—usually a relative—contacts the court and asks to open the estate for probate, whether or not there is a will. If there is a will, the family will have read it, and usually the executor named in that document will file the petition asking the court to open the will to probate.

If there is no will, the court appoints an administrator. (Because an executor and an administrator serve the same function, I'll use the term executor from now on to avoid confusion and save ink. You might want to keep in mind, though, that some courts use the generic "personal representative" for that individual. I'll still stick with executor.)

The executor collects the assets of the estate (a written list), pays the estate's debts and taxes, and distributes the balance to the beneficiaries or heirs. I'll talk more about those duties in just a little bit. Then the court terminates probate.

How do creditors know you've died? Well, not very likely by being invited to the funeral! The court places a death notice in your local or regional newspaper, asking anyone with a debt to come forward. I've reproduced a sample notice to give you an idea of what they look like. Incidentally, the fee to run that sort of news brief is paid by the estate.

NOTICE OF ADMINISTRATION

In the _____ County Superior Court_____
Probate Division_____
In the Matter of the Estate of_____
Joan Bradford, deceased

Estate Docket
    49D08-2006-EU0001

Notice is hereby given that on the 25th day of January, 2006, Matilda Swenson was appointed personal representative of the estate of Joan Bradford, deceased, who died on the 1st day of January, 2006.

All persons having claims against this estate, whether or not now due, must file the claim in the office of the Clerk of this Court within three (3) months from the date of the first publication of this notice or within nine (9) months after the decedent's death, whichever is earlier, or the claims will be forever barred.

Dated at _____, this 25th day of January, 2006.

    HENRY A. ABERNETHY
    Clerk of the _____ County
    Superior Court Probate Division

No Supervision? Great!

Some states provide for *unsupervised*, or *informal*, probate administration, which involves minimal court involvement. It makes the process quicker and usually less costly than the usual *supervised* administration, which frequently requires court orders and detailed accountings of assets and probate proceedings. If the estate is small, say less $25,000, many states permit simplified probate, which simply requires one of the heirs to sign an affidavit for the court agreeing to pay any of the decedent's debts and distributing the balance to the other heirs.

Words, Words, Words

Legatee is a word you might occasionally come across in preparing for, and reading about, a will. That is a person to whom money or property is left in a will. However, "beneficiary" is the more common term for that individual.

If you foresee battling beneficiaries, then it is probably safer to have supervised administration. The court orders protect the executor from frivolous challenges by disgruntled heirs or beneficiaries.

You might want to check with your attorney to see if unsupervised administration is advisable for your estate, and whether or not you need to request it in your will. In some states, heirs or beneficiaries in a will must consent to unsupervised administration.

Duties of Your Executor

Here is what an executor will be required to do with regards to the probate process:

- Petition the court to open probate
- Petition the court to admit the will
- Notify all beneficiaries to the will, or intestate heirs, of the administration of the will
- Notify all creditors of the deceased that probate administration is opened (that's the legal notice that will run in the deceased's local paper)
- Obtain a performance bond (check back in Chapter 7 for details on this)
- Collect the deceased's assets and list the assets in an inventory

- Seek court approval to sell any assets that might be necessary to pay debts (however, court approval is usually not necessary if a will is properly drafted and includes a power of sale)

- Determine and pay claims against the estate

- Pay any federal and state income taxes, federal estate, and state death taxes (there's more about these taxes coming up in Part 4 of this book)

- Distribute the estate's net assets, according to the court's order, to the will's beneficiaries, or to the heirs if there is no will

- Close the estate

Those are the basics. Of course, the estate might have complications that require additional work, such as operating a business for a time and/or selling it; defending a will contest; petitioning the court to interpret a will or determine the appropriate heirs; contesting IRS or state tax determinations; and accounting to the court and beneficiaries.

Because state probate laws vary, the executor might have additional duties, but the ones listed here are the primary tasks.

Selecting an Executor

It's common to name a spouse or adult child as executor. I'll discuss the pros and cons of family versus professional executors later, but keep in mind that the more complicated the estate, the less likely that your immediate family can or will want to serve as executor.

Here are some questions that might immediately pop into your mind about now regarding an executor. I've provided answers:

- *Should I ask the executor to serve before I put his or her name in my will?* By all means approach that individual to be sure he or she is willing to take on that responsibility.

- *Do I need a back-up executor?* Yes, definitely. The person you name as executor may not be willing or able to serve when the time comes, so always name an alternative executor.

◆ *Does an executor have to know about taxes to do this work?* He or she ought to have a minimal knowledge of paying taxes, although a lot depends on the size of the estate. If the estate is small, and the executor knows enough to do his or her own taxes, then that knowledge should be sufficient.

◆ *Will the executor be able to do the work required if he or she has a full-time, or even a part-time, job?* Certainly, although that, too, depends on the size of the estate. If the deceased has left a multi-million dollar business, feuding relatives, and complicated tax issues, there could be quite a job waiting for the designated person.

◆ *Does the executor have to put up any money to take on this assignment?* No, that performance bond you read about in Chapter 7 is paid out of the estate's assets.

Watch Out

One of the trickiest parts of an executor's job is tracking down all of the deceased's assets, and putting a dollar value on some of them, like antiques. Keep that in mind when preparing your will.

Quote, Unquote

What's a thousand dollars? Mere chicken feed. A poultry matter.
—Groucho Marx

You also need to consider the following when thinking about who might be best suited to handle your estate when you're out of the picture:

◆ **Organizational skills** If your candidate keeps a good checking account record, he or she should make out fine here. The executor is given a newly set up estate account, and writes checks and receives money through that account. The deceased's checkbook is rolled into the estate account.

◆ **Experience in managing assets** This depends on the size and complexity of the estate. You'll want someone who has at least written a check in his or her life, but the typical estate doesn't present especially tough challenges for anyone you're likely to be considering.

◆ **Investment expertise** Yes, you might want someone with experience in this area, if the estate is large enough so that money will have to be invested until probate is closed, which could be eight or nine months. Your executor will want to keep a close eye on your other investments, too.

◆ **Ability to get along with your heirs** This is very important. You want someone who will be contributing to the solution, and not be part of the problem. Choose someone who gets along with everyone involved here, or at least has the kind of temperament that can calm folks down if voices get a little shrill.

◆ **Fees to be charged** What, if anything, is your candidate likely to charge for performing an executor's duties? Take that into consideration.

Those are some qualities and points to look for in an executor. Sound like anyone you know? Here is a worksheet to help you determine who among your family and friends might fit the bill to handle your estate.

Selecting an Executor

Sometimes choosing an executor is easy: Your spouse wins that slot. Other times the choice can be difficult, as you mentally run down the list of family members and good friends. Here's a worksheet to help you decide whom you might ask—and who would be a good choice for alternate executor.

Name	Organizational Skills	Experience Managing Assets	Gets Along with the Family	Likely to Expect a Fee	Will Accept the Job

Best Choice(s)   _____

_____

_____

If you think the requirements are a bit heavy for those in your circle, you might want to consider hiring a professional. Keep reading to find out how.

Help! Bring in the Pros

Many commercial banks have estate departments that provide probate administration services. Instead of appointing a relative as executor, you could select Trustworthy Bank. You might also want to take that route if the assets of your estate are substantial, if there are business interests involved, or if tax issues are particularly complex. Probably a bank will only be interested in handling your estate if it has at least $500,000 in assets (not counting your home). They're likely to charge a percentage of the estate, maybe 5 percent, less if the estate is substantially larger, say several million dollars.

If the beneficiaries of your estate are likely to squabble, then you may well want to select an impartial and professional executor. After all, if Johnny and Janey haven't agreed on anything since they were in elementary school, there's no reason to believe they'll get along when handling your estate.

> **Tip**
>
> If you choose a bank to serve as the trustee for a family trust, then that same institution should be the executor for your will, to ensure continuity of management between the estate and the trust.

Ch-Ching: Probate Costs

Administering a probate estate costs money. Generally speaking, we are talking about the following expenses:

- **Court filing fee**   That's about $125, though it can vary significantly state to state.

- **Executor bond premium**   I've already talked about this in Chapter 7—maybe $150 or so.

- **Executor fee**   Probably free if the executor is a family member; as much as 5 percent of the estate if the executor is a professional.

- **Attorney fee**   If your executor chooses a lawyer, an uncomplicated estate should not take a lot of that attorney's time (many use paralegals to do most of the work). Some charge a flat rate, others a percentage of the estate. Again, I'll mention that 5 percent figure. Make sure you understand just exactly what will be included in that fee.

Keeping Those Costs Down

Your estate cannot do much about the filing costs, which are relatively minor anyway. But other fees can be reduced.

♦ Name a family member as executor, if that is appropriate in your situation, because he or she may serve for no fee, or at just a small charge.

> **Tip**
>
> If you are concerned that the institutional executor, such as a bank, will ignore your personal concerns, like dividing up family mementos, consider appointing a family member as co-executor to the corporate executor. This way, you get professional management with a personal touch.

♦ If you're dealing with a large estate and opt for a institutional executor, try to negotiate the fee. Many such fees are set, but it's worth shopping around a bit or at least asking the executor you've chosen if she or he will negotiate. As I have mentioned, the larger the estate, the more that fee should come down a bit. When factoring costs, consider that the institutional executor usually does not have to pay for a bond, which is a small saving to your estate.

The institutional executor also brings professional management and investment expertise that may enable the estate to earn more income than if it were managed by a family member. The institutional executor can use its tax department to make tax decisions, which could save the estate considerably in income and death taxes, too.

> **Tip**
>
> Some states, such as Indiana, permit small estates ($25,000 and less) to transfer estate assets by an Affidavit of Transfer. The Affidavit is a sworn statement made by one of the heirs that he has the authority and will transfer the assets to the other heirs, subject to payment of the debts and taxes. Check with your probate court to see if this is possible.

♦ If it's practical to do so, choose unsupervised, rather than supervised, administration. You will recall that earlier in this chapter I touched briefly on the two. Frequently unsupervised administration, or a local, similar version of it, is available and should be used in uncomplicated estates where all beneficiaries or heirs are agreeable toward each other. Unsupervised probate administration, where visits to the probate court only occur to open and close the estate, mean the executor and attorney have less work to do. Their fees should be reduced accordingly.

How to Avoid Probate

You say you'd like to skip the whole probate process, no matter how much money you can save here and there on expenses?

All you need to do is put your assets in a form of ownership that would not be distributed in your will at your death or go to your heirs, if you die without a will.

Here is a summary of ways you can avoid probate on your death:

◆ Co-ownership—whether as joint owners with rights of survivorship, tenants by entirety (spousal real estate), or community property. Keep in mind, however, that only avoids probate if an owner survives. Too often the surviving co-owner doesn't get around to putting another person's name on that document as a new joint owner. Then at the death of that survivor, the property goes into his or her probate estate.

◆ Life estate and remainder (see Chapter 2).

◆ Revocable or irrevocable trust (see Chapter 9).

◆ Life insurance, pensions, and annuities with named beneficiaries. Life insurance policies, many annuities, and pension plans permit the owner to name successor beneficiaries. As long as a beneficiary survives to receive the life insurance proceeds, annuity, or pension benefits, those payments will not be included in the deceased's probate estate.

> **Tip**
>
> Review beneficiary designations for life insurance, pension, and annuity benefits periodically to make certain that everyone you currently want to receive those proceeds is named.

◆ Stocks, bonds, and bank accounts paid on death to a person designated by the owner.

> **Quote, Unquote**
>
> A large income is the best recipe for happiness I ever heard of.
>
> —Jane Austen, *Northanger Abbey*

There's another way around probate: the living trust that you read about in Chapter 9. Using a trust avoids probate for all assets put in the trust, assuming that the beneficiaries named are living. Because most trusts go as far down as the second and third generation from the person establishing the trust, this usually isn't a problem.

Of course not all assets are suited for a trust, as you will recall. Too often we become so fearful of probate that we buy a "canned" living trust, fill it out, and then forget about it. We assume that our estate is in order. While it just may be, it is more likely we have created chaos for our heirs instead. Determining which property is and is not in the trust (and therefore in and not in the probate estate) can take a great deal of unraveling and be very expensive.

Trusts do have an important role in estate planning. You may certainly be a candidate for one. But avoiding probate shouldn't be your only goal.

Between having assets in forms of ownership that avoid probate, perhaps having a trust, and taking advantage of the money-saving tips just listed, your heirs' experience with probate shouldn't be that traumatic—or costly.

The Least You Need to Know

- ◆ All estates with solely owned property, with and without a will, must pass through a state's probate court, for distribution of assets and payment of necessary taxes.

- ◆ Many of the assets in your estate do not need to go through probate at all if they are jointly owned or have a named beneficiary.

- ◆ Choose an executor wisely, according to the demands of your estate.

- ◆ You *can* shave probate costs, and sometimes even avoid the process altogether.

Some Unique Probate Situations—Maybe Yours?

In This Chapter

- ◆ Bigamous marriages
- ◆ Surrogacy and similar estate puzzlers
- ◆ Getting an "advance" on an inheritance
- ◆ Crime *doesn't* pay

Now you know about probate and that court process. Hopefully it now all seems rather clear-cut to you.

Ah, but if probate court walls could talk! Many a twist and turn in estates have forced a probate judge into the role of present-day Solomon. Sometimes it's a grave Solomon, at other times, one fighting to hide a smile at a particularly amusing situation or folly of humankind. Here are some variations on simple inheritance issues. Perhaps one applies to you—or might one day.

Love and Marriage(s)

All states recognize solemnized marriages requiring a cleric or a judge; very few states recognize *common law marriages*. That is when a man and a woman do not have a legal marriage ceremony, but do live together as husband and wife for several years. Most states have passed laws abolishing common law marriage as a form of marriage for its residents.

Honey, Where Are You?

Throughout this book we have discussed spousal rights in a deceased's probate estate, and assumed, quite understandably, that the spouse was readily identifiable. Well, not every case is that simple.

I had a client I'll call Arnie, who was ready to retire from the military, but had a dilemma that called for legal advice. His pension required him to name his spouse as beneficiary. He had been in the Army, and over the course of his career had been stationed at about nine different bases around the country.

> **Quote, Unquote**
>
> Men marry because they are tired; women because they are curious. Both are disappointed.
> —Oscar Wilde

> **Tip**
>
> Remember, attorney-client privilege does exist. You need not fear talking frankly with your attorney about a tangled life that has perhaps even taken you down a legally questionable road or two.

It happened to have been Arnie's habit to select a new wife when he arrived at a new posting. He simply left the previous "spouse" and didn't bother with the formality of a divorce. Sometimes he went through a wedding ceremony with his new bride, but on other occasions the two just began living together as husband and wife.

I reminded Arnie of the law against having more than one wife at a time, and he acknowledged that yes, he had heard something about that. I told him whoever had come first was his legal wife, and the rest were void marriages, which means that no judicial action was necessary to establish that the marriage was invalid.

I thought that might have simplified his problem until I realized his first "marriage" was in a common law marriage state. It would be extremely difficult to determine if he were married or simply cohabiting, because there is no record of a common law marriage, whereas with a legal marriage there is, of course, a marriage certificate that can be produced.

The upshot of Arnie's case? We were never able to determine which "spouse" was which. Actually, Arnie couldn't even remember the names of some of his blushing brides at those new military assignments!

In the event of his death, could one—or more—of Arnie's wives apply to probate court for spousal rights? Of course, one can *try*. And maybe even win. There is at least one case of a so-called "wife" securing some part of her "husband's" estate, even though there was no marriage. So it isn't a foregone conclusion that the woman would be left in the cold financially on the death of her common law husband.

I know *you* will never enter into multiple marriages without making that little side trip to divorce, but keep in mind that bigamy violates civil *and* criminal law. The second "marriage" you enter into without a previous divorce is void. However, children born of a bigamous marriage are entitled to inherit from the father, even though the marriage was invalid. Some states may require alimony be paid to the innocent "spouse," too.

Oooh, That Cold Light of Day

Another client of mine—I'll call her Lydia—was at a party where she met a man who interested her. The feeling apparently was mutual because the two decided to get married that very night. They couldn't do so in Indiana because there was a statutory waiting period, so they drove from Indianapolis straight to Tennessee and were wed.

The next day, Lydia told me, she woke up with a nasty hangover. There was a man in the room with whom she seemed to have exchanged some serious vows, according to a marriage license on the table. She and her brand-new husband decided to discuss their future and quickly agreed they had none, at least not together. Because most states require the parties marrying to be sober (or at least not near-coma intoxicated), I suggested that an *annulment* of that marriage would be possible. Because Tennessee law controlled the marriage, Lydia would have to seek an annulment in that state.

Later, instead of obtaining an annulment in Tennessee, she decided upon divorce in Indiana.

My client's former husband of a few hours would have had have no claim upon her estate if she would have chosen to have the marriage annulled. If she had died after having the marriage annulled, the former "husband" could not

> **Words, Words, Words**
>
> Legally, an **annulment** is a court ruling that says a supposed marriage was never valid. The most common ground for annulment: fraud.

have showed up in probate court saying he was her spouse just because they were never divorced. An annulled marriage is no marriage at all; there's nothing left to get divorced from.

Pal o' Mine

You may recall that the actor Lee Marvin was engaged several years ago in a noted lawsuit brought by his live-in lover. She sued him to enforce an oral agreement purportedly giving her rights to support and one half of the property they accumulated during the seven years that they lived together. She argued that for all practical purposes they were living together as common law husband and wife; therefore, she should be entitled to "spousal" property rights. Ultimately the California courts denied her claim. However, some courts *have* awarded recoveries to former lovers on the basis of expressed or implied agreements.

There are two arguments for an award here: (1) palimony is like a marriage and (2) there is some kind of claim for services rendered. Of course, if you define that to include sex, there are laws against that! But it's possible to file a claim perhaps asserting some kind of management of the other person's career.

Marvin's lover could not claim an inheritance if he died without a will, because she is not an heir.

Marvin's lover's smartest move would have been to have him set up an irrevocable trust for her. Such a trust can never be changed, even if his affection for her someday did. Otherwise, to inherit from him she would have to have been named in Marvin's will.

Birth ...

Courts originally disagreed as to whether a child conceived by artificial insemination was legitimate. Fortunately, the statutes in almost all states have clarified that matter.

If artificial insemination is performed under the supervision of a physician, and with the consent of the husband (who is not the donor), the husband is treated as if he were the natural father of the child. The semen donor is not considered the father.

Medical science also makes it possible these days to extract ova from a woman and fertilize them with male sperm, then implant them back into the same woman. Inheritance, child custody, and support rights should not be at issue, unless participants other than a husband and wife are involved.

Surrogate motherhood for the most part focuses on the enforceability of the surrogate contract. That usually involves a woman who agrees to be artificially inseminated with the sperm of a man not her husband. The woman would then surrender her rights to the child to the donor and his wife.

Often these contracts involve payment to the surrogate mother of money beyond the birth expenses. Because many states have statutes that prohibit selling babies, this arrangement has been challenged. However, the statutes against baby-selling may not apply to the donor-father, because the baby is, after all, his biological child.

Quote, Unquote

The egg it is the source of it all.
Tis everyone's ancestral hall.
The bravest chief that ever fought,
The lowest thief that e'er was caught,
The harlot's lip, the maiden's leg,
They each and all came from an egg.
—Clarence Day, "Thoughts on Peculiar Dawns" (1921)

Obviously, inheritance, support, and custody rights of the child are not easily discerned under these circumstances, particularly as to the donor-father. The wife, for whom the surrogate mother is carrying the child, probably has certain rights. The gist of all this is that the law simply has not yet unraveled this tangled skein to anyone's complete satisfaction.

... and Death

Death used to be defined as the stopping of the heart. That is no longer an adequate definition in a medical era in which life can be artificially extended by machines.

Quote, Unquote

The art of will-making chiefly consists in baffling the importunity of expectation.
—William Hazlitt, "On Will-Making" (1821)

At the moment of death, the inheritance rights of the heirs or beneficiaries to that individual's will are fixed and determined. A moment sooner or later may make a difference.

I'm not about to discuss the "legal" moment of death—the date and time listed on a death certificate. However, I will examine here the problems involved when related persons die at the same time.

Nearly all states have adopted the Uniform Simultaneous Death Act. Under this ruling, if there is no evidence that one person survived the other (even for a brief time), then the Act applies as follows:

- **Wills and intestacy** The beneficiary or heir is treated as having not survived the deceased.

- **Life insurance** The beneficiary is treated as having predeceased the insured.

- **Jointly owned or tenancy by entireties** One half passes through each owner's estate.

- **Community property** One half passes through each spouse's estate.

Some states require a survival period of 120 hours after the decedent's death to inherit. If one person dies within 120 hours of another person, it is considered a simultaneous death for purposes of inheritance.

Unhappy with these provisions? You can get around it by stipulating in your will or life insurance policy that the Uniform Simultaneous Death Act will not apply in the event of a simultaneous death with a spouse. The will could state, "in a simultaneous death, my spouse is deemed to have survived me."

Let's Not Forget Greed

You might recall the biblical parable of the prodigal son (Luke 15:11). This younger son wanted his share of the family estate before his father died, an event that didn't look like it was going to happen any time soon (his father was in fine health and seemed nowhere near approaching his final days). The son wheedled his portion from the older man, left home, and proceeded to waste the money. Finally, after living in degrading conditions, he came to his senses and returned home. His father welcomed him and forgave him.

In modern legal terminology, the father of the prodigal son had made a gift to that man against his future inheritance (under intestate law). That is called the law of *advancement.* The law of advancement applies only in intestate situations, not to situations when there is a will, and it is usually proven by a written receipt from the individual advancing that money. If the father had a will and decided to leave equal amounts to both sons even though he had already given one son a sort of "advance" on his inheritance, the law of advancement would not apply.

Here is an example of how advancement is taken into account in dividing an intestate estate, again using our wayward son.

Assume that the young man received a $10,000 advancement. Then his father dies intestate, leaving a probate estate of $50,000. The prodigal son's advancement would be figuratively added to the probate estate for purposes of division between him and the elder son. That would make the probate estate worth $60,000. It's to be divided equally. Because the prodigal already received $10,000, he would be given only another $20,000 from the estate, with the older brother taking $30,000.

That should please the older brother. In the parable his nose was quite out of joint at his father's good humor—even celebratory feasting—over his brother's return.

If the father had made a will, he might want to follow the same division of his estate. But now that he's setting down his wishes on paper, he could explain a little. To his younger son, after his bequest he might add "I am reducing his share because I have provided for him, etc." The younger brother might have forgotten that gift or gifts over the years. Perhaps the other brother didn't. This is when the will calls for an explanation.

Quote, Unquote

A son can bear with composure the death of his father, but the loss of his inheritance might drive him to despair.
—Machiavelli (1517)

Tip

If there is any inequity in how you leave your children your assets—and you may well want to divide the estate in such a manner that would provide for the special-needs child—be sure to spell out your reasons, such as advancing money over the years to one of them. If you do not explain, you'll cause bad feelings among the kids and they will resent you.

Addressing Potential Problems Before They Come Up

This following worksheet can help you identify problems with certain heirs (over who gets what) or how property is held (jointly with only one of four children).

What Could Be a Problem for You in Probate

Is it real property that could cause you some concern about your estate? Is it a particular relative who might be concerned about an asset of yours? Or maybe there's a gray area in your estate you're just not sure about. Jot down where likely alarms might go off with your will, or later in probate, and what you can do to head them off.

Asset	Possible Problem in Will/Probate	Can I Handle It?	Better Check with an Attorney
_____	_____	_____	_____
_____	_____	_____	_____
_____	_____	_____	_____
_____	_____	_____	_____
_____	_____	_____	_____
_____	_____	_____	_____
_____	_____	_____	_____
_____	_____	_____	_____
_____	_____	_____	_____

Abandoned Spouses and Adultery

Abandonment and adultery can be tricky areas.

Some state intestate laws deny the spouse who deserts the other the right to inherit from that mate. Courts aren't particularly clear on what constitutes desertion, but most require substantial evidence of abandonment before they will impose its forfeiture provisions.

What could that evidence be? Well, if the departing spouse has set up residence elsewhere, especially if he or she is living with someone else, that could be considered abandonment.

Adultery has a different impact on an estate, or should I say, very likely no impact at all. Yes, there is probably in each state some appellate court division that has upheld a ruling in favor of a person's adulterous spouse. What you're no doubt looking at here is the adulterer who has set up permanent residence elsewhere. But the ones having, shall we say, a one-time fling? No, that is not likely to impact their estate.

The Missing Spouse

Not to be confused with the mate who has genuinely moved out, or abandoned, his or her spouse, the missing person is, well, just that. There are jokes about the husband who went out for a pack of cigarettes one evening and was never heard from again. On the far more serious side, there is the adult who disappears, perhaps not by choice. Has he or she met with foul play? Years go by with no answers.

The next of kin in those cases would probably ask the court, after the required period of time, to have that person declared legally dead, for inheritance and other purposes.

Murder and Profit? Never!

Most state laws bar anyone who feloniously and intentionally kills from receiving any inheritance from that victim. The statutes bar those found guilty of murder or voluntary manslaughter.

If you watch television news shows and notice a spate of parental killings from time to time, you will be interested to know that those who become orphans by their own hand cannot inherit from the parent-victims.

This bar applies not only to intestate laws, but also to wills and life insurance policies. The killer is treated as if he had predeceased his victim and gets nothing. In other words, if a killer is the beneficiary in a will of his victim, then the killer cannot inherit from his victim. The killer has no further claim to anything solely owned by the victim and his or her half of anything jointly owned. Obviously the majority of these cases and examples of problems in probate are pretty rare. The more usual probate estate is quite uncomplicated, causing hardly a flicker of interest in probate court. May your beneficiaries have just such an uneventful experience!

The Least You Need to Know

◆ No matter how strange or shady your story, your lawyer must keep it confidential through attorney-client privilege.

◆ Medical marvels in the area of fertility are still presenting puzzles to lawyers and courts when it comes to inheritance.

◆ An advancement to an heir will reduce his or her share of an intestate probate estate. It is usually proven by a written request.

◆ Abandonment and adultery occasionally, more correctly *rarely*, enter into a probate decision; both are difficult to prove.

Part

All in the Family—and Just a Little Beyond

What is all this planning for? Or should I say whom is it for? It's for your family, of course, immediate and extended, and perhaps a few very close friends.

So it's important that while you are being so diligent in this work, you anticipate what could call for more attention than usual. Everyone's life is different, of course, with ingredients not quite like the next person's.

In this part of the book, you'll learn about some special living situations that might affect you. You will also find out about a few specific, not run-of-the-mill, family circumstances that could have bearing on your will and estate. It certainly pays to anticipate what could go wrong and head off at the pass potential arguments among relatives or—heaven forbid—court decisions one day based on your choices now.

Chapter 12

Looking After Your Minor Children

In This Chapter

- The importance of naming a guardian
- Choosing the right person
- Setting up a trust to manage assets
- Determining a child's entitlements

Q: Kids—do we ever stop worrying about them?

A: No, probably no matter how old they—and we—are.

If we are already overwhelmed by all that could harm our minor children, the thought of what could happen to them if we are not even *here* becomes incomprehensible. What I'll help you with in this chapter is keeping your kids safe, or as safe as it's possible to be with the paperwork anyway, if by some chance you are not around to look after them.

Grim? Sure. But if you grapple with the issue now, you'll feel a lot better knowing your directives are written down and will be followed. Then you can get on with other things relating to the kids that are more fun, like figuring out where the money for college is going to come from!

A Minor Issue of Major Importance

You read in Chapter 7 how important it is to have a will, not just so that your assets will be passed on to whomever you choose, but also for arranging the care of your *minor* children. (If you have a special needs child of any age, that is certainly a concern to you, too. I'll cover that topic in Chapter 14, although you will still want to read this chapter because there's probably a good deal that will apply to your situation here as well.)

Words, Words, Words

A **minor** child is defined by law as one who has not yet reached a majority age. Okay, what's a **majority?** Well, that can vary in different states for different purposes. For example, it might be 18 for voting, 21 for drinking. Some states consider 18 a majority in wills and estates, while others say 21. Throughout these pages we'll use 18 as a majority.

Quote, Unquote

Rigid justice is the greatest injustice.

—Thomas Fuller, M.D., "Gnomologia" (1732)

A *guardian* is a person appointed by law to be responsible for the food, housing, and other needs of a child until he or she reaches legal age. (Of course, guardians are also named for adults who can no longer look after themselves. I'll talk about the elderly adult who becomes incapacitated in Chapter 23.)

Usually your will names a guardian, and the court appoints that person or couple, unless the court determines it is not in the child's best interest for the named guardian to serve.

Godparents are not automatically guardians; they need to be named in the will.

As you saw in Chapter 7, if you are a single parent and have no will, the state decides who'll get to raise your kids. That could be the other biological parent if he or she is living, or your parents or a sibling. If you're starting to hyperventilate about now just reading some of those choices, then you can see how important it is that your wishes are set down in a will. I'm sure you don't want your children handed about like so many parcels.

If a guardian does need to be appointed for your child, state law will specify a preference list for the judge to follow. Although laws do vary, it is common to follow this order:

◆ Any request in a will or other written instrument (if you have no will, then of course legally you've got no preference)

◆ Any request by a child at least 14 years of age

◆ A relative of a child (grandparents, aunts, uncles, etc.)

The court's overriding concern is the appointment of a guardian who will serve the best interests of the child. The court will do the best it can, but how much better it would be for your kids if the judge had your directives to consider.

If you are married, your spouse is likely to assume the legal and actual role of guardian over the property that your children inherit from you. But there are exceptions. If a surviving parent hasn't taken an active interest in the child or has outright abandoned parenthood, then he or she may not be the court's choice. A child with serious health disabilities calls for a guardian who will undertake extra duties.

The Guardian's Duties

A guardian for a minor has two primary responsibilities:

◆ Rear the child

◆ Manage the child's assets

The guardian appointed by the court performs one or both of these functions until discharged of them. More specifically, the guardian is responsible for …

◆ Petitioning the court for appointment as guardian.

◆ Securing a performance bond for him- or herself.

◆ Preparing an inventory of the child's assets, that could include property from your probate estate (through a will or intestacy), life insurance proceeds, and pension benefits, as well as Social Security payments due the child.

◆ Investing and managing the child's assets.

◆ Providing for the child's support, care, education, and training.

- Encouraging the child to be self-reliant and independent so that he or she becomes an adult capable of handling the money that will be inherited.

- Periodically accounting to the court about income, expenses, etc.

- Filing necessary federal and state tax returns on the child's income.

- Closing the guardianship when it is no longer needed.

Tip

If you want your home or any other asset kept in the family for your child's use, you need to specify that in your will. Most state laws require the guardian to sell assets that will not earn income.

The guardian is responsible for reporting all income and expenses both to the court and to the child. That accounting may be on an annual or biennial basis, depending on state law. The guardian is to use the funds for the child's livelihood, which includes necessities and perhaps amenities, like a first car for the youngster when he or she reaches driving age.

In many instances, the guardian is not paid a fee—usually it is a family member who takes on that role and does not expect payment.

When the child reaches age 18, the guardianship is terminated. The guardian files his or her final accounting and distributes the assets to the child.

At this point you may want to pause and contemplate your child receiving your estate at age 18. Is it likely to be large? Do you think he or she could handle the money? Is the child too young right now for you to be able even to guess?

A trust is likely the answer to any dilemma such an issue might pose. It can delay distribution of assets until the child becomes more mature. I'll explain how this works in a few pages.

How to Select a Guardian

Tip

It's wise to name an alternate guardian in your will, just in case the primary guardian is later unable or unwilling to serve.

Let me tell you, this is *hard*. My wife and I have four sons, all of whom have now reached adulthood. Over the course of the years in our various wills we have had five different guardians, and almost as many different alternates. Although a family member or friend might be willing to be guardian for one child, maybe even two, taking on four calls for a real martyr.

You want to select someone who will rear your kids the way you would, and manage their assets wisely. There are several factors to think about in selecting a guardian or guardians. Let's go over them one by one.

Age

The age of the guardian is especially important if you are considering your parents. They aren't as young as they once were (but, hey, who is?). You probably drove them nuts on more than one occasion, but they had the resiliency of youth then, and the energy to meet those demands.

As grandparents, they are wonderful. But they know that when the grandchildren start acting like kids they can be sent home. That can't happen if you appoint them as guardians. Your parents love your kids, but may want them around only part of the time. One generation gap is wide enough. Two could be a chasm.

> **Quote, Unquote**
>
> If men do not keep on speaking terms with children, they cease to be men, and become merely machines for eating and for earning money.
>
> —John Updike, "Assorted Prose" (1965)

On the other hand, grandparents *could* work if they have asked for the job of guardian (and you agree they would do a good job of it), and in some cases if the children are old enough so that your parents won't be raising small tykes. Taking in a 14- and 16-year-old brings its own, shall we say, challenges. On the other hand, it will be only a few years until those kids are grown. This is a decision that, as you can see, calls for serious thought.

You might prefer to consider a couple closer to your age with children. Their parenting skills, which you will have observed, are well honed by daily use and not, for the most part, out of practice by grandparenthood.

Marital Status

Your child needs to fit comfortably into a family environment. A husband and wife who have a solid marriage and children close to your child's age may be ideal.

We all know perfectly excellent single parents who rear their children to be what you would hope for yours. By all means if you know someone who fits that bill, don't

Tip _____

After you have made your tentative choice of guardian, observe the individual with your children, and discuss with the person(s) you've chosen as guardian how comfortable everyone would be likely to feel in that household.

exclude that individual from consideration. Or the single person with no children, perhaps a sibling of yours or your spouse's, who is particularly close to your child. However, two parents do make it easier on the child—and the guardians.

Here is something you will want to keep in mind though. If you are naming a married couple as guardians, consider the possibility of their divorce one day. Indicate who should be the guardian in that event, no matter how unlikely it seems to you now.

Lifestyle and Child Rearing Skills

Your child is used to you and your family life. If you want continuity, or as close as you're likely to find it in a guardianship situation, then you'll look for someone who is likely to fit within that pattern. That's not to say that the child can't succeed in a family that doesn't emphasize what matters to you in rearing kids. It's just that it's harder to do. For example, if religion is important to you and your family, you probably won't want the guardian to be an atheist.

Child rearing attitudes vary, of course. There is no one right way. But you have your own style, and probably want your guardian to follow that sort of system. If firm-but-fair is your style, you're not likely to look for a guardian who believes that children should be "free to do their own thing." Taking a child from a fairly structured family life to a guardian who plans only for the next few minutes could spell disaster for a kid.

Compatibility

As I mentioned, most courts will listen to a child's wishes if the youngster is at least 14 years of age. If your male teenager detests the very perfume that Aunt Maude wears when she gives him a big smooch at family reunions, and she gave him socks when he entered high school, for which he's never quite forgiven her, then you may want to rethink Aunt Maude.

Talk with your kids and find out whom they feel comfortable with. That may not decide it for you, particularly if your son likes oft-married bachelor Uncle Dave because he has plenty of "babes" around, but at least their input can move you toward a decision, as it would a judge.

Family Relationships

Your brother or sister may be your best choice. But if there are likely to be squabbles over which brother or sister, that's all the more reason to put your choice in your will.

Favoritism

Some folks do play favorites. If you have three children, and your proposed guardian dotes on one child, giving him more attention, consideration, and gifts than she gives to the other two, you might want to give second thought to choosing that person. At least have a candid discussion with the kids who aren't the favorite. They probably have noticed the different treatment and won't be inclined to give that person the benefit of the doubt if she becomes the guardian, especially when discipline is administered or money spent.

Managing Money

Some guardians make superb substitute parents and can manage money wisely. Others can fulfill one of those obligations, but not both. If your guardian choice will be a great parent, but always seems to be just one step ahead of the bill collectors, then take the tradeoff and go with him or her. Parenting should be your first consideration. You can turn to someone else to manage your child's assets. Which brings us now to your other choice: the trust.

First, though, is your head spinning about now with all the "perfect" traits you're supposed to look for in a guardian? Here is a worksheet to help you sift it all out. Perhaps your choice is an obvious one. If it isn't, putting your thoughts on paper should help you select an individual or a couple who could do a good job of caring for your child, should anything happen to you.

Choosing a Guardian

You've probably given some thought to your kids and a likely guardian, perhaps even before reading this chapter. Still, it helps to see on paper the pros and cons of various family members and friends who might be candidates for guardianship. Take a few moments—no, take as long as you need, this shouldn't be rushed—to set down your thoughts. Your work may lead you to answers that will be satisfying all around.

Name(s)	Good points	Any negatives?	Will they accept the job?	Can they manage money?	Do the kids like them?
_____	_____	_____	_____	_____	_____
_____	_____	_____	_____	_____	_____
_____	_____	_____	_____	_____	_____
_____	_____	_____	_____	_____	_____
_____	_____	_____	_____	_____	_____
_____	_____	_____	_____	_____	_____
_____	_____	_____	_____	_____	_____
_____	_____	_____	_____	_____	_____
_____	_____	_____	_____	_____	_____
_____	_____	_____	_____	_____	_____

Best guardian(s): _____

Best alternate(s): _____

The Trust Alternative

If your proposed guardian is a poor money manager, you might want to establish a trust to manage your child's assets.

You might want a trust anyway. It certainly should be considered by anyone who has significant assets to leave to a minor or special-needs child. By "significant assets"

I mean $100,000 or more in cash, life insurance, stocks, bonds, and other savings, not including the value of your house.

A trust can accomplish the following for you:

◆ Manage the child's property (stocks, certificate of deposit rollovers, and the like)

◆ Distribute the property later than age 18, if that is your wish

◆ Avoid a spendthrift child's problems

Chapter 9 has a complete discussion of trusts. In this chapter I talk about trusts as they specifically apply to minors.

The trustee you choose can be an individual or a corporate institution, usually a bank. If you choose a institutional trustee, then you will have the professional management and protection from risk that comes with that choice. Most trustees report to the guardian at least quarterly, and many will assist in filing the child's income tax returns.

You can establish a *revocable living trust* now, which would receive all your probate assets, life insurance, and retirement plan proceeds, or you can include a trust in your will—a *testamentary trust*—and accomplish the same thing.

> **Quote, Unquote**
>
> I'm still not sure what is meant by good fortune and success. I know fame and power are for the birds. But then life suddenly comes into focus for me. And, ah, there stand my kids.
>
> —Lee Iacocca, *Talking Straight* (1988)

Let's look at Carrie and Steve, who have two small children. The couple established a revocable living trust in planning for their kids, funded only by a life insurance policy on Steve's life, with the trust as the secondary beneficiary (Carrie is first beneficiary). Steve's and Carrie's wills provide for each other first, and then the probate estate goes to the children's trust.

The kids' trust could be structured like this:

◆ Trustworthy Bank as its trustee.

◆ The children are the primary beneficiaries of the trust, and will receive the income and as much of the principal as is necessary for their support.

Watch Out_____

A creditor might lend your child money, expecting to be repaid from income or principal distribution of that child's trust. The wise person preparing the trust includes a clause that orders the trustee not to distribute funds where the chief beneficiary is the child's creditor, thus protecting his asset in the trust. No trust should be without that clause.

◆ When the younger child becomes age 22, the trust assets will be equally divided and each child will get one third of those assets (upon written request). The balance of each child's share will be distributed when each child turns 25.

◆ If a child dies before final distribution to him or her, the other child receives that share.

You can establish similar distribution ages, or any ages you choose.

There are no tax breaks with a minor's support trust as above; it simply delays distribution of the inheritance until the children are more mature and can make better choices with your hard-earned money.

Special Requests

You can create trust terms that best fit your child, or make for differences between your kids.

The heroic woman who consented to be guardian for my four boys was a little concerned about housing the additional brood in her home. I told her we could provide in the trust that the trustee could allow some funds for home improvement.

She then asked about family vacations. We said the trust could specify that money could be used for her children, as well as for our kids, to get away. Indeed, the trust could provide for vacation money for the guardians to go off on their own without the children, a sort of reward for their efforts.

Like ours were, your particular concerns can be addressed in a trust.

Giving Your Kids Cash Gifts Now

You may have some spare cash that you want to give to your minor children, but don't want them to spend it now. You have some options:

◆ A gift to a custodial account

◆ Three forms of minor's trusts

Let's look at each in turn.

In Custody

Most states have a gifts-to-minors statute. The parent establishes a custodial account at a savings institution or transfers stock in the custodian's name (that'd be your name or that of any adult you choose) for the benefit of the child. When the child becomes of legal age, as defined by the statute, she receives the property outright. The child reports the income during the custodial period.

Federal law may require the income received from custodial accounts be taxed to the child at the parent's highest rate until the child becomes 14.

> **Tip**
>
> If you establish a custodial account or minor's trust, do not use the assets to support the child, because you will be taxed on its income. Remember, the child is the owner, not you (you are the transferor), so if you cannot afford to relinquish ownership of the property, do not establish a custodial or minor's trust.

The parent's gift will be excluded from federal gift tax if it falls under the $11,000 annual exclusion (one can give any person $11,000 or any married couple $22,000 each year without any tax repercussions). The custodial account will not be in the parent's estate and therefore will not be subject to federal estate tax if another person is selected as custodian.

To avoid inclusion of this property in your estate for federal estate tax, choose a close relative or friend to serve as custodian. (That individual can choose to do nothing except make minor investment decisions, such as rolling over a certificate of deposit.)

A Trusty Trio

The tax code and several court decisions have provided a few types of minor's trusts known as Section 2503(b), Section 2503(c), and Crummey trusts. There are minute differences among the three that would numb your mind if I were to explain them, but the gist of the three is ...

- ◆ They establish a trust.
- ◆ They make a gift for the minor to the trust, which receives the maximum annual gift tax exclusion for the transferor (there's that annual $11,000 again).
- ◆ They delay distribution to the minor until age 21 or later.

Each has variations on those themes that you may want to explore with your attorney.

Your Child and Your Estate: Entitlements

You read in Chapter 7 about a child's rights to inherit under state intestate laws when you have no will. In Chapter 8, you saw how to include your kids in your will.

If you are a divorced mom or dad providing child support, you may want to ask your attorney about your support obligations as they pertain to your estate. In some states the divorced parent's requirement to support a child is not terminated by that parent's death, but the amount of the support may be modified, revoked, or commuted to a lump sum by the court.

Quote, Unquote

A father is a banker provided by nature.

—French proverb

Most states have a family support statute that requires a specified amount—it can vary, but let's say, oh, $25,000—to be distributed to a surviving spouse and/or children, whether you had a will or not.

Also, divorce decrees may require the support-paying parent to maintain life insurance on his or her life, which may be the exclusive claim the child would then have against the deceased parent's estate. The child, of course, is the beneficiary.

The Least You Need to Know

◆ If you have minor children, you should name a guardian as well as an alternate.

◆ The guardian is responsible for rearing the children and managing their assets.

◆ Consider a trust to manage your children's assets should you die, because of its flexibility.

◆ Child support might be collected from a deceased parent's estate upon death, whether there is a will or not.

Chapter 13

Holy Wedlock: Sometimes a Deadlock

In This Chapter

- ◆ Property rights after "I do"
- ◆ Spousal election against a will
- ◆ Divorce planning and practice
- ◆ Prenuptial agreements in divorce court

It's bliss. It's a battlefield. It's both—and occasionally at the same time. That's marriage, all right, or so it would seem from all one hears and reads on the subject.

The law has many occasions to intrude into the lives of married couples, from good times to bad moments. All the legal paper shuffling that goes along with marriage, and then perhaps separation and divorce, can also affect an estate plan. Here's what can happen—and what you can do if distressing times hit you.

Spousal Rights

Before we get into the *sturm und drang* of much of this chapter, may I ask if you're planning to be married soon or even just eventually? Good for you. My wish is that none of what follows in this chapter will apply to you. Do me a favor, though. Here is a listing for you to refer to in order to make sure the estate paperwork for both of you is in order when you march down that aisle. It affects spousal rights. Keep it in mind and read it again just before you marry.

Getting Married? Check This Out

Congratulations! This isn't a very romantic suggestion, but before you make that trip down the aisle, you and your spouse-to-be need to review some estate papers, to get your house, figuratively speaking, in order. The marriage license is proof that you will soon become a new legal entity. It's time to look at some other documents that could or should be changed before you trade vows:

- **Your wills.** If you do not each have one, it's smart to have them drawn up so that you can provide for each other. Please, no joint wills, because a joint will may limit the right of the surviving spouse to change his or her will after the other spouse dies.

Tip

Until the law is clarified regarding same-sex marriages, this chapter is limited to the traditional marriage. The next chapter discusses same-sex unions under the topic "living together."

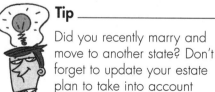
Tip

Did you recently marry and move to another state? Don't forget to update your estate plan to take into account requirements in your new state for a will and other documents.

- **Employee benefits, life insurance policy, Individual Retirement Account, and qualified retirement plan.** You will probably want to change the beneficiary for those investments to your spouse, or at least review the documents to be certain that you still want the beneficiary you have named.

- **Forms of property ownership.** Will you be buying a home? Do you already have one in your name? You might want to review Chapters 2 and 3, about ownership forms. Perhaps you'll want to hold real and personal property as "joint tenants with right of survivorship," the most common ownership form for spouses.

◆ **Prenuptial agreement.** Will you be having one? There's a discussion of pre-nups in Chapter 3 (with a sample agreement you can read over), and further discussion in this chapter. Remember to use separate attorneys for drawing up an agreement.

Now You Are Married

Now let's get back to the time after some marriages, when problems can crop up.

After the marriage ceremony, each spouse has certain legal rights. In states like California and Texas, the husband and wife have community property rights. In non-community property states—New York and Illinois, to take two examples—the law also specifies certain marital rights upon divorce or death.

Marriage is a fragile institution in our modern life, for a number of reasons. To ignore that fact is to proceed at your own risk—and possibly to the risk of your financial future. Read on and you'll see what I mean.

Electing Against Your Spouse's Will

It's your will. You can completely cut your spouse out, or leave only a small portion of the probate estate to him or her.

Of course if you intend to make either of those moves, I would suggest not letting your husband or wife view your handiwork unless a divorce is already inevitable, or you have a prenuptial agreement. I once had a client who was the wife of a friend. In the will I drew up for her she left one half of her estate to her parents, one quarter to her parochial high school, and one quarter to her husband. As far as I know, her husband was unaware of his relatively unimportant position in his wife's testamentary scheme. And of course I could not tell him. The couple eventually got divorced.

A spouse who is left out of his or her deceased spouse's will or given a small share of the estate has the right to *elect against the will*. It is a strategy for married couples only, and permits the party left out to go to court for a fairer shake. He or she is saying in effect, "Whatever he left me, it's not enough. I'm electing against that will." This isn't the same as a *challenge* to the will, which is open to any heir or beneficiary. An election is just for spouses, and already assumes some rights for the survivor.

The spouse who elects against a will must file that election within the statutory period of time. That time varies from state to state, but might be from three to six months after the estate is opened.

Most state laws allow a surviving spouse who elects against the deceased spouse's will to receive from one third to one half of his or her probate estate. Usually that is the same share that he or she would receive under intestate law.

If the election is untimely (presented beyond the accepted deadline), or improperly made, then the surviving spouse receives only what the will provides. However, any property jointly owned by both spouses, and any life insurance or pension with the survivor as beneficiary, would go to the surviving spouse, because those assets are not part of the probate estate.

Augmenting an Estate

Several states have laws that increase the probate estate for purposes of the spousal election, when certain transfers would otherwise diminish the part of the estate that the surviving spouse would receive. This increase is often referred to as the *augmented estate*.

Let me give you an example. Say that, for whatever reason, you don't want your spouse to inherit the bulk of your estate, or maybe not even a penny of it. So you set up a trust and place all of your property in that trust, thinking your spouse will have no access to that money, even if she or he decides to elect against the will.

Not so, at least in certain states. The court will take that trust property and deposit it right back into your probate estate, for spousal election purposes just where you didn't want it to be.

Let's look at another example. Meet Ray, who lives in a noncommunity property state and has the following assets in his own name:

◆ Three expensive cars

◆ A condominium in Florida

◆ A substantial savings account

♦ A significant investment portfolio

♦ A large life insurance policy

All except the life insurance proceeds would be part of Ray's probate estate.

But Ray intensely dislikes his wife Michelle, and the idea of her enjoying his property and money after he's gone drives him nuts. So he creates a trust and transfers all his solely owned assets, except the cars, into the trust. The trust provides nothing for Michelle. Ray changes the life insurance beneficiary to his daughter Eden. Shortly thereafter, Ray dies. His will leaves not a scrap to Michelle.

> **Watch Out**
>
> Consult an attorney before making any property transfers with the intent to thwart your spouse's election against your will. State laws vary as to what is considered part of the augmented estate.

Michelle can elect against the will and receive her share of the probate assets, which now consist only of the automobiles. This is a fine kettle of fish, the fuming widow thinks. But wait. State law may allow her to elect against an augmented estate, which includes the property in trust. Whether the life insurance proceeds are considered part of the augmented estate varies with each state. Most pensions are subject to federal law, which prevents a spouse from being cut out of benefits.

> **Quote, Unquote**
>
> In the multitude of counselors there is safety.
> —Proverbs 11:14

The laws in her state give Michelle the green light to elect against an augmented estate. She *runs* to a lawyer.

Actually, the election could bring a most satisfactory ending to this for Michelle. She could get one third of everything. As for Ray … well, we'll never know his response to Michelle's good fortune, will we?

It's important to note here that a surviving spouse may waive his or her rights to elect against a will by signing a prenuptial agreement. That's our next topic for discussion.

The Prenup as Love Flies Out the Window

They're called prenuptial, premarital, and antenuptial agreements, but they all mean the same thing: a document where prospective spouses settle certain property rights before the marriage, in the event of divorce or death of one party. I discussed prenups in Chapter 3 as they apply to property ownership. Now I'll tell you what happens when problems arise in a marriage.

They're for "Just Folks," Too

Prenups are not used only by millionaires and movie stars. Older couples, or indeed couples of any age, remarrying after the death of or divorce from a spouse, often are concerned about keeping for their children the assets they bring into that new marriage.

A prenuptial agreement will specify that each spouse waives his or her right to any intestate share (if there is no will) and waives any right to elect against the other's will.

The provisions of the prenup attempt to keep as separately owned any property brought into the marriage. Keep in mind, however, that spouses frequently convert each other's solely owned property into jointly owned property with right of survivorship. That results in the surviving spouse receiving the property, thus reducing the assets going to the deceased spouse's children and perhaps negating an important part of the prenuptial agreement.

> **Tip**
>
> If you have a prenuptial agreement that provides for the bulk of your assets to go to your children, then make sure the title to those assets remains solely in your name.

Prenuptial agreements are not irrevocable. Spouses can agree to modify or revoke their prenuptial agreement, but those wishes must be in writing, and signed by each partner.

If a married couple does not have a *pre*nup, they can, if they choose, make a *post*nuptial agreement, which could contain the same terms as a document drawn up before the wedding.

A prenuptial agreement can also get into questions of alimony, into wills and trusts and, as you saw in Chapter 3 and in the sample prenup agreement there, just about any area the couple wants.

Avoiding a Challenge to a Prenup

Joe is about to marry Angelina. It's his second marriage, the first having ended in divorce. Joe's concerned about a possible second divorce and its financial impact. He also wants to make sure that when he dies the bulk of his estate goes to the children from his first marriage. Angelina understands, and she agrees to the pact.

Joe should take the following steps to be sure there are no loopholes in his agreement with Angelina:

◆ Hire an attorney to draft the agreement.

◆ Completely disclose all his assets and liabilities to Angelina. Courts will more readily enforce a prenuptial agreement if it is clear that the spouses knew what rights each would give up in the event of a divorce or a death. Hiding assets will almost always guarantee a challenge to the agreement, perhaps a successful one.

Watch Out

The person who initiates the prenuptial agreement might be tempted to offer his or her lawyer's services to the other partner. Bad move. That would be a conflict of interest that the courts will probably not look kindly on when deciding whether to enforce the prenuptial agreement. Two parties call for two separate lawyers.

◆ Recommend to Angelina that she hire her own lawyer to review the proposed agreement. If she does not want independent legal advice, then the prenuptial agreement should clearly state that she was told to engage a lawyer but chose not to.

A well-drafted prenup, which is executed with complete financial disclosures and legal advice, is difficult to successfully challenge.

When considering upsetting a prenuptial agreement, courts retain the right to alter the effect of a prenup if it would result in extreme hardship for either spouse. For example, if both parties assumed that each would be self-supporting upon divorce or the death of the other, and injury or illness precluded that, then the court could specify support payments to the disabled spouse.

The American Way of Divorce

We are the marrying kind in America, yet about half of us later end up in divorce court. According to the U.S. Census, in 2001, 8.5 per 1,000 of us married, and 4.0 per 1,000 of us divorced. The divorce rate for 1999 and 2000 was 4.2 per 1,000.

Almost all states have a no-fault divorce (or dissolution of marriage) law. State laws usually have a residency requirement and a waiting period between the petition and the order granting the divorce. Several states require mandatory counseling before the decree is granted. But the marriage *will* be dissolved if one party desires it. For specific information on your state's marriage and divorce law, check with your local library for its statutes, or go to your state's website.

Watch Out _____

You don't see much of legal separation anymore. Folks seem to proceed straight to divorce. However, if you do seek a legal separation, it is certainly a move that calls for a review of your estate plan. Remember, though, no matter how separated you are, and how far away your estranged spouse, you are still married in the eyes of the law.

For detailed advice on divorce and child custody, I recommend Brent W. Terry's *The Complete Idiot's Guide to Protecting Yourself from Everyday Legal Hassles;* it's got several excellent chapters on these issues. But let me go into financial and tax consequences of divorce, and how divorce can affect your estate here.

Those areas can include …

◆ Property settlement.

◆ Child custody and support.

◆ Alimony or separate maintenance.

◆ The tax consequences of all of the above.

Remember that a prenuptial agreement may determine the terms of any property settlement, alimony, or separate maintenance for one party. Child custody and support will be set by the divorce court. What follows assumes there is no enforceable prenuptial agreement.

Property Division

Mark and Millie are splitting up. The couple has the following assets, with noted market values:

House	co-owned	$100,000 [net, or less mortgage(s)]
Household goods	co-owned	$30,000
Cars	co-owned	$30,000 [net, or less auto loan(s)]
Savings	co-owned	$10,000
His pension		$200,000
Her pension		$50,000

Most divorce courts would add up the assets and divide by two. Perhaps you've gone through a divorce and are saying "That didn't happen to me! I got the shaft and he (she) got the mine." Be that as it may, most laws require an equitable distribution of the marital assets.

Courts certainly can consider factors that could affect a distribution, such as …

◆ Who acquired the assets and how (gifts or inheritance).

◆ Income and property of spouses before marriage and at present.

◆ Duration of marriage and health of each spouse.

◆ Need of custodial parent to occupy the home.

◆ Spousal maintenance or alimony.

◆ Liquidity of assets.

◆ Financial future of each spouse.

◆ Spousal fault in wasting assets.

◆ Tax effects.

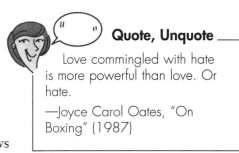

Quote, Unquote

Love commingled with hate is more powerful than love. Or hate.

—Joyce Carol Oates, "On Boxing" (1987)

This list is illustrative and not exhaustive. Certainly each divorce is unique, and state laws vary.

Remember, too, that community property states generally treat all assets acquired during marriage from either spouse's income as community property. This means that each spouse has a one-half ownership in those marital assets, no matter how the property is titled. This form of property ownership will affect the divorce. (You might want to review Chapter 3, which also talks about community property.)

Child Custody and Support

Courts award custody of minor children based on what they determine is in the best interests of the child. Naturally, parents should try to work together to establish an amicable custody arrangement that benefits all concerned.

Usually the noncustodial parent provides child support through minority, and often through age 21 if the child is attending post-secondary school (such as college or trade school). Many states have established child support guidelines to determine the amount of support to be paid.

Tip

If you think there might be a problem with your children having regular access to your parents after your divorce, you can make grandparental visits an issue in your divorce decree.

Income and Some Other Tax Consequences

Let's return to Mark and Millie's divorce. Mark is an accountant making approximately $75,000 a year; Millie is a public school teacher earning $30,000. They have one child, Manny, age 5.

If one spouse pays the other alimony, then the paying spouse gets a tax deduction and the recipient spouse reports the payment as gross income.

Mark, who is in the higher tax bracket, might be willing to pay alimony, perhaps as a form of property settlement, to get a welcome tax deduction. Millie, therefore, may receive more from the divorce financially because of the tax savings for Mark.

Words, Words, Words

We all know (and a few of us have experienced) **alimony** as a court-ordered payment from one spouse to another after a divorce. However, these days it is more common for money to be paid to an ex-spouse for property settlement; in other words, for a former spouse to buy out, in periodic payments, the other's share in real estate, investments, and so forth.

Watch Out

Thoroughly discuss the tax consequences of your divorce with your attorney and with your accountant, or you could wind up paying more to the IRS than you need to.

If the spouses split the property, they can determine which property each is to choose. Some choices have tax consequences if the property is subsequently sold. For example, if Millie keeps the house and eventually sells it, under the present tax law, the first $250,000 of profit from the sale (i.e., capital gains) is excluded from taxation.

If Mark relinquishes his share of the house in return for all of his pension (half of which his former wife would otherwise be entitled to), he will be taxed on all of the benefits when he receives the pension payments. (Chapter 20 offers a more comprehensive discussion of income tax planning.)

If Millie is awarded custody of Manny, Mark will pay child support. Tax law gives the custodial parent the right to the dependency exemption unless the parent waives that right. Because Mark is in a higher tax bracket, Manny's dependency exemption is worth more to him, and he may be willing to pay for that exemption with higher child support payments. Also, while Manny is living with Millie, she can file in the more advantageous tax status—head of household—while Mark will be relegated to filing as a single person.

Complicated, huh? Divorce isn't as simple as marriage. You ignore the tax implications at your own financial peril!

Gift Taxes

If Mark and Millie divide their assets during the process of divorce, the division will not result in any gift taxes as long as they are still married at the time they make the transfers.

Similarly, if a married couple had a postnuptial agreement that transferred assets from one spouse to another while married, there would be no gift tax. However, there might be a gift tax on any transfer made under a prenuptial agreement if the transfer occurs before the marriage.

For a more comprehensive discussion of gift taxes, see Chapter 17.

The Least You Need to Know

◆ If a surviving spouse has been left little or nothing in the deceased spouse's will, he or she can elect against that will and receive from one third to one half of the estate.

◆ A prenuptial agreement can limit the rights a spouse has against the other's assets in the event of divorce or death.

◆ Tax planning is an important part of the divorce process.

◆ A divorce calls for another look at your estate plan—specifically, your will.

Special Planning for Special Situations

In This Chapter

- ◆ Special tactics for taking care of disabled children
- ◆ "Living together" and same-sex unions
- ◆ Big wins and major financial losses
- ◆ Parenting your grandchildren
- ◆ Professionals and farmers

Not everyone fits neatly into any of the categories and circumstances that I've described so far in this book. Maybe after reading previous chapters, you've said to yourself, "Well, that's true for everybody else, but with me ..."

If you feel you're often the exception rather than the rule, then this chapter may be for you. In it, I address special situations, and you may well find yourself—and the answers you seek—here.

Planning for the Disabled Child—of Any Age

Statutes define an incapacitated person as one who has a severe and chronic mental or physical impairment that is likely to continue indefinitely. Needs certainly vary among the handicapped. Some require a guardian; others certainly do not and manage quite well on their own, although they will have certain medical needs throughout their lives.

The range of potential disabilities is so significant that no more than general advice can be offered here. Some kids will be able to earn enough to support themselves, others may be able to work at a minimal level, and still others will never be able to be gainfully employed. Clearly, any planning must account for your child's potential economic success.

If you have a child who is physically or mentally disabled, then you know most of such kids' needs are financial as well as personal. Parents provide a great deal of both, but sometimes the financial part becomes too great, and Mom and Dad must seek government assistance.

To preserve your estate for your other children, and enable the disabled child to receive needed support, it's often necessary to keep family assets from that child, especially as he or she grows to legal adult age. This is because government aid is often withdrawn or reduced when a child becomes an adult and has assets that can be used for his or her support.

For children, a number of programs are available. For example, federal law mandates special education programs to serve those with physical or mental disabilities. They begin at the pre-kindergarten level and continue through age 21. These entitlements are available at no cost to the family. Also, for those who are capable of post-secondary education, educational grants and special services may be available.

Words, Words, Words

Medicaid is a state-run health plan with federal government contributions, to help lower-income residents, which, in the context we're talking about here, would include your disabled child of any age, who has little or no income.

Several federal programs also provide financial support. The specifics are beyond the scope of this book, but you'll want to know, if you aren't already hooked up to them, that Supplemental Security Income and *Medicaid*, plus Social Security disability payments, might be available for your child.

Your Disabled Child's Assets

Because many entitlements have requirements that limit the income or asset resources of the disabled person, you need to take those limits into account in your financial planning. Consider doing the following:

- ◆ Review beneficiary designations in your will, life insurance policies, retirement plans and IRAs, trusts, and savings bonds to be sure your child isn't named in them.

- ◆ Avoid joint tenancy ownership of property with the disabled child, which creates more assets for him or her.

- ◆ Create a special trust for the child (for more on this topic, see the following section).

- ◆ Name a guardian in your will who is sensitive to the child's special needs.

> **CAUTION**　**Watch Out** _____
>
> Grandparents should consider *not* providing for the disabled child in their will if this would raise the child's assets to a level high enough to disqualify the child for public assistance.

A Trust May Be the Answer

Instead of giving your child money outright through a will or a life insurance policy, you might establish a trust. You would certainly need to consider the gift, estate, and income tax consequences. On the other hand, a well-planned practice of giving (see Chapter 18) and an independent trustee for a trust can avoid most tax problems.

Sara was a widow with several adult children. One of them, Alan, had medical problems that held him to a part-time, minimum-wage job, and would do so for the remainder of his life. Alan lived at home with Sara, and she was concerned that, when she died, Alan would need a house to live in and someone to handle his finances, even though he probably did not need a guardianship.

She established a revocable living trust and placed her house and investments in the trust for her life, and thereafter for Alan's life. Her grandchildren would receive the remainder of any assets left after Alan died. Sara consulted her other children before doing this so that they would understand why they would receive very little from her estate, although their kids would eventually benefit.

A trust is established to provide the amenities that government assistance cannot or will not. The goal is to provide a lifestyle for the child that best fits his or her needs. (The needs of Alan will, of course, differ from those of others with disabilities.) The trust must be drafted so that it keeps the assets for your child and does not reimburse the government for its basic expenditures.

Quote, Unquote

The joys of parents are secret, and so are their griefs and fears: they cannot utter the one, nor they will not utter the other.

—Francis Bacon, "Of Parents and Children" (1625)

Medicaid places severe limits on its aid for special-needs children who reach adulthood and have significant assets. To make sure your special-needs child is eligible for Medicaid, you might consider obtaining a court order appointing a guardian of your choice and naming that individual in your will. The guardian might be able to make certain gifts from the child's assets, or establish a support trust like the one Sara set up for Alan. If the child is institutionalized, and you are paying for that care, the guardian and trust can handle payments from your estate.

Medicaid-approved trusts have such specific requirements that the best advice is to use an attorney with an expertise in this area, particularly because the requirements vary among states.

When consulting an attorney about caring for your child with special needs, be sure to work with someone who fully understands the various federal and state entitlement laws.

Living Together/Planning Together

Living together is also legally called cohabitation, but we seldom see that expression anywhere these days. What we're talking about in these pages is a little more than living together. It's about life partners with a serious commitment on both sides, but where there is no marriage. With such long-term relationships there is often, maybe usually, the desire to share assets and, of course, incorporate the other person into one's estate plan.

Few laws apply to the legal rights of partners outside of marriage. Those with such living arrangements have no legal status. Contract law may apply to some arrangements, and the so-called "palimony" suits have been used as a means of trying to enforce support agreements. But the "significant other" has no inheritance rights under state intestate laws.

A few states, however, recognize common law marriages, where a man and woman cohabit for a statutory period and publicly acknowledge themselves as husband and wife.

At this writing, several states are determining the legality of gay or same-sex marriages. Until the law is clarified, the same-sex couple should follow the advice in this section of the text. The couple should consult an attorney and draft a contract that specifies the rights and duties between the partners. If children are involved, the couple should discuss custodial and support arrangements if the couple separates. As of this writing, only Massachusetts has permitted same sex marriages.

Certainly any couple, even if unmarried, can provide for each other in their wills if they choose. But remember, if you are not legally married, you do not have the right to elect against a will (see Chapter 13). Electing against a will is limited to a spouse.

Challenging your partner's will won't be a victory for you because if you are successful in having the will declared invalid, the deceased is considered to have died intestate (without a valid will). Then the state will decide who the heirs are—and none of them will be you.

Keeping Some Assets Out of Your Will

Joint ownership is a possibility for common law or same-sex couples, and it would provide the surviving half of the couple with the property immediately upon his or her partner's death. Keep in mind, though, that creating joint ownership in real estate gives both parties an interest in that property that is not easy to alter if the relationship changes.

You might also want to consider life insurance, with the partner named as beneficiary. Do the same with other investments, and they, too, will go directly to him or her at your death, avoiding probate and possible family squabbles.

Only a spouse has a right to the other spouse's qualified pension plan, but that plan could have any beneficiary you name. Consult a professional about any tax or other consequences.

Perhaps the wisest choice for unmarried couples would be a revocable living trust. You could establish the trust, fund it currently or in the future with life insurance and the assets from a pour-over will (those are assets that go through a will and then into a trust). The partner could be the current income beneficiary of the trust, or the future beneficiary, upon your death.

Any income from the trust would be taxed to the creator or grantor (that's you), and would be subject to gift tax to the extent the partner received income. (But the annual exclusion should be available; see Chapter 17 for more information about gift tax.) By setting it up as a revocable living trust, you can change the arrangement if your life changes.

Finally, the tax laws aren't much help to partners outside of marriage. The couple cannot file a joint return, which usually provides a lower tax rate, nor can one take the other as a dependent. There is no gift or estate tax deduction for a nonmarried partner.

Tip

Check with your employer. A growing number of companies are providing benefits for same- or opposite-sex life partners.

By all means, it's smart to have a written agreement regarding any financial or property ownership arrangement you have with your partner. That's for the protection of you both, to forestall litigation between the two of you, as well as between a survivor and the deceased's heirs.

The Role of Custodial Grandparent

According to 2000 U.S. Census Bureau figures, nearly 4.5 million children live in a household headed by a grandparent (although a parent might live in the house also). In 1.5 million U.S. households, there is no parent present.

Such arrangements can vary. Some grandparents are legally in charge of their grandchildren through adoption or guardianship. Others have taken on that responsibility informally, with their son or daughter's consent.

Are you raising, whether for the moment or until adulthood, your grandchildren? If you think you must have legal custody of your grandkids in order to be eligible for services and benefits for the child, that's not true. Many of them are available without you taking that step.

You'll want to do two things if you find yourself responsible for children at this stage of your life:

♦ Get as much information as you can about help available, both in the government and private sector, and through an appropriate support group in your area. The AARP (formerly the American Association of Retired Persons) website (www.aarp.org) can direct you to specific local and national agencies.

◆ Review your estate plan. You might want to change beneficiaries, even if just for a time. Or set up a trust for your grandchildren. If you are raising your grandkids because their parent(s) have problems with drugs or alcohol, those conditions might be different one day, and you may want to check your estate plan again. This could be a continually changing situation for you.

Eureka! We're Rich: Handling Sudden Wealth

I don't know your family, so I have no clue if you're likely to come into an eye-popping inheritance from your Uncle Forsyth. I don't know if someone's likely to ring your doorbell and declare you the latest $250,000 winner in the Publishers Clearing House Sweepstakes either.

In any event, you could wake up one morning to find yourself in the money. By all means allow yourself some champagne, and toast to your new fortune, while visions of sugarplums with all kinds of fancy price tags dance through your head.

Quote, Unquote

Wealth is known to be a great comforter.

—Plato, *The Republic* (fourth century B.C.E.)

More Money, More Taxes

Then, stop. Before you make another move, and after the champagne high wears off, think. Estate taxes, which were of marginal concern to you before, now loom ominously. You probably will be in a higher tax bracket, so "deductions" and "tax-exempt" become significant words. Yes, you have left behind your middle class tax concerns, and good riddance, you say. But now you have inherited the rich person's tax worries, which call for a whole new set of strategies.

What you need to do after absorbing your good news is run, don't walk, to your estate planning team (remember those men and women you engaged in Chapter 1?). Do not make any major expenditures or investments without their advice. More than one lottery winner, or inheritor of a small fortune, went from wealth to bankruptcy through unwise spending and investment.

You need immediately to do the following:

- ◆ Analyze all your assets and project your new income.

- ◆ Review your life insurance and casualty/liability insurance, now that you have more to protect.

- ◆ Revise your estate plan.

If you won the lottery, you have instant cash, but the payout is spread over as many as 20 years. If you receive a gift or inheritance, it may be in the form of assets that could be difficult to convert to cash, such as stock in a closed corporation, real estate, or valuable collectibles. Illiquid assets require special planning. Cash, on the other hand, can be invested in numerous ways to create high-yield, tax-exempt income, or growth in the investment. If you receive noncash assets, then the income flexibility is greatly reduced.

You may need to add more life insurance, particularly if estate taxes will bite into a cash-poor estate. Because you might buy and own more real property, visit your insurance agent and increase your casualty coverage. If you're involved in an accident with your expensive new car, a lawsuit will surely follow, so increase your automobile liability coverage.

Tip

You might want to direct the trustee of any children's trust to distribute funds to them based on certain incentives, such as gainful employment or a meaningful contribution to society. Inherited wealth need not create wastrel children.

Revising your estate plan may require rethinking your goals and the documents executed to further them. That includes who will benefit and by what means. Leaving everything to your spouse may have made sense before when the "everything" was relatively modest, but does it now? Or what about the children? You want to rear loving and responsible kids, not sponges. Perhaps giving something to charity is also possible now.

Often a well-drafted revocable trust can be used to manage assets for you and your spouse, and then continue to manage those assets for your children.

Tax planning becomes crucial at this time. A QTIP trust for the spouse and a credit shelter trust to take advantage of the estate's unified credit are important considerations. Making gifts that qualify for the annual exclusion and reduce your estate require proper training. All of these are explained in the next part of this book, about taxes. Transferring ownership of life insurance policies might be another option.

Finally, don't forget your will. All your planning may be for naught if your will is not an integral part of your estate file. Remember, everything you own solely is distributed by your will.

The most the federal estate tax can take is 47 percent of your assets as of 2005. Don't over plan to the extent that the tax tail wags the planning dog. First and foremost must be your goals for yourself and your family.

About Bankruptcy

Bankruptcy is growing in this country. In 1996 the jump in the number of personal bankruptcies was greater than it has been since the mid-1980s, when we were in the midst of a serious recession. Take at look at the statistics in the following table.

Annual U.S. Personal Bankruptcy Filings

Year	Total Non-Business Filings	Year	Total Non-Business Filings
1985	341,233	1994	780,455
1986	449,203	1995	874,642
1987	495,553	1996	1,125,006
1988	549,612	1997	1,350,118
1989	616,226	1998	1,398,182
1990	718,107	1999	1,281,581
1991	872,438	2000	1,217,972
1992	900,874	2001	1,452,030
1993	812,898	2002	1,505,306
		2003	1,650,279

Source: American Bankruptcy Institute

Financial distress has myriad causes. Some are self-inflicted, like running up credit card balances for unnecessary items. With other folks, the problem is corporate downsizing that might have led to a job loss. Or perhaps there have been enormous medical bills. Or a divorce.

Obviously the concerns of wealth transfer and high taxes don't apply when you're facing bankruptcy, but financial and estate planning are still important.

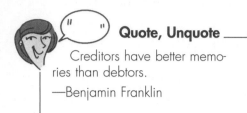

Quote, Unquote

Creditors have better memories than debtors.

—Benjamin Franklin

Budgeting, consolidating debt, cashing in assets, and reducing one's lifestyle expenses could be sufficient to turn things around without your turning to bankruptcy. Remember, bankruptcy does clear most of your debts, but it remains on your credit report for 10 years and can keep you from obtaining new credit for major purchases you may need down the road.

Help! And Perhaps Some Relief

Before taking that first step to filing for bankruptcy, by all means, first contact your local consumer credit counseling service; its telephone number can be found in your local directory.

If bankruptcy does seem to be the only answer for you, consult an attorney who specializes in that area of the law. You can find one by calling your local bar association and asking for the names of attorneys who handle such matters. Contact an attorney as soon as you have decided to file. Serious debt can threaten your health, marriage, and family, and needs to be quickly addressed.

Tip

Review your assets to determine how to maximize your bankruptcy exemptions, such as making a larger contribution to a qualified retirement plan. You will probably be able to afford it, as you will no doubt continue working, and will have the income to make that contribution.

Although bankruptcy exemptions vary from state to state, the debtor who resides in a state that uses federal exemptions (which are indexed for inflation) can keep from his or her bankruptcy creditors up to …

- ◆ $17,475 equity (fair market value) in his or her residence.

- ◆ $2,775 interest in a motor vehicle.

- ◆ $9,300 in household goods.

- ◆ $1,150 in personal jewelry.

In addition, qualified retirement plans and life insurance policies are exempt from bankruptcy creditors.

Better times *will* come. Keep moving forward with your estate plan, and don't for a moment think you do not need a will because you don't have that many assets. You still have some, and you might also need to provide guardianship for minor children.

The Professional: Different Planning Needs

Physicians, dentists, attorneys, accountants, and other professionals licensed by the state to practice have some unique estate planning needs. For example, they cannot sell their practice in the same way other businesses can be sold because, among other restrictions, the purchaser must also be licensed in that profession.

Usually the estate planning necessary for those with high incomes and substantial investments applies to professionals. If this means you, here are a few matters you'll want to note.

Choice of Business Form

At one time the larger qualified retirement plan benefits made operating as a C corporation the logical choice (see Chapter 6 for an explanation of C corporations). However, all forms of business organizations offer essentially the same retirement opportunities.

C corporations still have some employment fringe benefits, but these often can be obtained by other means, such as through the other spouse's employer. The choice of business entity can limit a professional's liability for an associate's negligence, but not for his or her own malpractice.

Disability, Retirement, Divorce, and Death

Because your employment income stops when you are no longer working, it's certainly smart to purchase disability insurance.

The limited marketability of your practice means that you should have a buy-sell agreement if you are practicing with others in a partnership or corporation (see Chapter 6). The agreement can cover both retirement and untimely death, and be a source of retirement income for you or an estate for your family.

If you're a sole practitioner when you opt to retire, you may have to hire a business broker to find a buyer for your practice. The major asset of your business—the client or patient list—may be of limited value to the purchaser. Adequate life insurance is vital to create an estate when the practice doesn't.

In several states, the value of a professional license is considered marital property for divorce purposes. I hope you'll have other assets to trade off. If not, divorce can seriously impact your estate planning here.

Down on the Farm: Also Special Needs

Are you a farmer? Then you probably know you have a unique position under the IRS Code and under some other government programs. I don't have the space in this book to go into all of them, but here are some planning opportunities:

- **Choice of business entity**   Many family farms have incorporated to take advantage of tax laws and more limited liability. For example, the farm home not only serves as your residence, but also as a deductible business office.

- **Accounting choices**   Cash and accrual basis accounting methods are permitted, and you can also use the crop method, which permits the deduction of crop expenses when the income is received. In addition, some capital improvements can be considered farming expenses, rather than depreciations, which must be spread over several years.

- **Federal and state programs**   Government loan programs are often available at attractive rates. Conservation and forestry incentives can provide cash for land that is not needed for crops. Certain crop reduction or diversion assistance can bring additional revenue. A number of states provide a lower property tax assessment for farmland.

- **Estate tax valuation and payment**   Under certain conditions, a family farm may be valued for federal estate tax purposes at its value as a farm, rather than at the *highest and best use* for that property. This is a term used by government and planning officials to mean the optimum use for a particular parcel of land, as they see it. For example, specific acreage might be seen as a shopping mall or a housing development, which would likely increase its value significantly. In addition, the estate may be eligible for the installment payment of the federal estate tax, which has interest-only payments for the first five installments, then the balance payable in 10 years.

> **Quote, Unquote**
>
> When tillage begins, other arts follow. The farmers therefore are the founders of human civilization.
>
> —Daniel Webster, "Remarks on Agriculture" (1840)

You have seen in this chapter how special health/living/work situations can bring concerns and problems not always easily answered. Still, if one of these situations applies to you, by going to the right sources you *can* find solutions—and the way to a valuable estate plan.

The Least You Need to Know

◆ Proper planning for the disabled child can protect him or her, as well as ensure assets for your other children.

◆ Having everything in written contracts can best protect the property rights of unmarried couples living together.

◆ There is help for the custodial grandparent, in both private and government sectors.

◆ Sudden wealth or financial reverses require immediate planning adjustments.

◆ Professionals and farmers qualify for tax elections and tax benefits unique to them.

15

Family Feuds: Avoiding One Over Your Estate

In This Chapter

- ◆ How wills can be contested
- ◆ Where the burden of proof rests
- ◆ Will writing dos and don'ts
- ◆ Making your will challenge-proof

It is the stuff of drama—challenging a will. "Then, Lieutenant, just as Great Uncle Simon was planning to change his will …" or words to that effect have turned up in dialogue in motion pictures and television dramas since both appeared on the scene.

Challenging a will isn't quite that dramatic in real life. It's families squabbling, threatening, seeing lawyers, not speaking—and continuing all of this sometimes for years. Naturally you don't want to see your loved ones carrying on like that about *your* will. Here's how to prevent it.

Challenging a Will: What'll Do It

Your will *can* be contested. Any beneficiary or heir can challenge it. What you need to know is the "why" and the "how" of will contests, so that you can prepare a nearly lawsuit-proof last will and testament. Read on.

The person contesting the will has the burden of proof. He or she must convince the court that the will should not be admitted to probate by proving one or more of the grounds (reasons) for finding that will invalid.

> **Quote, Unquote**
>
> Discord gives a relish to concord.
>
> —Publilius Syrus, "Moral Sayings" (first century B.C.E.)

If a will is successfully contested, the deceased's estate is distributed, according to state intestate laws, to his or her heirs. Or a contest may revive an earlier will of the deceased's.

I'll tell you first about the usual grounds for a will contest.

Plain Incompetence

The testator (that's the person who's writing his or her will) must be at least 18 years old and mentally competent. Courts look to several factors in determining mental competence. Those factors are whether a person …

◆ Knows that he or she is making a will.

◆ Knows the extent and value of his or her property.

◆ Knows the persons who would *ordinarily* be the beneficiaries of the will.

◆ Understands the disposition as to the beneficiaries in his or her will.

> **Tip**
>
> When signing a will, you may want to select credible witnesses who can readily attest to your mental competence. For example, if you are in a hospital, rehabilitation center, or nursing home, consider first using your doctor or a nurse as a witness.

If there is a contest based on competency, expert witnesses, such as the deceased's doctor, and friends and acquaintances who knew the deceased *toward the end of his life* (having last seen him five years ago won't count) will testify as to their observations.

Someone in the early stages of Alzheimer's disease, who fulfills the above-mentioned requirements, can have a will drawn that will stand up in court. So will a man or woman mildly mentally disabled who, again, can satisfy those requirements. It's not the illness per se that's in question, but rather the testator's degree of understanding while suffering from it.

If you, as testator, have a history of medical problems that can affect your judgment, then that would be relevant evidence for a challenge. But quirky behavior, such as cutting a child out of the will, in itself is not enough to mount a successful challenge.

Undue Influence: A Toughie to Prove

Undue influence is the concept of certain beneficiaries (those who receive more than the others) attempting to have the will made in their own favor by exerting inappropriate influence on the testator. Except in the most obvious of cases, undue influence is hard for a challenger to prove. The usual suspects for having undue influence include second spouses and favored children.

Anyone attempting to protest that will must prove …

- Undue influence was exerted on the testator.

- The effect of the undue influence was to overpower the testator's mind and will.

- It produced a will (or a provision on the will) that expresses the intent of the one exerting the influence, and not that of the testator, and the will (or provision) would not have been made if it weren't for that influence.

What is evidence of undue influence? Well, there are a few things one can look for here:

- The testator was in a weakened physical or mental condition, making him or her more susceptible to undue influence or domination.

- The testator is so isolated from other family members or friends that he or she is forced to listen to only one person.

Quote, Unquote

Go first class—your heirs will.
—Handstitching on a throw pillow

- The person alleged to have exerted the undue influence had the opportunity to exercise it.

- The disposition unduly favored the person exerting the influence on his or her family.

Often the person contesting produces evidence that the deceased's wishes were overridden by another, usually someone who was trusted by the testator. This trusted person, in essence, told the deceased who should benefit from his or her will.

The easiest cases of undue influence for the courts involve a confidential relationship that is perverted to divert the deceased's natural wishes away from his or her relatives, to another person or persons. Here's a good example. Lawyers, unfortunately, sometimes draft wills for clients that provide substantial devises to the lawyer or his or her family. Not only is that unethical conduct on the part of any attorney, but it also will probably result in a successful will contest by anyone who decides to take up that challenge.

> **Tip**
>
> Few wills are contested on the grounds that the deceased was forced into making one (duress) or induced to sign something that later turned out to be a will (fraud). Those illegalities do make for a good mystery plot, though. I highly recommend you read Agatha Christie's *Why Didn't They Ask Evans?*

What's harder to prove? That would be a situation involving some child or children receiving more than the others. There is no law requiring a parent to treat each child equally in a will. Still, some children deserve more, such as a special-needs child who will require long-term care (but it may actually be in the child's best interest to leave him *less*; see Chapter 14). Some children have more financial resources than others. Some children become alienated from their parents; others have had the burden of caring for them. There are many reasons why parents give preference to one child over another. Is that fair? In the case of the disabled child, yes, and the other children probably understand that. In the other instances, well …

If you are going to show some preference in your will, you should consider a letter or videotape stating your reasons for that choice. If Roberta is a doctor married to a multimillionaire and Clarissa is single and a sculptor with a fairly low income, you may get away with a discrepancy in what you leave. The letter or video may help Roberta understand why you left the bulk of your assets to Clarissa. That *could* help those who would otherwise feel shortchanged to understand and accept your decision. But don't bet on it. Not dividing equally among the kids is very likely to cause resentment among them—and toward you long after you're gone.

I once drafted a will for a woman who left half of her estate to her daughter; the other half was divided among her grandchildren. At the funeral the daughter's tears were freely flowing. But once the will was read, there was a dramatic change, and the daughter probably would have kicked the coffin if it had been there. A will contest was narrowly averted, but animosities lingered in that family for a long time.

Poor Execution

You know that your will must be signed by you, and your signature witnessed. Most states require two adult witnesses. Attorneys usually go through a little ceremony here:

> Attorney: Do you declare this to be your Last Will and Testament?
>
> You: I do.
>
> Attorney: Do you wish that we two (the lawyer and someone from his or her office) serve as witnesses to your will?
>
> You: I do.

You sign the will first, and then the witnesses do. If you are physically unable to sign, you can request that another person do so for you in your presence and in sight of the witnesses. In that case, your will would state that another person has signed for you. You must tell your witnesses that they are signing your will, but you don't have to allow them to read it.

Slip-ups do occur, often when a person writes and executes his or her own will. Common mistakes include ...

- ◆ No witnesses or poorly selected witnesses.
- ◆ Witnesses signing outside each other's presence.
- ◆ Failure to use a self-proving clause (there's a sample of that statement in Chapter 8).

Many states allow the person making a will to attach to it a self-proving document, where essentially the witnesses swear to having been present at the signing of the will and note that the testator was of sound mind and was signing freely.

Most will forms you can buy at a local stationery store, or those on a computer disk, will have a line for witness signatures, so if you do it yourself you probably won't miss that aspect of execution.

Your two witnesses (some states require three) must be at least 18 years of age and otherwise competent. If there is any question about the proper execution, or your competence, then those persons will surely be called to testify in any will contest. States don't require your will to be notarized, although I have seen at least one attorney who does so. All that a notary does is validate the signatures, which is seldom an issue.

Briefs

In the Line-Forms-on-the-Right-at-Probate Department: if you're a Grateful Dead fan, you certainly remember when Jerry Garcia, the group's leader, died in August 1995. In March 1997 the final tally on his estate came in: $9 million.

Immediately after the rock musician's death there was a scurrying for parts of those assets. It was also reported in March 1997 that lawyers for his third and last wife asked a judge to reverse his decision awarding a $4.6 million divorce settlement to wife No. 2. An assortment of business partners, former lovers, and acquaintances also filed more than $38 million in claims against the estate.

Witnesses, but Not Beneficiaries, Too

One other point: you shouldn't have anyone who's a beneficiary witness your will. Many state laws deny the witness his or her bequest in a will, or limit what he or she can receive to an amount that is no greater than what he or she would come into as an heir if the deceased died intestate. If the beneficiary is an unnecessary witness (a third witness when only two are required), then that rule does not apply.

Here's an example. Let's say Jacob leaves one half of his residuary probate estate to his son, Joseph, and divides the other half among his other 11 children, saving a little for his loyal servant Jim. Joseph was one of two witnesses to Jacob's will. Poor Joseph. Assuming that Jacob's wife does not survive him, but the other children do, Joseph's intestate share would be one twelfth, not one half, as stated in the will. And servant Jim, who happened to be the other witness, would be much worse off. He was left

Watch Out

Can a photocopy of a will cause a challenge because it is not an original? If the original has been lost, and a duplicate original, or a photocopy found, the contestant may well assert that the testator intended to revoke his or her will. So you and your witnesses should sign only the original will, which would make the challenged will invalid.

$10,000 in the will, but in fact he would receive nothing, because he was not one of the sons and was a witness. Jacob's will would be valid, but the witnesses much sadder for the experience.

"Messing Up" a Will

What looks to be a revoked will can also cause a court challenge. Mutilated or marked-on wills will cause a contestant to argue that the testator intended to revoke that document and the evidence is the torn will, or the one with handwritten notes on it. So be careful never to make handwritten changes on a will.

The "Don'ts" We Often "Do"

A simple will, which is all that most of us need, isn't that expensive. Save yourself worries and your family from a possible will contest: see an attorney and shop around for the best fee.

Now that my bias has been clearly expressed, let's consider some ways you could get into trouble, legally and otherwise, with a will. And I'll tell you how to avoid such trouble.

Making Abusive Remarks

The probated will is a public document, open to anyone who cares to see it. One of my clients wanted to vent her frustrations about her daughter, whose life, in the woman's eyes, had been less than exemplary. The phrases she proposed to put in her will were expressive and colorful, and derogatory in the extreme. She had every right to cut the daughter out of the will, but not to abuse her in public. Family disputes are tragic enough without that. I reminded her that she might reconcile with the daughter, but not get around to changing the will. In the end, she toned down her language.

Making an Omission Without Explanation

You can choose whomever you want to receive your probate estate (remember, however, a spouse may have a right to elect against the will). If you want to delete one of your four children as a beneficiary, that is your privilege. I mentioned earlier in this chapter that a letter or videotape explaining why you have chosen to do so might be a satisfactory way to allow the child to understand your motives. The same advice applies if the child doesn't get an "equal" share, and there is no special-needs child involved. In any event, explaining your reasoning can head off a will contest.

Tip

If you do want to reduce a particular child's "expected" inheritance, consider giving the child some memento that he will treasure, and then indicate that other considerations result in that child receiving nothing else from the will. That could soften the blow a bit. It might also give the child no grounds to contest the will if you clearly indicate why his interest is not what he might have expected.

Making Promises: Don't

Court decisions abound involving a deceased who allegedly promised someone that he would be left something in the will for services rendered.

For example, Ivan promises a neighbor, Sam, that if Sam handles the upkeep of Ivan's house and yard, then Ivan will leave him something in his will. Ivan dies, and—what do you know—leaves everything to his third cousin.

Sam is incensed. Is he going to see an attorney? Is the attorney going to take his case? Is he going to get anything from the estate? Answer: yes, yes, and maybe.

A better system for both Ivan and Sam would have been a written contract that specified Sam's duties and compensation, rather than a devise in Ivan's will. Sam can file a claim against Ivan's estate if the executor won't honor the contract.

Watch Out

Never use a codicil to reduce the amount a beneficiary is to receive from your will. You are almost guaranteed a will contest from that disappointed individual. Make a new will instead.

Making Codicils that Change Beneficiaries

A codicil (a separate paper amending a will) changing an executor or a guardian probably won't overly concern anyone and hardly ever results in a will contest.

The following is a sample codicil changing executors. As you can see, it is quite a simple form. Still, before you consider adapting it for yourself, be certain to check with your attorney or your state to make sure it meets requirements where you are.

CODICIL TO THE LAST WILL AND TESTAMENT OF

_____

I, _____, domiciled in _____, do make, publish, and declare this to be the First Codicil to my Last Will and Testament executed by me on the 31st day of July, 2001, in the presence of _____ and _____ as witnesses.

I hereby remove _____ as personal representative and substitute _____ under Article V of my Last Will and Testament.

In all other respects, I hereby ratify all of the provisions of my Last Will and Testament dated July 31, 2001.

IN TESTIMONY WHEREOF, I have subscribed my name to this my First Codicil to my Last Will and Testament consisting of one typewritten page, all in the presence of the persons witnessing it at my request on this _____ day of _____, 20___, at _____.

_____

Testator

The foregoing instrument, consisting of this page, was signed, published, and declared by _____ to be his First Codicil to his Last Will and Testament, in our presence. We then at his request and in his presence, and in the presence of each other, signed our names as witnesses to the Codicil this _____ day of _____, 20___.

_____ residing at _____

_____

_____ residing at _____

_____

(Note: A self-proving clause should be used with the Codicil, just as with a Will.)

A Joint Will? No!

Togetherness is fine, but there are some things you just gotta do on your own, you know? And making your own will is one of them. You and your spouse should have separate documents. The provisions can be reciprocal: everything to each other, then to the children. Or you can make different provisions.

Just don't have a joint will. When one of you dies, the surviving spouse may not be able to change the will without running the risk of a will contest. Those who were beneficiaries in the joint will, but are no longer in a subsequent will, may claim that the surviving spouse was legally bound to the provisions in the joint will.

Two wills really don't cost much more than one, and you can avoid that potential problem.

Making a Separate List of "Gifts"

Frequently we have several items we'd like to leave to a particular family member or friend, but we don't want to list them in a will. Most state laws allow you to prepare a list of that property, and the names of persons you want to receive those items. Many states require that such a list must exist at the time the will is executed and not subsequently be changed, and that the list be in the testator's handwriting or signed by him or her.

It's easier to decide what property to give a person and put that devise in the will. As to other items, consider making gifts now, or leave a letter to your beneficiaries asking them to distribute those mementos among your family and friends. The letter will not be legally binding, but your beneficiaries probably will honor your wishes.

Making Changes on the Will

That's right, *on*, not *in*, the will. As I have said, if you want to change your will, execute a codicil or prepare a new will. Don't line out cousin Calvin's name and replace it with niece Nancy's. Any changes on the will after it is executed will not be valid. You run the additional risk of the court treating substantial changes as reflecting your intent to revoke the will. A disgruntled heir may be tempted to contest the will on that basis; if he or she is successful, your estate would be distributed to the intestate heirs.

Families squabbling over an estate can be intriguing in mystery books, and funny in television sit-coms. But in real life, such feuds are not terribly attractive. You can easily avoid one by making sure your will is as challenge-proof as it can be. It's really not that difficult. When considering the use of a trust as a will substitute, be aware that the formalities of executing a trust are more lax than a will, but judges will consider the competency of, and undue influence on, the trust's creator if the trust is contested.

The Least You Need to Know

♦ A will can be challenged, but the burden of proof is on the challenger.

♦ To avoid a contest over your estate, take every step you can to make your will challenge-proof.

♦ Be careful, if you use a do-it-yourself will, to make no mistakes that a disappointed beneficiary can latch onto.

♦ Spouses should not execute a joint will.

Part 4

Taxes You Must Pay, and Those Maybe You Don't

Now we come to what you might not have been looking forward to reading about—taxes. You'll certainly find a variety of them here, from the federal estate tax to a tax levied by some states on what they call "intangibles," such as stocks and bonds.

Tax matters are important to your estate, of course, because the more you can legitimately hold back from the grabby IRS, the more there will be for you and your family. So while unfortunately I do have to tell you about all these taxes, I'll also have the pleasure of helping you keep them down to a minimum, and sometimes avoid them altogether.

That's about as good as the news gets in a tax section, and because we're talking about your hard-earned money, you should find that darned nice to hear. Let's get on with the savings.

Chapter 16

The Wonderful World of Federal Estate Taxes

In This Chapter

- ◆ Taxing estates more than $1,500,000
- ◆ Basics of computing the tax
- ◆ Marital and other deductions
- ◆ Transfers that skip a generation

Ah, so many taxes. Here is the first of them: the federal tax levied on your estate.

"Isn't dying bad enough," you're probably thinking, "without being hit with a new slew of taxes—in absentia, of course." I couldn't agree with you more. But for now that's the law of the land, and so here they are—estate taxes spelled out.

The Magic Number Is $1,500,001 (and Rising)

First you should know that officially the *federal estate tax* is a levy placed by the federal government on the transfer of property from the deceased to those who inherit. If $1,500,000 or less is transferred, then there is no estate tax, unless there have been prior taxable gifts, which I'll go into later in this chapter. Also, if you leave all your property outright to your spouse or to a charity, there is no federal estate tax at all (that's the marital deduction, which I'll also talk about). The excludible amount will be increased to $2,000,000 in 2006, to $3,500,000 in 2009, and in 2010 it will be unlimited. The law expires in 2010, which means that the excludible amount reverts to $1,000,000, unless a new law is passed. The law reduced the highest rate to 50 percent in 2002, and another 1 percent each subsequent year until 2008 when it remains at 45 percent until reaching 0 percent in 2010; thereafter it presumably reverts to 50 percent, unless the law changes.

The tax begins at $1 over $1,500,000 in 2005, $2,000,000 (years 2006–2008), and $3,500,000 (year 2009), with no tax in 2010, and reverting to the $1,000,000 thereafter.

If you're reading this and saying "Hah, I should only have an estate worth $1,500,000," then I urge you to stop feeling impoverished and do some fast math. Do you remember the assets form you filled out in Chapter 1? If you have, for example, a $300,000 life insurance policy and a home valued at $150,000 (although any mortgage would be a deduction from the gross estate), you're already at $450,000, and we haven't even touched on your pension and other assets. So do read on. All of this could apply to you.

Obviously, the exclusion increases will reduce the number of estates required to pay the federal estate tax, but the number will still be significant to your heirs if your estate is one of the estates over the exempt amount. In 2002 there were 114,000 such estates, which collectively paid $27 billion. If Congress feels the need to suspend the increased exclusion amounts, it will do so, if past history is any indication.

Spreading the Wealth to Avoid the Tax

There are ways of handling your "wealth" if you fall into the estate tax asset figure. Take Ted, as an example. When he died, his wife inherited one half of his property ($1,500,000), and the other half ($1,500,000) went to their children. Ted had made no substantial gifts in any one year. While his estate for federal estate tax purposes is $3 million, none of it is taxed, because $1,500,000 goes tax-free to his wife (remember, she's got that marital deduction) and the other $1,500,000 does not exceed the threshold figure of $1,500,000. Perhaps Ted did a bit of estate planning?

Tip

You can call the local IRS tax help line or obtain tax information from the IRS website, www.irs.ustreas.gov.

The federal estate tax, incidentally, is paid from the estate before any disbursements are made to beneficiaries or heirs.

What's in the Pot? Just About Everything

The federal estate tax includes the probate estate and property owned by the deceased where ownership transfers to another individual upon the deceased's death. (The spouse gets a marital deduction.)

Let's use Audrey, a single parent, as an example. She owned the following: her home (worth $200,000), and corporate stock, which she jointly owned with right of survivorship with her daughter, Paula (worth $300,000). She also had a life insurance policy ($300,000) with the proceeds payable to her other daughter, Diana and a pension (worth $800,000), also payable to Diana. The house is in her probate estate; the stock, life insurance proceeds, and pension amount are transferred to the daughters at Audrey's death. All of the estate is subject to the federal estate tax, because it totals $1,600,000 (although only $100,000 is taxed because of the exemption of $1,500,000), although if she died in 2006 or after, it would not because of the increased exclusion.

Another Important Figure: $11,000

The amount of $11,000 will be mentioned frequently throughout all of Part 4. It's a common tax break and a good one. Essentially, it is a *gift tax*. (Chapter 17 goes into much more detail about this gift tax.)

The first $11,000 of any gift you make to any person during any calendar year is excluded from taxation.

If you are married and have a child, you and your spouse can give that child a total of $22,000. Married couples can use those two annual exclusions (worth $22,000 per recipient), even if only one spouse owns the property. This is called *gift splitting*.

Take Mary for example. She gives her stock in ABC, Inc. to her son. The stock is worth $22,000. If Mary's husband joins in the gift (and files the appropriate gift tax return), there will be no tax because both parents are using their annual exclusions ($11,000 + $11,000). You'll see the words *annual exclusion* often in the next five chapters, too. They refer to this $11,000 gift.

The Gross Estate

This is where we'll begin calculating the federal estate tax. Basically, you take the gross estate, subtract expenses and other allowed deductions, and then add certain taxable gifts.

At the end of the specific explanations that follow, you'll see a worksheet. It will show you in numbers the explanations that follow.

Let's start with our base item, the gross estate.

The value of the property on the date of the deceased's death—the *gross estate*— generally determines the amount that is subject to federal estate tax. Here is a list of property that would be included in the gross estate:

- Property solely owned by the deceased

- Certain gifts transferred within three years before death (for example, a life insurance policy ownership transferred to another owner)

- Transfers where the deceased retains a life estate (see Chapter 2) or has the power to revoke the transfer, such as a revocable living trust (see Chapter 9)

- Survivor annuity and survivor pension (when the owner was the first to die)

◆ Jointly owned property: half included if jointly with spouse; all included if owned with another person (survivor has made no contribution to the property)

◆ Property over which deceased had *general power of appointment*. What's that? Look at it this way. I die and I own some property. I give my wife not the ownership, but the power to give that to herself or another individual whom she wants to have it. This is a rarely used transfer, confined for the most part to pretty sophisticated estate planning in the millions of dollars.

◆ Life insurance proceeds paid to the estate or where the policy was owned by the deceased (most of us own our policies, but someone else could also own an insurance policy on our life).

So essentially any property that someone else receives because of your death will be included in your gross estate.

Briefs

Artist Georgia O'Keeffe died in 1986 at the age of 98. Her estate included approximately 400 works of art. The executor and the IRS agreed that the total art valued individually amounted to $72,759,000. Because that was the value if all of the works were sold at once, both parties agreed that there should be a discount for federal estate taxes. The executor contended that the value should be discounted 75 percent, while IRS experts argued for a range of 10 to 37 percent. The Tax Court compromised: for tax purposes the art would be valued at $36,400,000.

I'll illustrate all of this with Anita's estate. Anita died in 2004. She was married and had two adult children. According to a prenuptial agreement, Anita's husband waived any right to her probate estate, so her will leaves the stocks/bonds to her church, and the farm to her children. She lived in a noncommunity property state (see Chapter 3). Anita owned the following:

Property	Ownership	Value
house	with husband	$200,000
household goods	with husband	20,000
savings/checking	with husband	20,000
stocks and bonds	Anita	200,000
farm	Anita	1,800,000
pension	(husband beneficiary)	200,000
life insurance	(children beneficiary)	200,000
	Total value of the property	$2,640,000

The gross estate for federal estate tax includes …

◆ Half each of the house, household goods, and savings/checking (the husband is considered to have owned the other half of each asset). That's a total of $120,000.

◆ The stocks/bonds, pension, farm, and life insurance proceeds. That's a total of $2,400,000.

Tip

Charities that qualify for federal *income* tax deductions will almost always qualify for the federal *estate* tax deduction. Chapter 18 contains several suggestions for charitable arrangements that could qualify for income tax deductions when made, as well as estate tax deductions.

Therefore, Anita's gross estate is $2,520,000 ($2,640,000 minus the spouse's $120,000).

Anita had not made any taxable gifts within the last three years, which would have been included in the gross estate such as a life insurance policy, nor had she established a revocable trust, both of which would have been included in her estate for tax purposes. (Most gifts made within three years prior to death are not in the gross estate, with a few exceptions noted above and the gift tax paid on a gift made within three years.)

She had not received from anyone a general power of appointment either.

If Anita lived in a community property state, marital property would be owned as community property, so the surviving spouse's half interest as his ownership interest in the marital assets would not be part of Anita's gross estate; it is already his one-half.

Great! Tax Deductions Allowed

The gross estate is, fortunately, reduced by certain allowed deductions. The most frequently used are the charitable deduction, the marital deduction, expenses of administering the estate, and the deceased's debts and certain of her taxes.

Let's examine them.

Charitable Deductions

As you have seen, Anita left her stocks and bonds in the amount of $200,000 to her church, which is, of course, a charity. That entitles Anita's estate to a charitable deduction. Gifts through a will or a trust, or through life arrangements that are paid by an estate or trust, qualify for this deduction.

Hooray for the Marital Deduction!

Here is a very popular deduction that includes all property that the surviving spouse receives outright or through certain qualified marital trusts.

Returning to Anita, we see that her husband received the following:

- Half of their house, half of their household goods, and half of their savings/checking account, because they owned each asset jointly with right of survivorship, and he survived her; altogether this property totaled $120,000. (He already owned the other half of each asset as co-owner.)

- $200,000 as survivor on her pension plan.

The total amount of the marital deduction here is $320,000.

> **Quote, Unquote**
>
> Wealth: any income that is at least $100 more a year than the income of one's wife's sister's husband.
>
> —H. L. Mencken

The QTIP and Credit Shelter Trust

Let me explain something else to you here briefly. Sometimes a spouse receives property in trust, where he or she is the only income beneficiary. If the surviving spouse elects to treat the amount left in the trust by her dearly departed as hers for her estate tax, then the marital deduction is available for the deceased spouse's estate tax. In effect, she receives the income from the trust during her life, then the balance of the trust at her death is included in her estate for the federal estate tax. The surviving spouse would be beneficiary of the trust income, and then the principal would go to others (e.g., children) at his or her death. This is an exception to the general rule that the spouse must receive the property outright to qualify for the marital deduction.

This qualified trust is often referred to as a QTIP (Qualified Terminal Interest Property). There must be an election (choice) to treat a QTIP trust as a marital deduction in the deceased's estate.

A spouse who has significant assets may want to establish two trusts:

- One trust involves a QTIP (for the marital deduction).

- Another trust, funded with $1,500,000, or the current amount of the exclusion, called a *credit shelter trust*, for using the unified credit equivalent amount. I'll explain that in the next few pages.

Combining the QTIP trust with the credit shelter trust could mean that the deceased's estate will not have to pay any estate tax.

The property transferred to the spouse's QTIP trust provides a marital deduction *and* the $1,500,000 that is exempt from the tax, which goes to the credit shelter trust, may equal the gross estate. Both trusts could be used to support the spouse during his or her life.

You can, of course, make a gift to your spouse and obtain the same result, except that you no longer have any control over what he or she does with the property given.

Deductible Expenses

The estate might have quite a few costs. There could be probate administration expenses (filing, executor, and attorney fees). There could be debts on the estate property, such as a mortgage on the home, and bills that were unpaid at Anita's death. Likewise, there may be taxes that Anita would have had to pay, such as income tax on earnings in the year before she died, or property taxes on her real estate. The state death tax credit expired as a *credit* in 2004, and became a *deduction* in 2005 and thereafter.

> **Quote, Unquote**
>
> The wisdom of man never yet contrived a system of taxation that would operate with perfect equality.
>
> —Andrew Jackson, "Proclamation to the People of South Carolina" (December 10, 1823)

Anita's estate actually had the following deductions:

Probate expenses	$150,000
Mortgage on her farm	$50,000
Income taxes due	$5,000
Property tax on her farm	$5,000
Total	$210,000

Tallying It Up

All of Anita's estate's deductible expenses include:

Charitable	$200,000
Marital	$320,000
Other (above-mentioned)	$210,000
Total	$730,000

Her whole tax computation looks like this so far:

Gross estate	$2,520,000
(less) deductions	$730,000
Taxable estate	$1,790,000

That's quite a reduction from the original figure, isn't it?

Anita did not make any post-1976 taxable gifts (gifts that are in excess of the annual exclusion of $10,000 per recipient, or $20,000 if the spouse joins in making the gift, increased beginning in 2002 to $11,000 and $22,000). Therefore her tax base is the same as her taxable estate.

If there are gifts in excess of the annual exclusion, then they would be added to the tax base. For example, if Anita had given $50,000 to one of her children in 1996 (and her husband joined in the gift), the taxable portion of the gift would be $30,000 ($50,000 gift less $20,000 annual gift exclusion for both of them).

How Does a 45 Percent Beginning Rate Sound?

Now we're getting to the important numbers.

The federal estate tax rate begins at 45 percent and goes up to 48 percent, but these percentages are changed beginning in 2003. (Anita's highest marginal rate, on the last $290,000 of her taxable estate is 45 percent.)

Anita's taxable estate is $1,790,000, so based on the following table, her tax computation looks like this:

> $555,800 (on the first $1,500,000) at 43 percent, which is, in effect, not taxed because it equates to the exempt amount of $1.5 million.
>
> $130,500 (45 percent of the next $290,000)
>
> $686,300 (on the taxable estate $1,790,000)

This tentative tax of $686,300 is computed using the IRS estate tax table on the next page.

The following table indicates the estate tax rates for estates over the exemption amount after the changes in the Tax Act of 2001.

Tax Rates and Exemptions for Federal Estate Tax		
2002	50%	$1 million
2003	49%	$1 million
2004	48%	$1.5 million
2005	47%	$1.5 million
2006	46%	$2 million
2007	45%	$2 million
2008	45%	$2 million
2009	45%	$3.5 million
2010	Top Individual Rate (for gift tax only)	Unlimited—Taxes Repealed

Tax Rates for Federal Gift Tax and Federal Estate Tax

If the Amount with Respect to Which the Tentative Tax Is to Be Computed Is:	The Tentative Tax Is:
Not over $10,000	18 percent of such amount.
Over $10,000 but not over $20,000	$1,800, plus 20% of the excess of such amount over $10,000.
Over $20,000 but not over $40,000	$3,800, plus 22% of the excess of such amount over $20,000.
Over $40,000 but not over $60,000	$8,200, plus 24% of the excess of such amount over $40,000.
Over $60,000 but not over $80,000	$13,000, plus 26% of the excess of such amount over $60,000.
Over $80,000 but not over $100,000	$18,200, plus 28% of the excess of such amount over $80,000.
Over $100,000 but not over $150,000	$23,800, plus 30% of the excess of such amount over $100,000.
Over $150,000 but not over $250,000	$38,800, plus 32% of the excess of such amount over $150,000.
Over $250,000 but not over $500,000	$70,800, plus 34% of the excess of such amount over $250,000.
Over $500,000 but not over $750,000	$155,800, plus 37% of the excess of such amount over $500,000.
Over $750,000 but not over $1,000,000	$248,300, plus 39% of the excess of such amount over $750,000.
Over $1,000,000 but not over $1,250,000	$345,800, plus 41% of the excess of such amount over $1,250,000.
Over $1,250,000 but not over $1,500,000	$448,300, plus 43% of the excess of such amount over $1,250,000.
Over $1,500,000 but not over $2,000,000	$555,800, plus 45% of the excess of such amount over $1,500,000.
Over $2,000,000 but not over $2,500,000	$780,800, plus 47% of the excess of such amount over $2,000,000.

Source: Internal Revenue Service

To Anita's Credit

But wait a minute. Anita has several tax credits available to reduce her tentative tax. First there is what is known as the *unified tax credit*. That's a lifetime tax credit of $345,800 on gifts or $555,800 on your estate in 2004 and 2005. Over the years, if you make gifts, that credit is reduced according to the size of those gifts. Indeed at your death you may have used up the credit, so that it is not there to benefit your estate. Please note that the unified credit increases with the exclusion, so, for example, this credit beginning in 2006 is $780,800 for the estate tax (gift tax credit stays at $345,800).

In addition to the unified credit, the federal tax allows a *state death tax credit* for years prior to 2005 based upon IRS tables (you can see the table here that spells that out). The state death tax credit expired in 2004 and the state death tax paid becomes a deduction beginning in 2005. The deduction will be part of the estate deductions.

State Death Tax Credit for Federal Estate Tax

(A) Adjusted Taxable Estate* Equal to or More Than	(B) Adjusted Taxable Estate* Less Than	(C) Credit on Amount in Column (A)	(D) Rate of Credit on Excess Over Amount in Column (A)(Percentage)
0	$40,000	0	None
$40,000	90,000	0	0.8
90,000	140,000	$400	1.6
140,000	240,000	1,200	2.4
240,000	440,000	3,600	3.2
440,000	640,000	10,000	4.0
640,000	840,000	18,000	4.8
840,000	1,040,000	27,600	5.6
1,040,000	1,540,000	38,800	6.4

(A) Adjusted Taxable Estate* Equal to or More Than	(B) Adjusted Taxable Estate* Less Than	(C) Credit on Amount in Column (A)	(D) Rate of Credit on Excess Over Amount in Column (A)(Percentage)
1,540,000	2,040,000	70,800	7.2
2,040,000	2,540,000	106,800	8.0
2,540,000	3,040,000	146,800	8.8
3,040,000	3,540,000	190,800	9.6
3,540,000	4,040,000	238,800	10.4
4,040,000	5,040,000	290,800	11.2
5,040,000	6,040,000	402,800	12.0
6,040,000	7,040,000	522,800	12.8
7,040,000	8,040,000	650,800	13.6
8,040,000	9,040,000	786,800	14.4
9,040,000	10,040,000	930,800	15.2
10,040,000		1,082,800	16.0

Adjusted Taxable Estate = Taxable Estate minus $60,000. The state death tax credit is reduced by 25 percent each year beginning in 2002 and will be eliminated entirely in 2005 and beyond.

Source: Internal Revenue Service, 2002

For Anita's estate the 2004 credit phased down to ¼

Because Anita's taxable estate is $1,790,000, her state death tax credit is $84,480 × .25 = $21,120, based on the IRS tables, with the year 2004 allowing only a 25 percent credit.

So Anita's final tax is as follows:

Tentative tax		$686,300
less credits of		
Unified tax credit	$555,800	
State death tax	$21,120=	$576,920
Federal estate tax		$109,380

Tip _____

There is a deadline for paying the estate tax. Usually it's nine months from the date of death. However, there are special installment payment provisions for certain family farms and small corporations.

That's the absolute bottom line. You think that's a lot to owe? Keep in mind the original amount of Anita's estate—more than $2.5 million.

If you are still unhappy with estate tax, you might read Chapter 20, which will, among other tips, provide you with some valuable estate tax avoidance information.

Now here is that worksheet I promised you earlier, which shows you in one place how these figures added up. Anita's death was in 2004.

Gross estate (transferred property)		$2,520,000
Subtract:		
Expenses, debts, certain taxes	$210,000	
Losses during probate*	$-0-	
Charitable devises	$200,000	
Marital deduction	$320,000	
		= $730,000
Taxable estate		$1,790,000
Add post-1976 taxable gifts	$-0-	
Tax base	$1,790,000	
Tentative tax (tax base × tax rate)		$686,300
Subtract:		
Unified tax credit	$555,800	
Other tax credits**	$21,120	= $576,920
Estate tax due		$109,380

*For example, casualty loss, such as fire destroying house
**Includes state death tax credit (see chart in this chapter)

Taxing Each Generation

The government will track you down, and your children, and your children's children and ....

Congress wants to tax each generation of yours if it can.

If you don't plan to make a gift in your will of more than $1,500,000 to your grand-children, then skip this section.

Suppose a taxpayer wants to skip the next generation (his child) and leave all of his money to the second generation (his grandchildren). He figures his daughter's estate is large enough already to be taxed when the time comes, so why leave his daughter money that will only be added to her estate tax?

Unfortunately for taxpayers, Congress has thought about that, too. The generation-skipping transfer tax (GSTT) is imposed when the next generation (children) is bypassed in favor of a later generation (grandkids). The tax applies to gifts and transfers by death. The current tax rate is 45 percent

Now, each person has a $1,500,000 *exemption* from the GSTT. A husband and wife could transfer $3 million through gifts and devises in their wills to their grandchildren free of the GSTT. Please note that the GSTT exclusion increases at the same amount as does the estate tax exclusion. Thus, in 2006, the GSTT exclusion increases to $2,000,000, and follows the estate tax thereafter. However, an estate or gift tax may still apply there.

> **Watch Out**
>
> Obviously it's wise to turn to the accountant who is part of your estate planning team before attempting to work around the GSTT. (No doubt you've been consulting the appropriate professional member of that team through major steps you've been taking with your estate plan any-way, haven't you?)

The Least You Need to Know

- After 2006 estates of $1,500,000 or higher may be subject to the federal estate tax.

- A gross estate for tax purposes includes all property transferred to someone else because of death.

◆ Thanks to the marital deduction, property going outright to a spouse is not taxed.

◆ The federal estate tax begins at 45 percent and rises to 50 percent, but the maximum rate is being reduced to 47 percent in 2005, to 0 percent in 2010, and then returns to the 2002 rate thereafter.

◆ Congress may suspend exclusion increases or rate reductions, so don't assume the federal estate tax will expire in 2010.

Chapter 17

Gifts—and Gift Taxes

In This Chapter

- Which gifts are taxed and how
- Where you're tax-free
- Ways around the tax
- Gifts to minors

A gift is a thoughtful, sometimes simple, gesture.

The IRS may see it differently, though, and can slap you or your estate with quite a tax. You might have done things differently if you had known the tax and estate ramifications of your generosity. Let's see how you can make someone else happy, while keeping a smile on your own face.

How to Present a Gift

Legally, there are certain elements of giving that make a gift a gift, as far as your estate plan goes, and also with the IRS when it comes to tax-paying.

Instead of my simply spelling them out, let's imagine this little scenario, which contains those necessary elements. I'll explain them later.

Aunt Agatha has promised you her antique oak chest, certainly a handsome piece of furniture, when she dies. Your aunt means well, but there are several "ifs" that could be impediments to your receiving that chest. You will receive that gift …

> **Words, Words, Words**
>
> *Merriam Webster's Collegiate Dictionary* defines a **gift** as "something voluntarily transferred by one person to another without compensation." In other words, no strings, ever.

♦ If she owns the chest when she dies.

♦ If she has a will specifically devising the chest to you.

♦ If her estate has enough assets to pay its debts (the chest might have to be sold to pay outstanding bills).

In this instance I would suggest you follow my advice and have Aunt Agatha make a gift of that chest to you now. Here, briefly, is why.

To have a valid gift, three things are required:

♦ The donor (in this case your aunt) has to have the intent at that moment to make the gift.

♦ The donee (you) has to accept the gift.

♦ The gift property has to be transferred from the donor to the donee.

Okay, now let's continue. You persuade Aunt Agatha to go along with this script.

Scene: The room in Aunt Agatha's house where the oak chest is situated.

Prop: Video camera, held by a third party.

Aunt Agatha: Joanie, I give you my oak chest *[points to chest as camera goes from aunt to chest]*.

You: Aunt Agatha McCleary, thank you so very much for this lovely oak chest. I accept your gift.

[Camera shows you patting the chest as Aunt Agatha moves—or appears to move—it toward you.]

You: But Aunt Agatha, this chest looks so right in this house. Please keep it for me as *bailee* until later.

Aunt Agatha: I will keep it for you as bailee.

End of script.

What you now have is a gift presented to you. When Aunt Agatha dies, you'll send a copy of the videotape to the executor of her estate to prove the oak chest is yours.

That's one way to handle a gift. As you have seen, it fulfills the three elements of gift giving, and there can be no mistaking the intentions of the donor, or the one accepting the gift. It's neat and clean.

> **Words, Words, Words**
>
> A **bailee** is someone who temporarily possesses, but does not own, a property. An example might be a parking garage near your office that has a copy of the key to your car. (This isn't a commonly used expression, as you have probably surmised because you no doubt have never heard of it. Most haven't.)

We don't have our camcorders always handy, of course. In this chapter we'll discuss some other giving styles, their benefits, and tax consequences.

The Federal Tax Nobody Knows

The *federal gift tax* is a levy on a transfer of property by gift. You must tell the IRS if you make any gifts more than $11,000 in cash or property.

Let's say you feel very generous today. Life has been good, so you want to spread the wealth (yours) around a little. Your spouse deserves something special, so you give her 100 shares of Huge Consolidated, Inc. (value $30,000). Junior and your little princess have matured more quickly than you'd expected, so you give each of them 50 shares of good old Consolidated for the holidays, with each gift worth $15,000. Shucks, it's just a little something.

> **Quote, Unquote**
>
> To give and then not feel that one has given is the very best of all ways of giving.
> —Max Beerbohm, "Hosts and Guests" (1920)

> **Quote, Unquote**
>
> What with your friend you nobly share
> At least a rescue from your heir
> —Horace, "Odes" (c. 23–15 B.C.E.)

When tax time comes around you ask your accountant if those gifts are deductible on your 1040 form.

Your accountant smiles. Deductible? In your dreams. You must file a gift tax return for both by April 15, which she will, of course, be happy to prepare for you at her usual fee. Your gift to your wife calls for no tax because of the marital deduction. But the stock to your kids? If your wife has gone in on the two $15,000 presents with you, then there is no tax because of the $11,000 annual exclusion available to each spouse, or $22,000 per recipient from both of you, even if the spouse does not own the gifted property. If she has not joined in the gift tax return, then you must compute the tax on each of the $4,000 amounts above the annual exclusion of $11,000.

A gift tax. What a wonderful country to come up with so many ways to be taxed!

Have you heard of this charge? Take an informal survey of your friends to see if they are familiar with it. Not many will be. When I was taking a graduate law class about 20 years ago, the lecturer, who worked for the gift tax section of the IRS, commented, not entirely facetiously, that they held a celebration every time a gift tax return was filed, there were so few of them.

So why do we have this tax? Well, for revenue of course, but mostly to protect the federal *estate* tax. If you could make a deathbed gift of all your property, without any tax, then the Treasury coffers would not get much in the way of estate tax revenue. So your gifts must be taxed.

Don't unduly worry. There are many exclusions to this tax. It's important, though, for you to understand the tax if it should be money you need to pay one day, and for you to know enough about it to be able perhaps to avoid it when estate planning.

When You Aren't Taxed

You might be thinking about all your gifts over the last several years. Were they *taxable*, for Pete's sake?

No, no, relax. Not every gift is subject to the federal gift tax. There is, of course, that $11,000 exclusion, and most of us give presents to family and friends that fall well below that figure. Gifts to a spouse (more about that coming up) or a charity can be made free of any tax. Because the gift tax is based on yearly gifts, the annual $11,000 exclusion and spousal gifts eliminate most gifts from taxation.

There is no tax levied on gifts of educational tuition, either, or paying another's medical expenses. Also, joint savings accounts, joint stock brokerage accounts, and joint U.S. savings bonds are not considered gifts and are not subject to the tax when they're established.

So if Mom opens a savings account with Trustworthy Bank, and puts her daughter, Fran, on the account as joint owner with right of survivorship, there is no gift to her daughter unless Fran withdraws funds for herself. If she does, Mom has made a gift.

Tax-Free Gifts to a Spouse

Outright gifts between husband and wife are technically subject to the federal gift tax, but the marital deduction reduces each gift to zero taxation. Therefore, spouses can shower each other with presents without any concern for the gift tax.

However—and isn't there always a however?—if a spouse is given only a life estate interest in property (meaning that it is hers only for her lifetime; see Chapter 2), or an irrevocable trust is created in which he or she is the life income beneficiary (see Chapter 9), then the tax law is a bit more complicated. Using a QTIP (Qualified Terminal Interest Property; see Chapter 16) avoids the gift tax. The election must be made, and then property would be included in the recipient spouse's estate for federal estate tax purposes.

For example, Jennie creates an irrevocable trust for her husband, who receives an income interest in the trust. If the QTIP is made, and his interest will be subject to federal estate tax upon his death (it wouldn't otherwise), then the marital gift deduction applies. That's because the QTIP is treated the same for gift tax purposes as an outright gift to a spouse—available for the marital deduction.

> **Tip**
>
> Gifts of services are not subject to the gift tax. For example, your receiving free advice from another, such as investment counseling, would not be taxable (but could, of course, be quite valuable to you).

The QTIP is fairly sophisticated tax planning and may not be useful for most couples, particularly those whose combined estate would not exceed $3 million.

A Variety of Gifts

The gift tax is imposed on taxable gifts made each year, accumulating those taxable gifts and imposing a progressive levy on the accumulating total. No tax is due until taxable gifts of more than $1,000,000 are made. Unlike the estate tax exclusion, the gift tax exclusion does not increase; it remains at $1 million.

If you have made annual gifts in excess of $11,000 to someone other than your spouse or charity, then you must file a gift tax return by April 15 of the next year reporting the gifts even if the lifetime exemption ($1 million) has not been exceeded. Because the gift tax applies to all gratuitous transfers, that is, one made without you receiving any tangible benefit, e.g. payment, from the recipient, you must carefully record all those over the $11,000 exclusion. Gifts may include …

◆ Outright transfers.

◆ Below-market interest rate loans or forgiven loans.

◆ Transfers to an irrevocable trust.

◆ Creation of co-ownerships in property or a remainder interest in property.

Let's consider these in a little more detail.

Outright Transfers—What's That?

It means that the person getting the gift has all legal rights to it, whether cash or property. There are no restrictions to ownership.

Let's say you give your child corporate stock worth $20,000, or $20,000 in cash. That is an outright gift, or transfer, and subject to the gift tax, because it is more than your $11,000 annual exclusion (unless your spouse is going in with you on the gift, with his or her $11,000 exclusion).

Below-Market Rate Loans

If you lend your son money interest-free, or below an established federal fund interest rate, then the amount of interest you *should have received* if the loan had the appropriate interest is treated as a gift of that interest by you to your son.

For example, let's say the loan was in the amount of $110,000, and had no interest attached. Assuming the federally prescribed interest rate to be 10 percent, then the first year's forgiven interest is $11,000.

If you have made no more additional gifts to your son in that year, the annual exclusion will apply and there will be no gift tax due. You will have come within your $11,000 figure.

Words, Words, Words

To **forgive** a loan, or interest on a loan, is to grant the one borrowing that money relief from payment of the debt. This should be in writing, of course, and dated.

However, the IRS may not be finished with you yet. It could require you to report the forgiven interest *as if it were* paid to you by your son, which means additional income to the donor. Why would the IRS do this? Because loans to children might be structured to minimize taxes. Interest might be low enough to use the annual gift tax exclusion, and a family member loan of $100,000 or less that isn't used to generate investment income might not be taxable income to the lender.

Let's say you want to lend your child money to help him or her buy a home. The loan is $100,000 or less, and you charge no interest. You could …

◆ Avoid the gift tax, assuming that it's determined that the interest, if charged, would have amounted to no more than $11,000 per year.

◆ Avoid the income tax, if your child had no more than $1,000 in net investment income for the year.

If you later completely forgive your child's loan, then that will also be a gift and will be subject to gift tax, minus your annual exemption in the year the loan is forgiven.

When the Revocable Trust Works Best

You learned about trusts in Chapter 9. Here's how they can work in a gift situation.

Hannah established an *irrevocable* trust for her daughter, Shirley, and contributed $100,000 to that trust. It was to accumulate income until Shirley was 25 years old.

Hannah's gift to the trust is indirectly given to Shirley; therefore, the transfer is subject to the gift tax.

However, if Hannah had established a *revocable* trust, where she retained the power to revoke, then the gift would not be complete and not subject to the gift tax. See what that slight difference in wording between "revocable" and "*ir*revocable" can do to a tax picture?

Co-Ownership: Togetherness and Taxes

Maria owns her home. She executes a new deed to the place with her son Yuri as tenant-in-common for one half of the property. Maria has made a gift to Yuri that is subject to the gift tax. The value of that gift is one half of the fair market value of the home at the time of the gift.

If Maria had made Yuri a joint tenant with right of survivorship, or had deeded the property to him and kept a life estate (you read about that in Chapter 2), the value of the gift would be the fair market value of the home at the time of the gift *less* an actuarially determined amount based on Maria's life expectancy.

Using IRS tables, Maria would compute the value of her interest, which then would be subtracted from the total value of the property, to determine the amount Yuri received subject to the gift tax.

Prior Gifts and the Unified Credit

Any prior year's taxable gifts are added to the current year's gifts to determine the total taxable gifts. Therefore you should keep copies of all your previous gift tax returns and records of any gift taxes paid, so that cumulative figures are available.

Remember that your gift tax unified credit is $345,800 (equivalent to $1,000,000 in taxable gifts). If you make any taxable gifts, then the unified credit is accordingly reduced.

Missy gave her son $1,011,000 in 2005. She had not made any prior taxable gifts. Applying her annual exclusion ($11,000) and her unified credit of $345,800 (equivalent to the $1,000,000 exclusion), she will pay no gift tax. However, upon her death, there will be a reduction of the unified credit by $345,800 to the federal estate tax credit; for 2004 through 2005 the unified credit for federal estate tax increased to $555,800 (equivalent to the $1,500,000 exclusion), and will increase to $780,800 (equivalent to the $2,000,000 exclusion) in 2006 through 2008. Note that the gift tax unified credit (and the excludible amount) does not change.

Taxable gifts that reduce the unified credit may be good estate planning if the gift is of appreciating property (in other words, if it's likely to increase in value). Without a gift, the property would be included in the estate at a much higher value, if kept until death. Be careful to consider the income tax law when you give appreciating property. See the accountant member of your estate planning team.

Briefs

There are gifts, and then, of course there are gifts. There was a merchant named Guyot, who lived and died in Marseilles, France. He amassed a large fortune by working hard and saving most of his money. His neighbors jeered at him, considering him a miser, and avaricious. Local boys threw stones at him.

Eventually, M. Guyot died, and in his will was found the following: "Having observed from my infancy that the poor of Marseilles are badly supplied with water which they can only purchase at a high price, I have cheerfully labored the whole of my life to procure for them this great blessing, and I direct that the whole of my property be laid out in building an aqueduct for their use."

Estate and Gift Taxes Go Hand in Hand

Each of us has one unified credit ($345,800 for gifts), which, again, is the equivalent of making $1,000,000 in taxable gifts. After 2003, the estate tax unified credit increased to $555,800, and will increase to $780,800, as previously indicated, but the gift tax credit stays at $345,800. Jim, who is divorced, gave his daughter, Kelly, $261,000 in 2005. He had made no other taxable gifts to date. His taxable gift was $250,000, because of the $11,000 annual exclusion. Applying the tentative tax to that $250,000 means a gift tax of $70,800. Jim has a unified credit of $345,800, so there is no gift tax due. However, he has reduced his unified credit for gifts to $275,000 ($345,800 less $70,800) and reduced the unified credit for federal estate tax to $485,000 ($555,800 less $70,800). If his federal taxable estate exceeds $1,250,000 ($1,500,000 less $250,00), then the estate will begin paying an estate tax at a 45 percent rate (see the federal tax chart in Chapter 16) for 2005. Any gifts above the $750,000 left as available for the gift exemption ($1,000,000 minus the gift of $250,000) will require payment of a gift tax, because its credit remains at $345,800; however, as previously noted, his estate tax credit does increase after 2003.

Take a look at the calculations here to see how the numbers applied to Jim.

Gifts during the year (at fair market value)	$261,000
Subtract	
Deductions:	
Marital	$-0-
Charitable	$-0-
Annual exclusion (per donee)	<u>$11,000</u>
Taxable gifts for year	$250,000
Add: Taxable gifts from all prior years	<u>$-0-</u>
Total of current and past taxable gifts	$250,000
Compute gift tax (use tax rates for gift and estate tax)	$70,800
Subtract:	
Prior gift taxes	$-0-
Unified credit	<u>$345,800</u>
Gift tax due	$-0-

That takes care of Jim's 2005 gift. If in 2006 Jim makes a taxable gift to his daughter of more than $750,000, the unified gift credit will be exhausted and he will have a tax on any amount more than $750,000 at 41 percent. When he dies, all those taxable gifts and any subsequent ones will be added to his taxable estate to determine his federal estate tax.

Gift Giving from the IRS Perspective

Here are some situations where you might be handed a present, perhaps quite a handsome one. What are the tax implications? That won't matter to you because the donor is responsible for paying gift tax. But these examples will give you some idea of how you will be taxed when you feel the urge to give someone close to you a little something.

Gift	Donor's Tax Situation
On your birthday Aunt Maude gives her diamond earrings and brooch, valued at $4,500	No tax due—gift falls under $11,000 you allowed exclusion
Your Dad gives you $15,000 toward the down payment on a condo	If Mom doesn't go in with him on the gift using her $11,000 exemption, Dad will be subject to gift tax on $4,000
Your godfather gives you his $12,000 stamp collection	Subject to gift tax on $1,000
Your spouse gives you a $20,000 automobile for your birthday	No tax due—an outright transfer, marital deduction
Your significant other gives you a $20,000 automobile for your birthday	$9,000 of that is subject to federal gift tax

Deferring Gifts for Minor Children

What if your child is a minor and you don't want him or her to have the money right away?

To take advantage of the annual exclusion, you recall that you must give a current ownership in cash or property. Putting the gift in the typical irrevocable trust won't do. However, the tax code does provide three possibilities I introduced you to in Chapter 12, on minor children, that can help you obtain the annual $11,000 exclusion for your gifts:

♦ A trust with *Crummey* powers (an irrevocable living trust that allows the beneficiary or his or her guardian to withdraw the contribution within a specified period of time)

♦ An Internal Revenue Code 2503(c) trust

♦ A custodial account

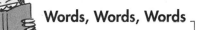

Words, Words, Words

A **Crummey trust** takes its name from the court case involving a gift to a minor child and whether it would qualify for an annual tax exclusion. Crummey is the name of the taxpayer who brought suit. He won his case.

To give you an example, let's look at May. She creates an irrevocable living trust that provides that her minor child, Tim, cannot receive any income or principal from the trust until he becomes 25 years of age. The trust allows her son's guardian (his father) to withdraw the annual contribution of $11,000 if done so within 30 days of the gift. The father wisely chooses not to exercise that right. This transaction qualifies for the annual exclusion.

Instead, May could have established a similar trust, with Tim as the sole beneficiary if the principal and income would be distributed to him outright upon becoming 21. This is a Section 2503(c) trust and likewise qualifies for the annual exclusion.

Watch Out

Use a custodian for your minor child's account that is neither you nor your spouse, because the custodial funds could be included in your or your spouse's estate at death. Choose instead a trusted relative or friend.

Or May could have established a custodial account for her son under the Uniform Gift to Minors Act (or Uniform Transfer to Minors Act) and make an annual contribution that would qualify for the exclusion. Tim would be entitled to the account when he became of legal age to receive it under state law (either age 18 or 21, depending on the state). May should consider naming a relative or friend as custodian, thus keeping the account out of May's estate for income and death taxes.

The Least You Need to Know

- The federal gift tax applies to taxable gifts more than $1,000,000.
- Gifts of $11,000 or less per year may be made to anyone free of gift tax.
- Husband and wife can add each of their annual exclusions together so that they can give a combined nontaxable gift of $22,000 per year per recipient.
- A loan given tax free or at a reduced rate may be subject to tax because the interest *not* paid is considered a gift to the loan recipient.
- Giving away appreciating property will reduce the estate tax.

How Charitable Donations Can Save You Money

In This Chapter

- ◆ The benefits of giving
- ◆ Many varieties of gifts
- ◆ Good, and better, tax implications
- ◆ Gifts after retirement

If you are generous to family and friends, and can afford the money, you are probably also generous to your favorite charities.

Can you save money while giving to a worthwhile cause? Yes, indeed. Planning allows you to arrange charitable contributions in a way that will maximize your personal objectives with appropriate tax incentives. Read on.

Tax Savings and Philanthropy

Americans have always been a generous people. Our religious institutions, universities, and local United Way agencies and civic organizations, among other groups, have all prospered with our gifts.

Tip ___

Not all charities qualify for income, estate, and gift tax deductions. Public charities such as churches, educational institutions, hospitals, and government offices (any of them— U.S. Treasury Department, State of Nevada, etc.) *do*. To see which others qualify for such deductions, check with the IRS; it has a list of qualified charities.

Take a look at the following list, showing how generous we have been to national charities. Have you contributed to some, perhaps many, of them?

Charitable Giving in 2003

Total charitable giving was $241 billion.

Individual charitable giving was $179.4 billion.

Bequests accounted for $21.6 billion.

Foundations gave $26.3 billion and corporations $13.5 billion.

Religious organizations received $87 billion and education $31.5 billion.

Here are some of the benefits of planned giving:

- Fulfilling your charitable goals
- Providing income tax deductions for the value of the charitable gift
- Avoiding the capital gains tax when giving appreciated property
- Retaining income rights to the property donated to the charity
- Increasing lifetime income by converting low-yielding assets
- Supplementing retirement income
- Obtaining professional asset management
- Reducing federal estate and state inheritance taxes

Clearly, charitable donations should be considered part of your estate planning. The following pages point out several different methods to make them fulfill your goals, from outright gifts to charitable trusts and pooled income funds.

Briefs
Lilly Endowment, Inc. is an Indianapolis, Indiana–based, private philanthropic foundation with assets of about $10 billion. It was established in 1937 by three members of the Lilly family through gifts of 17,500 shares of stock worth $280,000 in their pharmaceutical business. Lilly Endowment is usually in the top five largest U.S. endowments (measured by assets).

Which Assets to Give

What you choose to give to charity has important tax implications. After all, doing good does not preclude doing well for oneself.

The tax deduction for charitable gifts is usually the fair market value of the property given. But the law requires that certain types of property be deducted at what it cost the donor to purchase, not its current market value.

To explain the difference, consider Willie. He bought ABC, Inc. stock in 1995 for $40,000. It is now worth $60,000. He gives the stock to State University. He wants to deduct from his income tax the full value of the stock contribution, rather than just the amount he paid for it.

The tax code permits individual taxpayers to deduct charitable contributions if they itemize their deductions (Schedule B, form 1040). However, there are some limitations regarding the deduction:

- ◆ No deduction can exceed 50 percent of the taxpayer's Adjusted Gross Income (AGI).

- ◆ If you are giving appreciated property, then you may be limited to 30 percent of your adjusted income.

- ◆ Ordinary income assets (inventory, for example) are deductible at the inventory cost.

Confused? Here's an example that should help.

Assume that Willie had an AGI of $100,000. If he wanted to take the full value of his contribution of $60,000, he would have to spread the deduction over two years because he would be limited to 50 percent of his AGI ($50,000) in the year he made the gift in all events, and, in this example, 30 percent of his AGI ($30,000) because that is the yearly maximum for capital gains assets such as stock.

Words, Words, Words

The **tax basis of property** is the taxpayer's investment (cost plus improvements *less* depreciation).

Or he could take the gift's cost (or *tax basis*) of $40,000 as a deduction in the year he gives it because the 50 percent of AGI rule applies when he limits his deduction to what the stock cost him. The amount of deduction that Willie cannot take in the year of contribution because of the maximum percentage rules will be available for him to take in the next tax year.

Back to Willie, who is certainly generous to his alma mater. He is a professional landscape artist, and now donates several of his own paintings to the university. Because the sale of his works would create ordinary income to him, he can only deduct his cost in producing the works, up to 50 percent of his AGI.

Here is another consideration. Willie purchased XYZ, Inc. stock in 1990 for $20,000. The stock is now selling for $10,000. If he gives the stock to the university he will get only a $10,000 deduction. However, if he sells the stock, and then gives the proceeds to the university, he will receive a tax loss deduction of $10,000 *and* the charitable deduction of $10,000.

Like Willie, you might consider selling property you own that has depreciated and taking a tax loss (if available). Then make a charitable contribution of the proceeds.

Quote, Unquote

Posthumous charities are the very essence of selfishness when bequeathed by those who, when alive, would part with nothing.

—Charles Caleb Colton "Lacon" (1825)

Finally, consider giving your tax deferred IRA, 401(k), or defined contribution pension to a charity, if you have a choice of assets to give. Consider Bill, who has two assets—stock worth $200,000, and a 401(k) worth $200,000. Bill wants to make a $200,000 contribution. Bill gives the 401(k), takes a current charitable deduction, reduces his estate, and never has to report the tax deferred income in the 401(k), because the charity is tax exempt and has become its beneficiary.

This is an estate planning area where you will certainly want professional help. In this case, of course, that will be the accountant who is a member of your planning team.

Getting Donations in Order

Timing is everything, even here. A charitable donation saves you more in taxes when your tax rate is at its highest.

Olive gave $10,000 to Healthy Hospital in 2004, her last year of employment, when she made $100,000 (her tax rate was 28 percent). In 2005 she gave another $10,000, but her only income then was earned from investments of $20,000 (her tax rate was 15 percent).

Her contribution in 2004 saved her $2,800 in taxes ($10,000 gift *times* 28 percent tax rate), while her 2005 contribution saved her $1,500 in taxes ($10,000 gift *times* 15 percent tax rate) for a total tax savings of $4,300 in two years.

> **Tip**
>
> Do you like a particular charity, but are not certain you want to give them a sizable sum? If you have the time, do some volunteer work for that group first, to make certain you agree with its policies and programs, and how it spends its money.

If Olive had made a $20,000 gift in 2004 , she would have saved $5,600 in taxes ($20,000 gift *times* 28 percent tax rate). By making the gift in the year she had her highest earning she could have saved $1,300 in taxes.

Some Years You Give, Some You Don't

Alternating years when you make charitable donations could also save you in taxes, particularly if you don't have many other itemized deductions (e.g. mortgage interest, state taxes). You *can* choose between a standard deduction or itemizing each year.

For instance, one year you would not itemize but take the standard deduction, which is $9,700 in 2005 for married persons filing jointly. Then the next year you could make the bulk of your charitable contributions and itemize deductions.

That's what Art and Susan did. They regularly give $4,000 a year to their synagogue. Each year they have approximately $2,000 in other itemized deductions. In 2004 they gave nothing to the synagogue, but in January 2005, gave $4,000, then an additional $4,000 later in the year.

The couple did not itemize in 2004 (and wouldn't have anyway, even with a charitable donation because the standard deduction was greater than their itemized deductions), but did so in 2005 because their charitable contributions plus other itemized deductions ($10,000) exceeded their standard deduction for 2005. Thus they saved taxes by alternating years for charitable contributions.

Lots More Ways to Donate

The tax law provides for a myriad of ways to make charitable gifts and take income, gift, and estate tax deductions. Here are some:

- ◆ Outright gifts
- ◆ Charitable annuity
- ◆ Charitable remainder trusts
- ◆ Charitable lead trusts
- ◆ Pooled income funds
- ◆ Charitable remainder in residence or farm
- ◆ Charitable bargain sale

Tip

Keep in mind the charitable deduction is only available for the net value of property transferred to the qualified charity. If the donor retains some interest in the property, the amount of the deduction will be reduced by the value retained by the donor, or given to another noncharity, such as a relative.

The first way to make a charitable contribution has been amply illustrated in previous pages. Most of us simply give our money to a charity, but perhaps we should consider some of the preceding alternatives.

The Charitable Annuity

Maureen decides to give some land she owns to a favored charity. In turn the charity agrees to pay her an *annuity* for her life. In essence Maureen has made a transfer, or sale, of one asset (her land) for another asset (the charity's annuity). You can use IRS tables to make your calculation (www.irs.org); you can compute how much of the value of the gifted property will be returned to her in the form of the annuity (nondeductible) and how much of its value the charity will keep (deductible). Maureen can only deduct the net value of what the charity gets.

Charitable Remainder Trusts

The tax deduction for a *charitable remainder trust* operates on the same basic principles as the charitable annuity.

Charitable remainder trusts have a noncharity as an income beneficiary, with the remainder (the principal) going to a charity when the income interest terminates.

The person creating the trust (the grantor) often will be the income beneficiary. Frequently the spouse is included as a joint/survivor income beneficiary. There is no tax for the gift to the spouse because of the marital deduction. However, if anyone other than a spouse is an income beneficiary, then there is a gift tax (but the annual exclusion of $11,000 per donee may be available).

There are two types of these remainder trusts: *annuity* and *unitrust.*

The annuity trust is required to pay a set percentage of the *initial value* of the assets to the noncharitable beneficiary. The unitrust must pay a set percentage of the trust assets *valued annually.*

The minimum percentage of payout for each is five percent. Additional assets can be contributed to the unitrust, but not to the annuity trust. The income tax deduction will be based on actuarial and income tables prescribed by the IRS.

Let's say Carl establishes a charitable remainder trust with $1,000,000. He and his wife, Jennifer, are income beneficiaries. When they die, the trust will terminate and the charity will receive the remainder of the trust assets.

If this is an annuity trust, then the amount Carl and Jennifer will receive as income will be fixed, based upon the payout percentage and the initial contribution to the trust.

But if this is a unitrust, then the amount Carl and Jennifer will receive as income will vary each year, based upon the payout percentage and the annual valuation of the assets.

The unitrust can be structured more flexibly than the annuity trust because later contributions and contributions of appreciating assets will increase the income available, and could be timed to increase the payout when the donor has retired and is in a lower tax bracket.

Quote, Unquote

A small gift is better than a great promise.

—German proverb

Words, Words, Words

To **endow** a hospital, college, or similar public or charitable facility is to make a grant of money providing for the continuing support or maintenance of that institution.

Charitable Lead Trust

A charitable lead trust is essentially the flip side of the remainder trust. In the *lead trust*, the charity gets the income for a set time period, and the donor or some non-charity receives the principal after that time period. The longer the term for the income payments to the charity, and the higher the payout, the greater the income tax deduction.

Beth establishes a charitable lead trust and contributes $500,000. Her church is to be the income beneficiary for 10 years. Then the remainder will go to her daughter.

The income from the trust will be taxed to Beth only if it exceeds the amount of income paid to the charity. Because the daughter receives the remainder interest, there is a gift to her that is subject to the gift tax (but there is no annual exclusion because she does not have a present right to the property).

Pooled Income Funds

Many charities have established *pooled income funds*. Here the donor gives cash or property to the fund, which is made up of contributions from other donors, and in return receives income for life (or lives, if a spouse is included). This is similar to the gift annuity you read about earlier.

A pooled income fund may provide several advantages to the donor in addition to the tax deduction. The charity provides professional management, and there is now a diversified investment portfolio, which could mean a higher return if the donor contributed a low-income yielding asset.

CAUTION

Watch Out

There's a way to learn as much as possible about your favorite charity—its history; programs; use of funds; tax exempt status, if any; percentage of fundraising that goes toward programs and percentage used for administrative costs; and more. The BBB Wise Giving Alliance publishes its "Tips on Charitable Giving" on its website, www.give.org.

Other Charitable Gifts

The list goes on. Tax law permits you to deed your personal residence or farm to a charity, while you retain a life estate in that property and receive an income tax deduction for the actuarial value of the charity's remainder interest. The personal residence doesn't have to be the home in which you are currently residing either.

Tony, for example, lives most of the year in Ohio, but spends a good part of each winter in Florida.

He may deed either or both homes to a charity, while retaining a life estate so he can use that residence and receive a tax deduction.

Here's another way to give: if you have an asset that you would like to convert to cash, keep some proceeds, and give the rest to charity, then you might enter into a *bargain sale* with a charity.

A bargain sale is a sale of property to a charity or another person for less than its fair market value so that the difference is a gift to the purchaser.

If Tony, for example, sells some land he purchased several years ago to his college for less than its appraised fair market value, he will be taxed only on a portion of the gain (the difference between what he paid for it and what it's worth now) and also receive an income tax deduction on the "gift" portion of the sales price.

Any mortgage on the sold/gifted property will increase the bargain seller's gain. It's treated as if the debt is released when the seller transfers it to the charity, that is, the charity assumed his debt.

Retirement and Beyond

Most of us buy life insurance to protect our families while the children are growing up. As we grow older, the life insurance becomes more expensive and less important, particularly if our estate will be ample for the rest of our lives.

If you like, you can change the primary or contingent beneficiary of the policy and name a qualified charity.

If the charity is the primary beneficiary, you can receive a charitable deduction for the premiums you pay. Upon death the charity will receive the proceeds. So for a relatively modest premium payment, you can leave a substantial amount of money to charity. (The charity must be the owner of the policy for you to receive the tax deduction.)

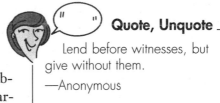

Quote, Unquote

Lend before witnesses, but give without them.

—Anonymous

Perhaps you can't spare anything now to give to a charity, but after your death your estate could part with some money. You can leave a specified amount or a percentage of your probate estate to one or several charities.

The Least You Need to Know

◆ Gifts to charities may qualify for an immediate income tax deduction.

◆ Charitable gifts are usually valued at their fair market value at the time of the gift.

◆ Gifts in a charitable trust or pooled income fund can create income *and* a tax deduction for the donor.

◆ Life insurance policies and devises in a will allow the donor to make a substantial gift at little or no expense.

State Taxes: When and How You Can Be Hit

In This Chapter

◆ Inheritance tax

◆ Gift and income taxes

◆ Choosing a permanent residence

◆ State taxes affecting that choice

Too often we focus on the big dog (the IRS) and forget about the little puppies (state taxes). In estate planning it's important to consider all taxes as obstacles to building wealth. That goes for real estate taxes, sales tax, and a number of other "pups."

Here's what your beautiful, much-loved state can do to you, tax-wise (although in all honesty there are some states that can do something *for* you as well).

Inheriting? The State Has Its Hand Out

There's good and bad news here. About one-half of the states have some form of death tax (inheritance or estate).

On the other hand, death tax rates are considerably lower than the federal estate tax rate (which ranges between 45 and 48 percent), although many begin the tax at a much lower estate value than the federal estate tax, which starts at more than $1,500,000.

First, a few definitions so we all know what we're talking about here:

An *inheritance tax* is a state levy on what each beneficiary receives from the estate.

A state's *estate tax* is similar to the federal estate tax because it is a tax upon the *net* estate of the deceased, based on the right to transmit property from the deceased's estate to its beneficiaries.

Transfers (e.g., assets distributed through a will) that are subject to state death taxes typically include those that are subject to the federal estate tax. That would be a will, intestacy, life insurance, retirement plans, jointly held property, and the like.

The inheritance tax usually has *graduated rates* that vary in amount for different classes of beneficiaries, with those of a close relationship to the deceased subject to lower rates than those of more distant relationships. For example, the tax rate on an inheritance by the deceased's child would be lower than the rate on an inheritance by a cousin.

Tip

Who pays the inheritance tax? Well, technically it is the beneficiary whose interest is reduced by the amount of the tax. However, you could provide in your will that your estate pick up any death tax for your beneficiaries. Consult your lawyer about the wording for handling those taxes the way you want in your will.

Watch Out

The time allowed for payment varies from state to state. Most state laws make the executor personally liable if the tax is not paid. There also may be a tax lien imposed on estate property transferred to a beneficiary if the tax is not paid.

Frequently a *state inheritance tax* will have several exemptions, such as transfers to a spouse or to a charity, and varying exemption amounts for transfers to estate beneficiaries (again, often based on their relationship to the deceased).

The state estate taxes are imposed in a method similar to the federal estate tax, or by using the state death tax credit on the federal estate tax return. State death taxes usually allow certain deductions, such as debts, funeral expenses, and estate administrative expenses.

Where Did You Say You Live?

I asked you that question once before, a few chapters ago, when I suggested that you decide what state to consider your permanent residence for any number of purposes. In this chapter, that purpose is state death tax.

Legal residence, or *domicile*, of the deceased determines which state can impose its death tax. Real estate and tangible personal property are usually taxable in the state where they are located, while all other property is typically taxed by the state in which the deceased had legal residence.

I am an Indiana resident, and I co-own a house, cars, savings accounts, etc., in Indiana. Therefore my property will be subject to Indiana inheritance tax upon my death. If I also owned a farm in Nebraska it would be subject to Nebraska death taxes.

I'll mention the subject of permanent residence again at the end of the chapter, in another context.

One, Two, Three—Ways of Taxing You

Here is a brief summary of the three different types of state death taxes:

- ◆ Estate tax based only upon federal state death tax credit

- ◆ Estate tax

- ◆ Inheritance tax and tax based upon federal state death tax credit (pick-up tax)

Let's look at them in more detail. Nine states: Connecticut, Indiana, Iowa, Kentucky, Louisiana, Maryland, Nebraska, Pennsylvania, and Tennessee have an inheritance tax.

All other states that have a death tax, except Ohio and Oklahoma, base their death tax on the federal state death tax credit (as it existed prior to 2002). A caution is in order. The federal state death tax credit was phased out over four years beginning in 2002; therefore many states that wish to continue a death tax will need to modify their death tax. I suggest that you visit your state's Department of Revenue website to determine current law. For example, for New York residents the site is www. tax.state.ny.us.

Estate Tax Based on Federal State Death Tax Credit Without Phaseout (Applying State Death Tax Credit as It Existed in 2001)

Illinois, Kansas, Maine, Massachusetts, Minnesota, New Jersey, New York, North Carolina, Rhode Island, Vermont, Washington, and Wisconsin have a death tax based upon the federal state death tax credit before the phaseout began in 2002. Whenever a federal estate tax is payable, these states have an estate tax that equals the amount of state death tax credit as it existed in 2001. For example, using the IRS tables (Chapter 16) for a taxable estate of $1,600,000 in 2001, the state death tax credit would have been $70,800.

Estate Tax

Ohio and Oklahoma have their own estate tax, with their own specific deductions and rates, which determine what tax is payable by their decedent's estates.

Briefs
John Dorrance, once the sole owner of Campbell Soup Company stock, died in 1930, leaving a $115 million estate. He had a residence in New Jersey but lived most of the year in Pennsylvania. Upon his death, his estate was probated in New Jersey, and that state taxed the estate. Pennsylvania claimed his legal residence (domicile) was there and also taxed his estate. Whoa, said the estate. They appealed to the United States Supreme Court, which refused to accept the appeal. The estate was taxed in both states.

Inheritance Tax and Additional Tax Based upon Federal State Death Tax Credit

Whew, these headings are getting long. What this one means can be explained quite briefly, though. Indiana and most of the other states that have an inheritance tax (see the list) also have a tax based on the federal state death tax credit (usually with the credit tax based on the full state death tax credit applicable in 2001). Unlike the estate tax, the inheritance tax is computed on who receives the estate. Again, it's the closer relatives who have more sizable exemptions and are taxed at a lower rate than distant family.

If the inheritance tax is less than the federal state death tax credit, then an additional tax is imposed to pick up the difference.

For estates of $1,500,000 or less, the most advantageous tax is the one solely based upon the federal tax's state death tax credit, because it is determined by the taxable estate, which is zero.

Some States Even Tax Your Gifts

Just a handful of states have their own gift tax. (Again, the best advice is to check your state's Department of Revenue website.) They must feel compelled to do so to "protect the integrity of the estate tax," which is the same reasoning the feds use.

In many instances, state gift taxable transfers are similar to the federal gift tax, which you read about in Chapter 17. North Carolina, for example, allows an annual exclusion of the first $11,000 to any donee each year, and a lifetime exclusion for parents, children, grandchildren, and other close relatives.

If a state has a gift tax that has a lower rate than its estate or inheritance tax, then gifts can reduce death taxes later.

In states that do not impose a gift tax, gifts certainly can reduce the state death tax.

Not to be outdone by the IRS, most states that use the federal state death tax credit also impose a generation-skipping transfer tax, so if you plan to give your grandchildren more than $1.5 million, beware of this state tax. The tax is usually the maximum state tax credit allowable under the Internal Revenue Code. My advice is not to try this without benefit of counsel. Recall that the GSTT exclusion is increasing with the federal estate tax exclusion. Whether your state follows the federal changes can best be determined by visiting its website.

> **Quote, Unquote**
>
> Taxes, after all, are the dues we pay for the privileges of membership in an organized society.
>
> —Franklin D. Roosevelt, in a speech, Worcester, Massachusetts, October 21, 1936

Pesky State Income Taxes

Still more taxes, folks.

Here are those fine states that do not have a personal income tax: Alaska, Florida, Nevada, Texas, Washington, and Wyoming. The rest of our states tax our income at various rates.

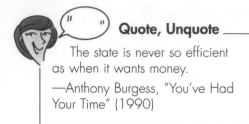

Quote, Unquote

The state is never so efficient as when it wants money.

—Anthony Burgess, "You've Had Your Time" (1990)

The top five states where income is taxed the highest are New York, Maine, Ohio, Hawaii, and Rhode Island.

Many state income taxes begin with the Adjusted Gross Income figure on the federal tax return, and also have deductions similar to those on your federal return. Federal and state income tax planning can provide a double reduction in your taxes.

State income tax is imposed on any legal resident of the state, and often upon income earned in the state by those who live elsewhere. Some states also tax income if you have resided in the state for several months during the tax year. What is taxable income for one state is not necessarily the same for another, although many states use the federal income tax definition (usually by taking the federal Adjusted Gross Income amount).

But that's not all: many states allow cities and counties to impose a local income tax. Does it ever end? It doesn't seem to!

A Retirement Residence

Estate planning tip for the day: Be sure to die a resident of a low-tax state.

Your work may dictate where you earn your income, but retirement is another matter. Consider the entire tax burden when selecting a state for retirement. The state income tax you pay should be less as your income decreases, of course, but the property tax on your home may be onerous.

States just love to collect taxes, as you have seen. Many are delighted if you decide to live within their borders—income taxes now, death taxes later. As I noted earlier, legal residence is important. For one thing, it matters in determining your heirs (some states have intestate distribution that is different from others), the validity of your will, and state taxes.

You should have only one legal residence (domicile), but often the evidence about which is your permanent home is mixed, particularly if you are retired and living in different states during different seasons of the year.

Briefs
Edward Green's estate was more fortunate than that of John Dorrance, described a few pages ago. Green was a wealthy resident of Maine who died in the mid-1930s. Four states claimed his legal residency and the right to tax his estate. Their cumulative taxes and the federal estate tax exceeded his estate of $42 million! The Supreme Court took the case because the states were suing one another. The court awarded the inheritance tax to only one of the states, claiming a person can have only one legal residence.

Florida has a Declaration of Domicile form. If you want the Sunshine State to be your legal residence, then execute that document. Even if your state has no provision for a similar declaration, you may want to execute such a form for your state and keep it among your important documents. Your lawyer can help here.

If you have not clearly established one state as your legal residence, then your estate could be taxed by any state in which you have residency at the time of death.

Make sure that the following are evidence of your legal residence:

- Driver's license and license plates
- Income tax return
- Mailing address
- Proof of membership in local organizations
- Will, trust, and other estate planning documents mentioning that address
- Voter registration card

Ideally, upon retirement you should give up any former residence and transfer all your assets to what you want to be considered your domicile.

Some Other State Taxes to Consider

If you are planning a move to another state upon retirement, you will want to consider what's waiting for you there in the way of state taxes. It can make quite a difference in your retirement lifestyle and budgeting.

Some of those taxes include state sales tax, which the overwhelming majority of states do charge. Sales tax ranges from three to seven percent, but sometimes the effective rate is higher because it's combined with local sales taxes. In many states, prescription drugs and food not eaten on the premises are exempt from sales tax.

All states have property taxes, or real estate taxes. However, some states have programs that can help seniors with a property tax burden. The two most common are …

◆ The homestead exemption or credit, which reduces the property taxes on a homeowner's primary residence.

◆ The deferral program, which allows older or disabled Americans to put off paying property taxes until after death or upon sale of their property. This is not entirely free, however. Usually a somewhat below-market interest rate is charged on the taxes that are being deferred. The tax deferral and all accumulated interest usually are represented by a lien on the property.

Quote, Unquote

His money was twice tainted: 'tain't yours and 'tain't mine.
—Mark Twain

Tip

In deciding where to move, you might visit the website of the Department of Revenue of the state that interests you to learn about taxation there. Other sources of information: the local tax collector's office in the community you're considering, your real estate agent there, and the reference department of the local library.

Chipping Away at Your Social Security

The states that tax your Social Security benefits are Colorado, Connecticut, Iowa, Kansas, Minnesota, Missouri, Montana, Nebraska, New Mexico, North Dakota, Rhode Island, Utah, Vermont, West Virginia, and Wyoming.

And …

Some states also levy a tax on what is known as intangibles, such as stocks, bonds, cash and bank deposits, accounts receivable, patents, and licenses.

You can see how important it is to give careful thought to where you'll live after you retire. All of those taxes, small and not-so-small, can eat away not only at your estate, but also on the money you've got to live on—don't call the moving van until you've worked out all the numbers!

The Least You Need to Know

♦ Most states have an estate tax or inheritance tax and a "pick-up" tax equal to the federal state death tax credit. These taxes likely will change, so visit your state's Department of Revenue website.

♦ Only a few states have their own gift tax, which is similar to the federal gift tax.

♦ State income tax planning should be coordinated with federal income tax planning.

♦ Legal residence determines which state imposes its death tax on everything except real and tangible personal property.

Chapter 20

Income Taxes and Tax-Saving Tips

In This Chapter

- ◆ Kids and tax savings
- ◆ Negotiating divorce settlements for tax benefits
- ◆ Business deductions
- ◆ Timing estate income and distribution for tax savings

I'll tell you this: you're probably paying too much federal income tax. And I'll tell you something else: the IRS isn't about to set you straight.

Naturally the more money you keep from the government over the years, the larger your estate will be. What follows are some income tax savings that build wealth. So use these tax strategies to your—and your family's—advantage.

Round Up Those Dependents

Come April 15, your dependents are worth something ($3,100 in 2004), and the amount increases yearly, depending upon the rate of inflation. The tax code provides a long list of possibilities from your children to your parents and in-laws (sorry, your dog doesn't count—yet). There are certain dependency qualifying requirements, though, such as the following:

- ◆ Dependent's gross income must be limited to $3,100 (as of 2004).

- ◆ You must supply over one-half of the dependent's support.

- ◆ Dependent cannot file a joint tax return with his or her spouse.

- ◆ Dependent is a U.S. citizenship or resident.

> **Tip**
>
> If your dependent child is to marry late in the year, ask him or her not to file a joint return with the new spouse so that you can have that exemption one last time. Your child and his or her spouse should file separate returns. This works best if they don't have a high income, of course, because then the deduction might be far better for you to take.

Fortunately, many of these requirements have some exceptions.

For example, if you have a son or daughter who is ready to graduate from college in May, and who is under 24, then the gross income test doesn't apply. Just keep track of all the money you spent on him or her that year because it must be over one-half of what the child has spent on him- or herself. College tuition, room and board, and room and board at home—it all adds up for you quite nicely.

For another example, say you and your siblings are supporting a parent, but no one is providing over half of that support. Any one of you who contributes more than 10 percent may receive the dependency exemption. Just enter into a written multiple support agreement with your brothers and sisters. Because just one of you can claim the deduction for each tax year, you might rotate the exemption every year or allocate it to the sibling in the highest tax bracket.

In addition to the dependency exemption, the tax code allows a child tax credit for children under age 17 of $1,000 in 2004.

Kiddie Craftiness

The tax code requires a child under age 14 who has more than $1,600 of unearned income (e.g., dividends, interest) to pay a tax at the parent's rate for unearned income over that amount. This is the so-called "kiddie tax."

If you want to exploit your child's lower tax bracket by avoiding the kiddie tax, you have several possibilities to consider:

♦ Savings bonds where income can be deferred.

♦ Growth stocks with small dividends but substantial capital gains potential.

♦ Wages to the child for working in your business; earned income is not subject to the kiddie tax and the payments are deductible by your business. (Make sure you keep track of the work performed because the IRS may claim this was sham employment.)

Divorce and the Dollar

All states have some variation of "no-fault divorce," so the primary issues in most contested cases are child custody and support, and property division. Tax planning is important. Included in the custody and support issues is the question of who gets the child's dependency exemption.

The parent awarded custody is entitled to the child's dependency exemption unless that right is released under a written agreement (for example, a divorce decree) and that custodial parent files the required tax form.

Property settlements between spouses usually do not result in any tax to either at the time of the divorce settlement. But who gets to keep which assets may have significant tax implications in future years. For example, the higher bracket taxpayer might want to transfer to the other person marital assets that have significantly appreciated and will soon be sold.

Tip

A higher-bracket taxpayer/ parent should consider negotiating for the dependent's exemption. It's more valuable to that parent.

Take Cliff and his soon-to-be-ex-wife. They purchased stock several years ago for $10,000 that is now worth $60,000. It's estimated that Cliff's capital gains tax bracket after the divorce will be 15 percent, hers, 5 percent. If he receives the stock and sells it, he will pay $7,500 ($50,000 gain × .15) in taxes, while if she receives the same property and sells it, she will pay $2,500 in taxes.

Also, alimony may be negotiable. Usually alimony payments are taxable income to the recipient and a deduction from gross income to the payer. The deduction may be more valuable to the higher bracket ex-spouse than the income tax paid would be to the recipient.

Try, if at all possible, when negotiating child support/dependency exemption and property settlement/alimony to consider tax advantages that will benefit both parties.

Taxpayers' Twelve Biggest Mistakes

Do you know that there are some taxpayers who don't take into account all allowable deductions when filing taxes? They're literally giving a gift to the IRS! Take a look at this list, and check the common mistakes made by those who file. Do you recognize yourself anywhere here? Some of these errors result in additional paperwork for the taxpayer that, in the long run, might not really be worth the bother. But others, as I said, can sometimes cost him or her sizable amounts of money.

In my years of counseling clients engaged in estate planning, I've noticed some of them have made serious—and expensive—mistakes in paying taxes. Here are the worst:

1. Not using the proper IRS forms (tables, schedules, etc.)

2. Not keeping records (receipts, auto mileage, etc.)

3. Not doing mathematical calculations correctly

4. Having too much money withheld each paycheck, so that the government is holding on to your money interest-free (Some, on the other hand, view such extra withholding as a form of forced savings, and they look forward to the refund check.)

5. Not keeping up with tax news if you're preparing your own return—what you don't know can cost you

6. Not seeking professional help when stumped (and it's tax-deductible!)

7. Not being forthcoming with answers to a tax preparer

8. Not properly reporting tax refunds from your previous year's state income tax refund if you itemized last year

9. Not deducting gambling losses, to the extent of winnings, including lottery tickets (save those tickets!)

10. Not deducting employee-related expenses—such as professional journals, memberships, uniforms not for everyday wear, etc.

11. Not including payment with a return if tax is owed (being billed incurs a late charge)

12. Not signing the tax form(s) before mailing—forms might be returned and you'll pay a late charge

Exclusions and Deductions Worth a Look

Did you know that not all income is taxable? Municipal bond interest, for example, is tax exempt. High-bracket taxpayers invest in municipal bonds. Maybe you should consider diversifying your investment portfolio to include some tax-exempt bonds, too.

Rob is at the 25 percent tax bracket. His average taxable investment return is 5 percent, so 25 cents of every $1 goes to the federal government. Or, to put it another way, his after-tax return is 3.5 percent. (If his investment is $10,000 and he receives $500 income, then his tax on $500 income is $125; therefore, his after-tax return is $500 minus $125, which nets him $375, or 3.5 percent.) If he were to invest in tax-exempt bonds, returning 5 percent or more, he would be money ahead.

Investing, then selling, appreciated capital gains property (corporate stock, for example) could be another alternative to anyone in the 28 percent or higher tax bracket, because capital gains are taxed at 15 percent or lower, depending on your tax bracket.

As an employee, you'll find your employer may provide a number of fringe benefits. If group term life insurance is among them, sign up. The rates usually are the least expensive and the premiums the employer pays for up to $50,000 face value are tax-free to you. And if the coverage is greater, the tax tables specify a very reasonable amount of premiums you have to report. That is one tax free fringe benefit.

Here are some further exclusions that can enhance your estate:

- Gifts and inheritances

- Personal injury compensatory damages awards

- Employer-paid medical and dental insurance premiums, and employer-paid educational assistance

- Lodging and meals furnished on employer premises for employer convenience

- Some employee discounts and no-additional-cost services

- Scholarships for tuition and fees

> **Quote, Unquote**
>
> The ceiling on taxation of capital gains reflects the national belief that speculation is a more worthwhile way to make a living than work.
>
> —Calvin Trillin, *Uncivil Liberties* (1982)

> **Quote, Unquote**
>
> It is necessary to work, if not from inclination, at least from despair. Everything considered, work is less boring than amusing oneself.
>
> —Charles Baudelaire, "Mon Coeur Mis á Nu" (1887)

Employers can provide benefit plans to employees that allow them to choose between cash, such as a bonus, and some other form of compensation, such as a nontaxed fringe benefit. A plan that allows employees to choose from a selection of benefits is called a *cafeteria plan*.

Joy works for an employer who provides such a program. Among other choices she can take cash or have her employer pay for her medical insurance. Joy's husband has adequate family medical coverage, so Joy opts for the cash.

Consider enrolling in a health savings account with your employer. The plan allows you to take a salary reduction and use the money to pay for medical expenses not covered by your employee plan. The reduction in salary lowers the income tax and permits you to pay for medical and dental expenses that you may not be able to deduct as an itemized deduction because of the 7.5 percent of adjusted gross income threshold requirement. In 2004, the amount contributable to the plan is $2,600 (single) or $5,150 (family); the amount is adjusted for inflation each year.

Dandy Business Deductions

If you work for yourself or own a business, you had better hire a good tax accountant or study the books carefully because there are a number of excellent deductions out there. Take a look at Schedule C, form 1040, if you are a sole proprietor, or at the corporation or partnership tax forms.

The tax code is obviously too complex to discuss every possible deduction, so I'll highlight just a few here:

♦ Consider a business vehicle as a means of private transportation. The company gets to depreciate the car, and you get to drive it, perhaps including a few personal miles.

♦ Self-employed persons may deduct up to 100 percent of their medical insurance premium.

♦ Think about attending a business conference. They're usually held in warm, scenic locales, making the mixture of business and pleasure a quite attractive "twofer." The airfare is a business deduction if the primary purpose of the travel is business.

♦ Remember, timing is important. If your tax accounting is on a cash receipts and payment method, you can manipulate the timing of income and expenses. For cash basis taxpayers, waiting to mail out bills until the end of the year for work done during the year, or accelerating the purchase of supplies, are possible ways to save on taxes.

♦ Generally, you have to depreciate capital expenditures, which spreads the deduction over several years. However, the tax code does allow you to write off in one year up to $102,000 (limit in 2004); the amount is adjusted for inflation each year. You could buy that new computer system for your business, and pay and write off the $10,000 cost of the system in the year you purchased it.

♦ Take care, though, if you have a business that has been losing money. Beware of the IRS hobby loss rules, particularly if you don't spend a great deal of time in that business.

> **Quote, Unquote**
>
> In America, it is sport that is the opiate of the masses
>
> —Russell Baker, "Observer," *The New York Times* (1967)

> **Quote, Unquote**
>
> The income tax has made more liars out of the American people than golf has. Even when you make a tax form out on the level, you don't know when it's through if you are a crook or a martyr.
>
> —Will Rogers

Ally, for example, is an accountant with a strong love of horses and a devotion to the racetrack. She buys a horse, hires a trainer and rents a stable, all of which costs money, and quite a bit of it, too. This is an intriguing but not inexpensive enterprise.

Ally's horse wins some and loses some, but every year the operation shows a tax loss.

Ally can bet on an audit. The IRS has a clear philosophy on this: No deductions for any activity that gives the taxpayer any enjoyment whatsoever.

Well, that's not quite true. There *is* a presumption that an activity is not a hobby if it has shown a profit in at least three of any five consecutive years (two of seven if horse racing).

Tax regulations require that the taxpayer show that he or she entered into the activity for the purpose of making a profit. The IRS looks at several factors, the most important being whether or not the activity is conducted in a businesslike manner. Therefore you should spend sufficient time running your interest like a business and hire experts if you lack expertise in certain aspects of the operation. If you are strictly a dabbler, interested in recreation, then forget deducting losses.

The Home Office

The IRS is concerned about all of us who have offices in our homes, because we can then deduct expenses related to the office.

Lois, for example, is a law professor during the day, and at night practices law out of a room in her house, where she sees clients. Let's see what deductions are available to Lois:

◆ Lois deducts—and you can, too—a portion of the cost of utilities for the whole house, depreciates the room, and allocates some of the real estate tax and mortgage interest to the office.

◆ Employees and the self-employed may also deduct any related expenses for an office in the residence if it is used exclusively, on a regular basis, as either the principal place of business for a trade or business, or a place of business used by clients, patients, or customers. Are you putting in a new roof on your house? A percentage of that bill can be deducted as an office expense.

◆ No, decorating doesn't count as a deductible expense for your home, but it does for your home office. Don't forget not only the obvious deductions, such as a desk, chair and computer equipment, but also lamps, pictures for the wall, bookcases, and rugs.

◆ Remember if you are operating a business from your home, and you don't show a profit in at least three of five years, your deductions for that enterprise can be questioned.

Limits on Itemizing

In addition, check Schedule A of the 1040. Use it as a checklist for your deductions. Several require amounts in excess of a certain percentage of your Adjusted Gross Income (AGI). For example, medical expenses must be in excess of 7.5 percent of AGI. Again, timing is important. Delaying, or advancing payment of medical expenses or job-related expenses may allow you to alternate itemizing one year with taking the standard deduction the next year.

Estate Tax Savings

If you don't have an estate worth more than $1,500,000 (and haven't made taxable gifts), then the *federal* estate tax won't bother your estate. However, *state* estate or inheritance taxes might. Reducing or escaping death taxes means more money passing to your loved ones, rather than to the state or IRS coffers.

Avoiding death taxes is simple: die poor. Or die and leave everything outright to your spouse, a charity, or a combination of both—not always viable solutions. I offered many suggestions for tax avoidance in Chapters 16 through 19. Here are some special strategies that take a broader view of the subject:

◆ Give it away. Not all at once, but enough each year to take advantage of the annual gift tax exclusion ($11,000). Very often children need money when they are rearing your grandchildren. You can accommodate their needs better now than at your death.

◆ Establish an income trust for you and your spouse, with the remainder going to a charity. You get income to live on, a current charitable deduction, and the rest goes to charity at your deaths.

◆ Create a QTIP (Qualified Terminal Interest Property; see Chapter 16) trust for your spouse and also a credit shelter trust for him or her (equal to the estate exemption equivalent of $1,500,000), which would impose no federal estate taxes at your death and provide income for the spouse; the remainder could go to your children; the QTIP will be taxed in the estate of the spousal beneficiary.

◆ Buy life insurance and transfer ownership to someone else, probably in the family (or have another person, for example, your child, purchase a policy on your life). If your spouse doesn't need the money and your children are all grown, you can give them a substantial legacy at very little expense to you.

◆ Review your estate assets, because the federal estate tax law allows installment payments if, for example, more than 35 percent of your adjusted gross estate consisted of a farm or stock in a closely held (usually family) business.

Briefs

Could you use a smile about this time, with all the talk of your own mortality? An insurance office was naturally surprised when an elderly gentleman of 97 stopped in and asked to take out a life insurance policy. His application was turned down. The oldster stood up, shook his head at the agent who had given him the rejection, sighed and said "You folks are making a big mistake. If you look at your statistics you'll find that mighty few men die after they're 97."

Savings by Your Executor

The executor administers the probate estate, which means he or she has certain power over the property and timing of its distribution that can have beneficial tax implications.

There are several ways an executor can do this:

◆ Reducing estate taxes by appropriate tax elections or deductions

◆ Reducing income taxes to the estate and its beneficiaries by manipulating income distributions

◆ Encouraging the use of inheritance or jointly owned/survivor disclaimers

Let me explain some of these tax-saving strategies to you.

Tip

The executor can choose to value the estate assets at death or at an alternate valuation date (up to six months after death). The alternate valuation can only be used if it results in a decrease in the estate tax. Also, an estate's value can change based on market conditions. The higher valuation may save taxes for the beneficiary because of a stepped-up (higher) basis, but would also mean more estate taxes. If the beneficiary is going to sell an asset right away and is in a high tax bracket, to minimize the income tax, the executor probably should value the asset at its highest level, because the gain is based on the difference between the selling price and the basis.

Timing Income

Every estate that has any property-generating income (e.g., stocks, savings accounts, rentals) will have to file income tax returns for the income earned …

- During the deceased's life (individual's last return).

- During estate administration (estate's *fiduciary* tax return).

Some estates may have to file federal estate tax returns and state death tax returns. If both income and estate tax returns must be filed, then some expenses may be deducted on one or the other return, such as probate administration costs (e.g., legal and executor fees) and casualty losses. A comparison of the highest rates on each return will usually dictate where the greatest tax savings will be.

Because there are at least two income tax returns to be filed (deceased's last return and fiduciary return), manipulating the timing of income may be possible.

Brian is a sole proprietor. He knows he is dying. He can accelerate income and have it apply to his last return by billing and collecting income before death, or delay collection and have the executor report the income. Brian also owns some land he considers selling. If he entered

Words, Words, Words

Fiduciary means trust. In the context here it means the estate has income it's earned and has to file a tax return.

Words, Words, Words

Basis is a tax term usually related to the cost of an asset, and used to determine gain on the asset's sale. Tax gain is determined by subtracting the basis from the selling price. Tax law allows the basis to be stepped up (increased) to the fair market value of the asset at the taxpayer's date of death.

into a contract to allow the purchaser an option to buy the property after his death, then when the option is exercised and the land sold, the estate's stepped-up basis (appreciated value from time of purchase until death) will wipe out most, if not all, of the taxable gain.

Timing Estate Distribution

The executor usually has the authority to time estate distributions to beneficiaries. When income is earned by the estate, it may distribute that income to a beneficiary, which would result in the estate income being taxed to the beneficiary and not the estate. For example, if Jon Jones is the residuary beneficiary of a will and the estate makes a partial distribution to him of $10,000 when it has $10,000 or more in taxable income, then the income tax law treats Jon's distribution as receipt of its income, and he has to report it as income. If the estate had not made its distribution, the estate would have been taxed upon its income.

> **Quote, Unquote**
>
> If Patrick Henry thought that taxation *without* representation was bad, he should see how bad it is *with* representation.
> —*The Old Farmer's Almanac*

There is an exception to this distribution rule for a special devisee. Jon's sister, Jane, was given stock in the will. Even though the estate has income when it makes the stock distribution to Jane, she will not be treated as having received that income. There is a special income tax rule to protect Jane's distribution.

The executor therefore needs to be aware of income tax rules that apply to estate distributions when the estate has taxable income.

Timing deductions may allow a splitting of income between the estate and the beneficiary and could save taxes if there is a tax rate differential.

No, Thank You

Sometimes an estate beneficiary does not want the inheritance or a surviving joint owner does not desire to own the asset. State law and federal tax law permits a *disclaimer* in those situations, which is a refusal to take the devise or joint ownership. Generally that refusal must be put in writing within nine months of the deceased's death. In addition, the person disclaiming the interest cannot benefit from the property before executing the disclaimer.

Cam, for example, inherited all the estate from her husband, so nothing is taxable, but Cam's estate will be taxable on her death, so she wants to reduce what she has inherited. She executes a disclaimer of property worth $1,500,000, which then goes to the alternative beneficiaries (or intestate, if there are none).

A joint savings account that is just in one child's name may be disclaimed by that child so that the money in the account is put in the probate estate and available to the other children. That makes for less family feuding and may be what the depositor-parent had intended.

Finally here, the executor may have cash to invest during administration. Tax-exempt bonds or growth stocks would be helpful to high-income tax beneficiaries. But a word to the wise executor: Discuss all this with the beneficiaries who may have diverse needs, or just want their share as quickly as possible. It is their money, after all.

The Least You Need to Know

- Before filing, scrutinize your income tax return for more tax deductions. There are likely to be some.

- Time your income and deductible expenses to take advantage of different tax rates in different years.

- A will can maximize estate income and death tax savings.

- A good executor will seek advice about ways to save taxes on your estate.

Chapter 21

Keeping Your Wealth Within the Family

In This Chapter

- ◆ Partial gifts
- ◆ Selling to the family
- ◆ Gifts to youngsters
- ◆ The family business

Let's assume that you want a family member, or perhaps the whole clan, to inherit from your estate.

That can be done—to everyone's benefit. Here are some suggestions; a few you may have read about briefly in other chapters, plus some new strategies. All are designed to keep your assets in the bosom of your family. Match them up one against the other to see which might work best for you. Just as important as keeping wealth in the family, of course, is how to make that transfer at the least cost to you (or them). I'll tell you how right now.

Charity Begins at Home

Probate and taxes take time and toll, so our goal is to minimize both.

The transfer laws are fairly simple and you've read about them earlier in these pages. For example, making a gift requires only that the donor intends to make that gift, the donee accepts, and a physical transfer occurs. Likewise, upon death the will distributes probate assets to the named beneficiaries, or the living trust continues to provide principal and interest for its beneficiaries.

The rub in all of this, of course, is taxes. Let's see what we can do about that.

The Next Generation

Most couples with children quite naturally want to pass on their assets to those kids, either now or through their estate. There are a number of ways to do this:

- Outright gifts
- Section 529 Education plans
- Trusts with split income and remainder interests
- Rearranging business assets
- Purchasing life insurance, annuities, or other easily transferable assets
- Creating joint interests, or "paid on death" accounts
- Gifting property but retaining a life estate in it for the donor
- Below-market rate loans or gift loans (the latter might be a loan to a child that is then forgiven)
- Bargain sales of property or installment sales with annual forgiveness of payment
- Employing children in the family business
- Wills

All of these require planning and thorough consideration of the tax consequences. You can read about some of them in earlier chapters of this book and can, of course, discuss them with your accountant.

Tip

All transfers during your life require you to determine how much less money you can afford to live on. You don't want to give away too much; one day you may need some of that money for your own purposes.

Certainly transfers to your spouse are considered within the purview of this chapter, because they are most easily made, with little tax consequences, and are likely to result in your property ultimately going to the children after your spouse's death. (Of course that assumption may not be true if the spouse is not the parent of your children.)

Giving Something—and Keeping It

Perhaps you'd like to make a gift—but only sort of. How about a partial transfer of property to someone else?

Bonnie owns a condominium in Florida. She wants to keep ownership and use it during her lifetime, and then wants the title to go to her daughter. Bonnie could deed the condo to her daughter and retain a life estate that would accomplish her goal. (There's more about life estates in Chapter 2 and Chapter 18.)

Retained interest in property is subject to federal estate tax, and may be liable for state death taxes. The interest given up (for example, the remainder after a life estate) is subject to federal gift tax (but with no allowance for the annual exclusion because it is a future interest).

You may want to create a 529 Coverdell education plan for your child's college education. Put money into the plan account, and then when your child is ready for college she may withdraw money from the account for her college expenses entirely tax-free.

Trust Them

You can establish a trust for yourself (and your spouse), reserving the right to the income and withdrawing the principal, with the remainder going to your child upon your (and your spouse's) death.

Ken created a *revocable* living trust for himself and his spouse, deposited assets in the trust, and lived off the income. Upon the death of Ken's wife, and then Ken, the assets went to his adult children outright.

Income from revocable trusts is taxed to the grantor, or creator, who established the trust. There is no gift tax to the children because they receive nothing until the parent's death. But the children will have to pay federal estate tax when their parent dies and they get the trust's assets.

If you create an *irrevocable* living trust, then there is a gift to beneficiaries of the trust. The annual gift tax exclusion is available for a gift to income beneficiaries.

Dina transferred $200,000 into an irrevocable living trust for the life of her four children, and then the remainder to her grandchildren. If Dina's spouse joins in the gift, then their annual exclusions will amount to $88,000, assuming the actuarial value of the income interest is at least $88,000 (4 [one for each of the four children] times $22,000 [$11,000 exemption for each of the two parents]), and the balance would be subject to gift tax (but a unified credit, the equivalent of which is $1,000,000, would first apply).

Watch Out

Be sure you talk over with your children any gifts or investing you want to make for your grandkids now rather than later. What you have in mind might conflict with your children's ideas and plans.

The value of the grandchildren's remainder interest, which may be small if their parents are young, might be subject to the generation-skipping transfer tax, but only if it exceeds $1.5 million (which is the exclusion limit, which increases with the estate tax exclusion).

An irrevocable trust, with the grantor retaining no rights, will not be included in the grantor's estate, and income from the trust will be taxed to the trust and its beneficiaries.

Considering Co-Ownership

You might want to own property, such as bank accounts or stock, with another person. When you create jointly owned property that transfers an undivided interest at the time it is created, the survivor receives the entire interest at the other's death.

Quote, Unquote

If wisdom were offered to me with the proviso that I should keep it shut up and refrain from declaring it, I should refuse. There's no delight in owning anything unshared.

—Seneca, "Letters to Lucilius" (first century)

In case that isn't completely clear to you, I'll give you an example. Grant adds his son to his savings account as joint owner with right of survivorship. He also owns a house, and executes a deed in which his daughter is joint owner with right of survivorship.

No gift tax occurs in creating a joint ownership in a savings account (only withdrawal by the non-depositor is a gift). A gift is considered complete only upon withdrawal from the bank account. But the creation of a joint ownership in other property such as a house, is an immediate gift. The annual exclusion (that $11,000 you've been reading so much about) is available when the gift occurs. All this means that Grant owes no tax for the savings account with his son, when established, but he might owe on the property he now owns jointly with his daughter if its value at the time the new deed is drawn exceeds $11,000.

The gift tax does not apply to the creation of the savings account because the son only has a "right" to withdraw the money, while the daughter owns the house, just like her father.

Jointly held property is subject to the federal estate tax. Income is taxed to the income recipient.

As an alternative, you could establish "paid on death to …" accounts. You solely own the account. Upon death, the person named as the payee receives the account without any probate, thus avoiding that expense.

Life Insurance

You might want to purchase life insurance, particularly group term, and then transfer policy ownership to a child.

That could provide a substantial benefit to the child at little expense to you, and may be appropriate when you don't need the coverage to protect your family in the event of your untimely death.

A life insurance policy transferred more than three years before the owner-insured's death is not subject to estate tax, and gift tax applies only to the value of the policy (e.g., term value is the cost to purchase a policy on the insured's life, and whole life value is a variant of its cash surrender value). Because of special IRS rules, the transfer is a gift, but the value of the gift is limited to its cash value at the time of transfer, which may be for less than the face value proceeds collected later.

Loans Within the Family

Loans to family members aren't that unusual (naturally we're not talking about the can-you-let-me-have-twenty-until-payday variety), and can be an excellent means of shifting wealth to a child.

Casey lends his son $100,000 at 0 percent interest per year, with installment payments of $10,000 each year. There is a promissory note evidencing the debt and a mortgage on the home his son purchased with the funds. While Casey has never indicated any plan to do so at the time of making the loan, he has for several years completely forgiven those annual $10,000 debt payments.

Gift tax applies to below-market interest loans because the borrower doesn't pay the same interest he would on a commercial loan. Thus, he is, in effect, "given" the interest by the lender. However, the annual exclusion ($11,000) is available for the gifted interest.

> **Words, Words, Words**
>
> Merriam Webster's *Collegiate Dictionary* says to **document** is "to provide with factual or substantial support for statements made or a hypotheses proposed." An example of that would be a promissory note.

The federal income tax treats the waiver of interest income as if the lender has received the interest, but only to the extent of the borrower's net investment income (interest and dividends received by the borrower from the invested money) when they exceed $1,000 and if the loan is for $100,000 or more. This is called the "imputed interest" rule.

Don't forget to *document* this loan, and enforce its provisions the way you would any other. The IRS is not particularly happy with this type of arrangement, so you'll want to cover yourself.

Your Family as Buyers

Selling an asset to a family member keeps it in the family. You can structure the sale on an installment basis or as part gift and part sale, which is what is called a *bargain sale*.

> **Tip**
>
> You might want to consider the sale of appreciating property to a family member, because the appreciation occurring after the sale will not be included in the seller's estate. Only the proceeds from the sale when the property had a lesser value will be included.

Alex sold some land to his son for $100,000, payable in 10 equal installments, with a 10 percent per annum interest rate. The property had cost him $10,000 when he first purchased it. He also sold another parcel to his daughter for $50,000 (it was worth $100,000 at the time of this sale). That property originally cost Alex $10,000 as well.

Alex's installment receipts and interest will result in taxable income. Each installment of $10,000 from his son involves $9,000 of gain and $1,000 of nontaxable return of his original cost. Alex may want to forgive some of the installment payments, which would be a gift (but the annual exclusion is available). He must be careful to do so in a manner that would not allow the IRS to claim a tax avoidance scheme.

Alex's bargain sale to his daughter is one half taxable gift, the other half a taxable sale, with the income tax amount reduced by one half of Alex's original cost of the land. He may want to structure the bargain sale with installment payments to take advantage of the annual gift tax exclusion.

Gifts to Minors

Outright presents to minor children are all right for birthdays and holidays, but only when they come in gift-wrapped packages or are relatively small amounts of cash.

For any sizable amount (more than $11,000), consider one of the following:

◆ A custodial bank account

◆ Custodial property (stocks, bonds)

◆ A minor's trust

◆ A living trust

You don't want your child to waste your hard-earned cash, so it's important to keep his or her hands off the money while still young.

Nan establishes a custodial account at her local bank for her daughter and deposits $11,000 in the account each year. She purchases stock for her son for the same amount and names a custodian. Her choice of custodian for both is her brother, Bob.

Custodial accounts and property are in custodianship until the donee reaches the age of majority as indicated by that state's gift to minors law. Gift tax law applies, with the annual exclusion. Custodial accounts are not included in the donor's estate if he or she is not the custodian. Income is taxed to the minor.

An alternative to custodial accounts, which are usually bank or stock accounts, that have basically the same income, gift, and estate tax advantages is a *minor's trust*, which is a formal trust established, usually by parents or grandparents to benefit the child.

> **Quote, Unquote**
>
> Put not your trust in money, put your money in trust.
>
> —Oliver Wendell Holmes Sr., "The Autocrat of the Breakfast Table" (1858)

Ben creates just such a trust for his daughter, age 2. The trustee is the Trustworthy Bank. The trust will distribute all income and principal to the daughter when she becomes 21; if she dies before then, all the trust property will be in her estate. (A minor's trust can also be extended beyond 21.)

The gift to a properly designed minor's trust qualifies for the annual exclusion. The trust assets are not subject to the donor's estate tax if he or she maintains no control over the trust, and the income is taxed to the trust and beneficiary.

Another example of a trust that allows the annual gift tax exemption is the so-called *Crummey trust*, which gives the child or his or her guardian a brief period to accept an outright gift before it goes into the trust. That is useful if the grantor wants to continue the trust beyond the beneficiary's twenty-first birthday. (See Chapter 17 for more on Crummey trusts.)

A irrevocable living trust, which is not specifically designed to qualify for the annual gift tax exclusion, would reduce the donor's unified credit for each gift. While its terms may be very flexible (as contrasted with the prior custodial accounts and minor's trusts), it can be expensive because of the reduction in the credit. If a long-term trust is considered necessary because of a child's disability, you might want to refer to Chapter 14, which discusses that particular situation.

Splitting It with Your Spouse

If you're looking to save on taxes (and who isn't!), mind the annual gift tax exclusion. As I've explained more than once already in this book, you can give $11,000 to anyone outright and not pay a single penny in taxes on that money. And if your spouse joins in the gift, then your exclusion automatically doubles. Your spouse need not have an ownership interest in the property given (that is, the money for the gift can come from the other partner).

Sherry gave her son $100,000 from her own funds in 2005. Her husband joined her for gift tax purposes. The two annual exclusions reduce the taxable gift to $78,000, and each spouse can use his or her unified credit to apply to his or her taxable gift of $78,000.

The split-gift election is particularly helpful to transfer the maximum property at minimum gift tax when one spouse owns very few assets.

Your Business for Your Benefit

You own a business, whether it is a sole proprietorship, partnership, limited liability partnership, limited liability company, or corporation. If you control the company, you may want to pass it on to your children. You want to leave behind your little niche of capitalism to those who can most appreciate it—your family.

Often the parent/owner wants to retain control while gradually transferring ownership to the next generation. Usually that is easier to structure with a corporation than with a partnership, limited liability partnership, or limited liability company, but it is certainly available for the latter three business entities as well.

Watch Out

Be realistic in determining whether your children are interested in owning your business, or are indeed capable of running it. Also be prepared to compensate those who *don't* want the business, especially in ways that will not interfere with those who do.

Transferring Company Stock

Jay owns all the outstanding stock in House Calls, Inc., a repair service. He could give 40 percent of the stock to his 2 children and still control the corporation. Or he could restructure the stock and create voting and nonvoting common stock, retaining all or a majority of the voting stock so that he stays in control of the business.

Gifts of stock are subject to the gift tax, but the annual exclusion and wise use of the unified credit may significantly reduce that tax. This is especially true if you can justify a substantial discount in the value of the gift because it involves owning only a minority interest in that stock. Periodically giving stock to your children as it becomes clearer that they will be responsible can significantly reduce the parent's estate and income taxes.

Watch Out

Corporation stock restructuring may have adverse income tax effects. Consult a tax expert before making any move.

S corporation (a corporation where the income is taxed to the shareholders) tax laws changed in 1996 to permit a variety of trusts to own S corporation stock. This can provide additional planning opportunities for S corporation owners.

Tip

Children-shareholders could purchase life insurance on the life of the parent-shareholder and use that money to fund an estate stock buyout upon the death of that parent.

Buy-Sell Agreements

Another way to transfer your family business to a member or members of your family is through a buy-sell agreement. In such an agreement family members would purchase your interest in the business at your retirement or upon your demise. This would provide cash during retirement years or for your estate survivors and would keep the business within the family.

Employing Your Kids

Wealth can also be transferred through the employment of your children. Many family businesses have done this. Children, even when still in their teens, can earn spending money from the business. Full-time jobs there allow parents to share the wealth (and responsibilities). And reasonable wages are deductible business expenses. Income can be shifted from the higher tax bracket parent to the lower-bracket children.

Rich, and Staying That Way

The very wealthy are probably not spending a lot of time reading this book. They probably have droves of tax lawyers doing their estate planning for them. On the outside chance that one or more of you who are reading this do fall into that category, I offer this brief section of tips.

GRATs, GRITs, GRUTs, CRATs, and CRUTs are the heady stuff that excite tax planners who have clients able to pay hundreds of dollars per hour in fees. The first three GRs are trusts that have forms of annuity payments. The trust grantor, or creator, transfers assets into an irrevocable living trust, which pays him or her income. Upon death the trust principal goes to the remainderman (the person designated to receive the trust fund when it ends). The transfer is subject to gift tax and the trust asset will be partially included in the grantor's estate for federal estate taxes.

GRs can be used to transfer appreciating property to the next generation, who will benefit from the appreciation, while the grantor receives some income from the assets. The same or better results may be achieved by other means discussed in this chapter.

The CRs involve charitable trusts, which have been discussed in Chapter 18. The advantage is a charitable deduction, but the disadvantage for the children is that they won't see a penny—the charity gets it.

Likewise, you could sell your children property in exchange for an annuity, which would have much the same effect as the GRs without the complications. The parent receives income, and the property is kept in the family. The income tax impact is reduced because the gain is spread over the term of the annuity.

My personal favorite involves gifts in trust to grandchildren (thus skipping one estate-taxable generation and saving those taxes). Properly structured, the gifts may qualify for the annual gift tax exclusion and minimize the reduction of the unified credit. The generation-skipping transfer tax (GSTT) can be avoided for transfers of $1.5 million or less.

Jack gave his wife $1.5 million because she doesn't have much money in her own name and any gift to a spouse, as you know by now, is not subject to gift taxes. Because the couple's children are well provided for, Jack and his wife have now established a well-crafted plan to transfer $3 million to the grandkids without incurring the dreaded GSTT (her brand-new $1.5 million, plus $1.5 million from Jack).

If you like the idea of skipping your children because they do not need the money, and want to pass everything, or nearly everything, on to your grandchildren, following is a diagram that will show you at a glance some of your options.

> **Quote, Unquote**
>
> Nothing is more admirable than the fortitude with which millionaires tolerate the disadvantages of their wealth.
>
> —Rex Stout

> **Words, Words, Words**
>
> A **tontine** is a sort of annuity gimmick. It's named after Lorenzo Tonti, an Italian banker who died in the mid-eighteenth century. Basically, it's a joint financial arrangement whereby the participants contribute usually equal amounts of money to a prize that is awarded entirely to the participant who outlives all the others.

Leaving Your Assets Directly to Your Grandchild(ren)

You

|

Your Child(ren)
(skip this generation)

|

Your Grandchild(ren)

You can leave your assets in any of these:

Will   Living/Testamentary Trust

Crummey Trust   Gift

Life Insurance Policy   2503(c)Trust

* Be careful of the generation-skipping transfer tax (GSTT) if you are transferring more than $1.5 million. Remember that the exemptions increase in the same amounts as the estate tax exemption, e.g., $2,000,000 in 2006, etc.

The Least You Need to Know

◆ Gifts in the form of a trust can create income for the grantor and keep assets in the family.

◆ Gift loans can shift income and assets to children.

◆ A parent can purchase a life insurance policy and give it to a child, providing significant death benefits at little expense.

◆ Family businesses can be restructured to form an orderly transfer to the next generation, and to reduce taxes.

Part 5

Retirement, Elder Issues, and the Broad Planning Picture

Time marches on. Perhaps you're just a handful of years from retirement. Or maybe that time in your life is so far into the future it seems almost science fiction: retire in 2030? Will there actually be a 2030? Will there still be a life passage known as retirement then?

You'd better count on it. And count it into your estate plan.

As you will see in the coming chapters, there is some good news ahead for retirees in the form of help with some bills. But there are some shaky happenings, too, with familiar, dependable programs that appear to be in trouble. The bottom line for all of us seems to be: save, get organized, and don't count exclusively on government aid in your retirement years.

Here's a closer look at what can be going on in your life as you approach—and then pass—65.

22

Bring 'Em On: Social Security and Other Retirement Benefits

In This Chapter

- ◆ Collecting Social Security
- ◆ Who else is eligible for your benefits
- ◆ Medicare—its coverage and gaps
- ◆ Medicaid's requirements

We huff and we puff—figuratively speaking—through much of our working lives. And then when we hit 65, government programs kick in to give us a hand with expenses. Thank goodness for Social Security and Medicare, which are government programs available to those who qualify (in government jargon, an *entitlement program*)! They'll still be around, won't they, when *we* retire? And the coverage will be at least adequate, won't it?

Hmmmm. There's some good and some iffy news ahead.

What You Can Expect at Social Security Time

If you're employed, you pay a Social Security tax (FICA) of 7.65 percent of your wages and the employer matches that percentage. The percentage has varied over the years and now includes a 1.45 percent Medicare tax. If you are self-employed, you pay slightly less than the combined employer and employee tax.

Of course you are not thrilled about all of this, but the silver lining is that you might get some of that money back when you reach age 65, or later, because the retirement age for full benefits increases gradually to age 67 for those born in 1960 and after.

Words, Words, Words

Social Security is an **entitlement program** because Congress has set certain criteria for eligibility that, when met, automatically qualify workers to receive benefits. Workers pay special payroll taxes into the fund, unlike Medicaid or food stamps, for example, which are financed out of general revenue and have income requirements for eligibility.

Fully vs. Currently Insured

Social Security retirement income will be paid to a worker (or his or her survivors) if the worker is fully insured, which requires that he or she has at least 10 years, consisting of 40 quarter years, of coverage. *Fully insured* means entitled to full Social Security benefits.

Rich is now 51 years old. He has worked full-time since he was 21 (30 years consisting of 120 quarter years of coverage, paying *FICA* tax). Rich's work experience entitles him to full Social Security old-age retirement income when he reaches Social Security retirement age. Rich is fully insured.

Words, Words, Words

What do the initials **FICA** mean—that abbreviation we see on our paycheck stubs as we grumble about the amount of money being withheld there? FICA stands for Federal Insurance Contributions Act.

Being only *currently insured* entitles a worker to disability benefits but not to old-age retirement payments. To be currently insured a worker must have been covered in 6 quarters of the last 13; however, for persons in 2004 who are age 24 or older, the requirements are increased, and may require 20 or more quarters. Then he can claim benefits, or his family might be granted survivor benefits.

Earl just began working 5 years ago, so he has earned 5 years consisting of 20 quarter years. He must work another 20 quarter years to be covered by Social Security old-age retirement. However, Earl is *currently insured* and if he dies his family could receive Social Security benefits. Likewise *he* could receive Social Security disability benefits. All of his credits as he continues to work, of course, go toward his old-age benefits.

Why do they use quarter years? That's a good question. I suppose it gives those who work for only part of a year a better chance to qualify.

Adding Up Your Benefits

If you were born in 1937, and are fully insured, then you are now old enough to begin receiving your full old-age Social Security benefits, but if you were born later, say 1943, you will begin full benefits at age 66.

Tip

Social Security will send you a computer printout annually that gives you a year-to-year breakdown of your earnings, the amount of Social Security taxes you have paid, and the current dollar estimate of retirement benefits you are likely to receive. If you don't receive your statement, you may contact them through their website: www.ssa.gov.

Benefits are increased by cost-of-living adjustments. There are also overall benefit limits.

You *can* take old-age Social Security payments as early as age 62, but at a 20 percent reduction (or more as the retirement date increases) of what you could count on at 65.

Your old-age benefits can be reduced if you work (if you receive wages or self-employment income) while getting the benefits:

◆ Age 62 to 64—your income is limited to $12,000 (2004 limits, indexed to inflation)

◆ Age 65 or full retirement qualification to 69—no earning limits

◆ Age 70 on—there are no earning limits

What if you earn "too much"? Some benefits will be withheld. For people under 65, $1 will be withheld for every $2 earned above the limit. In any year that you think you will earn more than the limits, you must give the Social Security Administration an estimate of those earnings.

If you delay receiving old-age retirement benefits beyond the time you are entitled to them, then when you do start, your benefits will be greater than if you had taken them at 65 or when fully qualified.

Medicare, incidentally, is not affected by your decision to delay receiving old-age payments. That still kicks in at 65.

When the time comes, you can apply through your local Social Security office for retirement payments and other benefits.

A Beneficiary Other Than the Covered Worker

Your Social Security does not have to be paid to you; you can designate another beneficiary or split it with another person. Here are your options:

- ◆ **Spouse or Divorced Spouse.** Basically, this person will receive one half of the benefits of the covered worker while the covered worker is alive. An ex-spouse is only entitled to benefits if he or she was married to the covered worker for 10 years and has not remarried.

  Cal, for example, is 66 years old, retired, and receiving a monthly Social Security check in the amount of $1,660. His wife's share of his Social Security is based on one half of that benefit, or $830.

  (Cal's wife must choose between her own benefits—if she's entitled to any—and those that would accrue to her as Cal's spouse. She can't have both—no "double-dipping" allowed here.)

- ◆ **Children.** If they are under age 18 (19 if still in high school), children can receive one half of the covered worker's benefits when he or she is alive (and either currently or fully insured), and 75 percent when he or she has died. An adopted child will qualify, and a stepchild may under certain circumstances.

- ◆ **Widow or Widower.** This individual can receive the covered worker's entire benefit if he or she is at retirement age, and, if not at the retirement age, up to 75 percent of the covered worker's benefit if the surviving spouse is caring for the covered worker's child who is under age 16.

- ◆ **Grandchildren.** If both parents of the grandchild are dead or disabled, and the grandchild is a dependent of a covered worker, then the grandchild receives the same benefits as the child of a covered worker.

Tip

The Social Security website has a benefit calculator, which you should consult because it contains the most current information.

In addition, a surviving spouse or child receives a lump sum death payment of $255 to help with burial expenses.

If a young worker with a spouse and children dies and is covered by Social Security, the family survivor payments can amount to hundreds of thousands of dollars. Consider that when computing your insurance needs. You might want a lesser amount of coverage knowing that Social Security payments will be available.

Yes, You're Taxed on Benefits

"Let's see if I get this straight," you're probably saying, "I paid taxes on my Social Security retirement earnings while I worked, and now I'll pay taxes on them again when I receive them. Talk about double-dipping! Only in America!"

Once upon a time Social Security old-age retirement benefits were not taxed. Then Congress saw that that was a vast untapped resource and decided to tax those moneys. What Congress giveth, Congress can taketh away.

If a taxpayer's income after the age of 65 exceeds one of two specified base amounts ($32,000 or $44,000 for joint filers; $25,000 or $34,000 for taxpayers who file as a single person or head of household status), then from 50 percent to as much as 85 percent of the Social Security retirement benefits must be included in the gross income and declared for tax purposes. Note that tax-exempt income is included in the tax base calculations for determining taxable income. The 1040 instruction booklet has a form for calculating the taxable amount.

The computation involves two different calculations, which are not too difficult to determine by using the form in your 1040 tax packet. That's the package you receive in the mail each year around the holidays (Happy New Year!).

So ... Will Social Security Be There for Us?

Yes, in all likelihood it will. If you were born before 1938, you have begun receiving benefits. If you were born after 1937 well, you might still have to keep working for two more years before claiming benefits, and there are likely to be other changes in the program as well.

The federal government is *very* nervous about this system, as it waits for the huge crush of Baby Boomers (those born between 1946 and 1964) to begin claiming benefits in 2012. Also, following the Baby Boom was the Baby Bust, which means fewer working Americans coming up behind the boomers to pay into the fund. And we're all living longer these days, not just a bit but into *really* old age. That's great news! But it's also another growing drain on Social Security.

The system will endure. But there are a few things we might keep in mind. Social Security was designed in 1935 by the administration of President Franklin D. Roosevelt to be a sort of ... well, actually, almost a welfare program for America's neediest during the Depression. Remember, too, in those days 60 was considered old age, and not that many lived much beyond to claim Social Security benefits.

The system was never expected to grow the way it has. Today we look on Social Security as our right, and of course, to an extent it is. Something like 6 out of 10 workers in private industry have no pension other than Social Security.

But for all of us, a comfortable retirement must also depend on saving money during our working years. We can't let ourselves depend exclusively on Social Security.

Medicare for Your Aches and Pains

What about health benefits after that magic number 65?

Medicare is a federal health insurance program for ...

◆ Persons age 65 and older.

◆ Persons of any age with permanent kidney failure. (This illness was included in 1972 amendments to Medicare because of the interest of a few senators who believed many Americans requiring renal dialysis would be unable to afford that treatment.)

◆ Certain disabled persons under age 65.

I'll bet the latter two categories came as a surprise to you. Yes, Medicare is not just for the 65-plus set, although they make up by far the greatest number of users of the program.

If you are receiving Social Security benefits when you turn 65, you are enrolled in Medicare automatically. (If it's not automatic, then contact your Social Security office.)

You will receive a Medicare card. That card shows the Medicare coverage you are entitled to—Hospital Insurance (Part A) and Medical Insurance (Part B), as well as the date your coverage begins.

If you or your spouse is entitled to Social Security benefits, you do not have to pay a monthly premium for Part A Medicare coverage, which generally begins at age 65.

You *will* have to pay a monthly premium to be covered by Part B, however. In 2005 that charge is $78.20 a month. Initial enrollment may be made three months before you become 65.

Medicare doesn't pay all your hospital and medical bills—not by a long shot. You have certain premiums, deductions, and co-pays on your medical expenses. Coverage under Part A and Part B is limited (insurance may be purchased for more extended coverage, which I'll talk about later).

Medicare Part A helps pay for medically necessary inpatient care in a general hospital, skilled nursing facility, psychiatric hospital, or hospice facility, as well as medically necessary home health care and certain other costs. The important words here are "helps pay for." For updated inpatient and other coverage by Medicare, consult its website at www.medicare.gov or the Social Security website at www.ssa.gov.

Medicare Part B pays for a number of medical services and supplies, most significantly your doctors' bills. For current deductibles and costs, consult the Medicare website noted above.

> **Quote, Unquote**
>
> Use your health, even to the point of wearing it out. That's what it is for. Spend all you have before you die; and do not outlive yourself.
>
> —George Bernard Shaw, *The Doctor's Dilemma* (1913)

> **Tip**
>
> Do you have questions about Medicare coverage? Go to the Medicare information website at www.medicare.gov or visit the AARP web site at www.aarp.org.

Filling Those Gaps

Medicare leaves some significant gaps in its health care coverage. You can purchase insurance for some of your expenses not covered by Medicare.

These various policies are referred to as "Medigap" insurance, more formally as Medicare supplement insurance. They are specifically designed to fill in what Medicare excludes, and are regulated by federal and state law. The standard policies range from Plan A, which is a basic policy, through Plan J, which includes the basic

Watch Out

You need only *one* Medigap policy, no matter what insurance salespeople tell you. It is a federal offense to sell policies that duplicate a buyer's existing protection. Once you turn 65 you might find yourself bombarded by telephone calls from eager insurance salespeople trying to sell you such coverage.

plan plus significant other benefits. Obviously the more you pay in insurance premiums, the more coverage you get.

You might also want to consider managed care plans with a health maintenance organization; continuation of your employer's health insurance, if that is available after your retirement; a long-term care policy (there's an explanation of that coming up); or any regular medical insurance coverage that pays all or part of hospital stays.

Compare the costs and benefits of various policies. Your state insurance department is a solid source of no-cost consumer information. Also consult with appropriate professionals who are knowledgeable about Medicare. You might wind up paying too much for too little insurance if you're not careful. Also, visit the U.S. Department of Health and Human Services website (www.os.dhhs.gov) for information on Medigap policies.

Good Grief, Will Medicare Be There When We Need It?

You might not know this, but Medicare is a relatively new program, quite a bit younger than Social Security. It was founded by President Lyndon B. Johnson in 1965 and was aimed at the one third of the elderly in the nation who were then living in poverty, with little or no access to health care. The program, like Social Security, just grew and grew. Again, Americans are living longer and medical technology has gotten very costly, which all adds up to a huge expense each year.

Quote, Unquote

The trouble about always trying to preserve the health of the body is that it is so difficult to do without destroying the health of the mind.

—G. K. Chesterton, "On The Classics" (1930)

In 2003, Medicare cost $255 billion and covered 35 million Americans, and it is estimated that Medicare now pays about 50 percent of the medical costs for the elderly. Congress, around election time, looks concerned about the escalating cost and even looks for solutions. Americans know about this concern and realize changes will have to be made to the system. We're seeing one already: the adoption of managed care, for example, such as HMOs instead of the fee-for-service setup of the Medicare program we've always known.

Managed care looks like it could be a partial solution to rising costs. No matter how imperfect, it would probably be better than no Medicare at all.

Long-Term Care Insurance

Long-term care insurance, also known as LTCI, is a private insurance coverage that has become increasingly popular over the last several years as older Americans realize the limitations of Medicare, especially when it comes to nursing home costs. The average annual cost of nursing home care is between $40,000 and $55,000. Medicare does not cover this cost.

By covering ongoing and/or high-priced expenses, LTCI can keep you from total loss of your assets, such as you might find with long-term nursing home costs, for example. But as good as it might seem, approach LTCI with caution.

On the one hand, a policy like this can offer you security you would not otherwise have as you grow older, and most of these policies are guaranteed renewable even if your health worsens. The flip side of the coin is that the insurance is quite expensive. Some folks just do not have enough assets to justify carrying such coverage.

How much money are we talking about? Well, a healthy 50-year-old may pay at least $1,000 a year in LTCI premiums, and a 70-year-old may pay at least $3,000 annually, with premiums going higher and higher as the birthdays pile up.

Don't buy LTCI until you have researched the subject thoroughly, which I'm afraid I can't help you do in the limited space here. Talk with your estate planning team. You might also find these sources of information helpful in determining the benefits of LTCI in your particular situation:

◆ *The Shopper's Guide to Long-Term Care Insurance* is a free publication, available from many state insurance departments.

◆ Again, the AARP has several articles on its website regarding Long-Term Care Insurance (www.aarp.org).

Medicaid These Days

Medicaid is not a variation of Medicare. It is an entirely different program. For one thing, it is a *state*-run plan (with federal funding) that provides certain minimum medical benefits to persons who are financially needy. Those recipients primarily include the aged, blind, or disabled who are eligible for supplemental Social Security (benefits tied to need, not to earnings coverage), and certain low-income families with children. Each state has its own rules about who qualifies and for what benefits.

Health-care costs can be so catastrophic, they force some of us into Medicaid. In 2003, the cost for Medicaid was $154 billion and covered 34 million recipients.

> **Tip**
>
> For more information about Medicaid, call your state Medicaid office, which is listed under the state Department of Social Services or Human Services.

Once an individual qualifies for Medicaid, the government pays his or her health-care bills. The qualifications for coverage basically require the person to spend down his assets to $2,000. (That's an example. Dollar amounts may vary from one state to another.) The Medicaid beneficiary can exempt his or her principal residence (if a spouse is living there), certain household, and other minor possessions. These exemptions vary slightly from state to state.

Medicaid has special rules for married couples if only one of them is to receive benefits. The spouse not using that coverage may keep up to one-half of the marital assets, generally not to exceed $95,100 in 2005. He or she is also entitled to have at least $1,562 per month in 2004 to live on, drawn from his or her own income, income-producing assets, or from the Medicaid spouse's income.

If both spouses are to receive Medicaid, then the spend-down provisions apply to all spousal property.

A few states—California, Connecticut, Indiana, and New York—have developed plans that combine the purchase of Long-Term Health Care Insurance with asset protection from Medicaid spend-down provisions. Indiana, for example, specifies that a person who purchased such a policy could keep all his assets should he later be required to go on Medicaid.

Please keep in mind that Congress sometimes changes the amount and type of exempt property here. You'll need to consult with your financial planner about current income and resource limits to see if you qualify.

Uh-Uh, You Can't Give It Away

When an individual applies for Medicaid, he or she is tempted to give away enough property to the children so that they feel they are "inheriting" something. Congress has considered this and imposes a "penalty" for gifts made within 36 months of the individual's accepting Medicaid benefits (60 months if the transfer had been to a trust).

Dwight, for example, transferred $100,000 to his son 37 months ago. There is no penalty. However, if he transferred $100,000 one month earlier so that it was within the last 36 months, then that amount, which may be reduced by a complex state Medicaid formula, would have to be applied to his medical bills before Medicaid would kick in.

CAUTION

Watch Out

Do not transfer assets to avoid the Medicaid spend-down requirements without professional advice. Gifts over a period of time may trigger new 36-month "look back" periods when the person making the gifts applies for Medicaid, which penalize you for the recent transfer.

In addition, a gift tax may have to be paid, and there could be unintended income tax consequences.

The Least You Need to Know

◆ Social Security old-age retirement income begins at age 65 or later, although you can take payments as early as age 62 with a 20 percent reduction in benefits.

◆ Medicare benefits begin at age 65 and partially pay for hospitalization and doctor services.

◆ Medigap insurance policies are available to help with costs not covered by Medicare.

◆ Medicaid is available for those with certain property limits set by that government program.

Chapter 3

Who's in Charge? Arranging for Others to Take Over If You Can't

In This Chapter

- ◆ A durable power of attorney
- ◆ Health care directives
- ◆ Organ donation
- ◆ Funeral prepayment

How do you know you're *really* getting older? That flip kid behind the counter at the fast food place automatically gives you a senior citizen discount!

It happens to all of us (aging, not the discount, although that, too, may be a commonly shared sign that the years are piling up). Estate planning now calls for a few more steps to bring you peace of mind—and the continuing preservation of your assets. There's some paperwork still to be done, some of which may be unfamiliar to you.

Guardianship, and Why You Wouldn't Want It

No adult likes to be dependent on anyone else, much less on their children, if they have them. Unfortunately, as some of us get older, we don't function as well physically or mentally as we once did. That's life, and there isn't a lot we can do about it. But we *can* plan for the possibility that at some time we might not be able to manage for ourselves.

When an individual becomes incompetent and cannot manage his or her affairs, then state law requires a guardian be appointed. Most states call for evidence that that individual, because of a physical or mental disability, can no longer cope alone.

Here is how that process works:

1. Usually a close family member petitions the court to be appointed the guardian.

2. If a guardian is appointed, then he or she (or it, because a financial institution could serve in some instances) must inventory all the incompetent person's assets and file that list with the court.

3. The guardian is responsible for the care of the incompetent and must account to the court for all income and expenses.

4. Upon the incompetent person's death, the guardianship is closed and the remaining assets are released to the deceased's executor.

Quote, Unquote

Old people are dangerous. They have no fear of the future.
—George Bernard Shaw

Quote, Unquote

No one is so old not to think he can live one more year.
—Cicero

A guardianship situation is not only intrusive, it can also be expensive. Attorney fees for all court filings, guardian's bond, and guardian's fees could add up to several thousand dollars over the life of the incompetent person.

In addition, the individual you may want to serve as guardian might not be the one the court appoints. Second marriages in particular have the potential for guardianship battles between the second spouse and the children of the first marriage. This is the stuff that front-page news is made of, particularly if there's a prominent person involved.

Not all guardianships can be avoided, but you should nonetheless determine whether having one will be in your best interest.

Here are two alternatives that are better:

◆ A revocable living trust (you've read about trusts often in this book, particularly in Chapter 9)

◆ A durable power of attorney, which I'll talk about next

In any event, plan ahead for this possibility. Don't let a guardianship occur by default.

Durable Power of Attorney

A power of attorney authorizes an agent to act on behalf of the grantor of the power (you). My wife has my durable power of attorney, and she can execute legal and financial documents for me. That could be especially important if I am not available or not competent to act.

A durable power of attorney continues to be valid even if the grantor becomes incapacitated. It terminates when revoked by the grantor, or when the grantor dies.

Within the last few years, states have enacted laws creating durable powers of attorney, and this might mean that a power of attorney executed several years ago may not contain the durable authority (authority continues even if the grantor is not competent) and should be re-executed, because the old power of attorney would not be effective when the grantor became incompetent. You should look for that word *durable* in the document.

If there is no durable power of attorney and the grantor becomes incompetent, then a guardianship may be required.

The durable power of attorney usually lists the various powers granted to the agent. They are quite broad and all-encompassing. Here is a sample durable power of attorney.

> **Tip**
>
> You might occasionally need a *limited* or *special power of attorney*. It's been given that name because it's usually in force for just one transaction, such as executing a real estate deed when the seller is not available for the closing. Your attorney can tell you more about these one-time documents.

> **Quote, Unquote**
>
> Love all, trust a few.
> —Shakespeare, *All's Well That Ends Well*

A word to the wise: don't use this form for yourself without first learning if it is acceptable in your state.

DURABLE POWER OF ATTORNEY

1. I, (name of principal), hereby appoint (name of chosen agent) to serve as my Attorney-in-Fact to exercise the powers set forth below. If (name of chosen agent) is unable or unwilling to serve, then I appoint (name of second-choice agent) as my Attorney-in-Fact.

2. (Use only for a standby power of attorney, in conjunction with Alternate Clause 4.) THIS POWER OF ATTORNEY SHALL BECOME EFFECTIVE ONLY UPON MY DISABILITY OR INCAPACITY. I HAVE NOT AUTHORIZED MY ATTORNEY-IN-FACT TO UNDERTAKE ANY ACTS UNLESS THE EVENTS DESCRIBED IN CLAUSE 4 HAVE TAKEN PLACE.

3. I authorize my said Attorney-in-Fact to take all actions and perform all acts in my name concerning my affairs as my Attorney-in-Fact may deem advisable or necessary in his (her) absolute discretion. I give to my Attorney-in-Fact full power to act in the management and disposition of my person and property the authority that I might exercise were I present, including, but not by way of limitation, any or all of the following:

a. To manage my affairs, handle my investments, arrange for the investment and disposition of funds, exercise all rights with respect to my investments, establish, use, and terminate brokerage accounts, collect amounts owed or payable to me, endorse checks or other instruments drawn to my order and cash them or deposit them to any account in my name, make withdrawals from any account in my name, open bank accounts in my name, enter my safe deposit box and add to or remove from there any or all contents;

b. To exercise all rights to securities and bonds, including the right to buy, sell, transfer, encumber, pledge, and vote and to establish, use, and terminate brokerage accounts;

c. To buy, sell, transfer, lease, subdivide, alter boundaries, mortgage, encumber, pledge, manage, improve, and maintain real property, including the power to erect, repair, or demolish buildings;

d. To buy, sell, transfer, lease, mortgage, encumber, pledge, manage, improve, maintain, repair, or alter personal property;

e. To pay claims and debts, borrow money, and create security interests for the repayment;

f. To disclaim any interest in property, renounce fiduciary positions, claim an elective share of the estate of my deceased spouse, make gifts, create trusts, and make additional gifts to trusts;

g. To exercise all rights of mine under insurance and annuity policies, including the right to change beneficiaries, to borrow, to assign, to change owners, and to surrender the policies;

h. To expend and to distribute income or principal for the benefit of my spouse and dependents;

i. To file tax returns, including a joint tax return with my spouse;

j. To engage and dismiss agents;

k. To pay my bills and to pay for all things necessary for my physical care, protection, and well-being and for that of my property;

l. To authorize my admission to medical, psychiatric, nursing, residential, or similar facilities and supervise and agree to my care, and to authorize or withhold consent to medical and surgical treatment and procedures;

m. To consent to, or to withhold consent for, my medical and surgical treatments and procedures, and to authorize, revoke, modify, or change consent to medical and surgical treatments and procedures as my Attorney-in-Fact shall deem appropriate, including the discontinuance of life support systems. In the exercise of this power, my Attorney-in-Fact shall take into consideration that if at any time my attending physician should determine that I have a terminal condition or if I should become permanently unconscious, it is my desire that life-sustaining treatments, to include but not be limited to antibiotics, cardiopulmonary resuscitation, artificial ventilation, artificial hydration or nourishment, should be withheld or withdrawn when the application of such procedures would serve only to prolong the process of dying and that I be permitted to die naturally with only the administration of medication or

continues

(continued)

the performance of any medical procedure deemed necessary for my comfort or to alleviate pain;

n. To designate another person or persons, including a financial institution, to serve as my Attorney-in-Fact in the place of (name of agent).

4. This Power of Attorney shall not be affected by my disability or incapacity.

Alternate Clause 4 (for a standby power of attorney). This Power of Attorney shall become effective only upon my disability or incapacity. My incapacity shall be deemed to exist if I have been declared incompetent by a court of competent jurisdiction or upon a notarized affidavit signed by two licensed physicians stating their opinion that I am mentally or physically incapable of caring for myself and managing my financial affairs. This Power shall become effective on the date of such a judicial finding of incompetency or on the date of the said notarized affidavit signed by the two licensed physicians.

If this Power of Attorney becomes effective, it shall be suspended if I shall regain capacity. I shall be deemed to have regained capacity if there is a finding to that effect by a court of competent jurisdiction, or upon presentation to my Attorney-in-Fact of a notarized affidavit signed by two licensed physicians that I am capable of caring for myself and managing my financial affairs. This Power shall become effective again if I should subsequently become incapacitated again as provided above.

5. I HAVE READ THE PROVISIONS OF THIS POWER WHICH AUTHORIZE MY ATTORNEY-IN-FACT TO REFUSE OR WITHDRAW MEDICAL AND SURGICAL TREATMENT AND PROCEDURES. I UNDERSTAND SUCH PROVISIONS AND THEY EXPRESS MY DESIRES.

6. If I should be declared incompetent by a court of appropriate jurisdiction and should the court decide to appoint a guardian to care for my person or property, it is my preference that (name of Attorney-In-Fact) be named as my guardian.

IN WITNESS WHEREOF, I have signed this Power of Attorney on this _____ day of _____, 20___.

_____   _____
                                            (name of principal)
_____
Witnesses

STATE OF _____

COUNTY OF _____

This personally appeared before me, (name of principal), who signed and acknowledged the foregoing Power of Attorney to be his (her) free act and deed, on this
_____ day of _____, 20___.

                                            _____
                                            Notary Public

My commission expires on: _____

As you can see, you certainly need to have complete confidence in a particular
relative or friend before giving him or her authority under a durable power of
attorney. Because the powers are extensive and there is really no court supervision,
the possibility of abuse always exists.

The law requires that an agent act faithfully on behalf of the grantor. If there is a
violation of that standard, which is known as the *fiduciary duty*, then the court, upon
petition, may remove the agent and, if funds are misused, require an accounting.

Laws vary about the need for recording a power of attorney in a county recorder's
office. If you do so, then you must also record a revocation. Whether or not you
record your power of attorney, if you wish to revoke it, then you just notify the agent
in writing and request that he or she return the original document.

Words, Words, Words

A **proxy** is the agency, function, or office of a deputy who acts as a substitute for another. A proxy might also be a document giving such authority, such as a power of attorney authorizing a specific person to vote corporate stock. Or, in the context of this chapter, the power of attorney to make business and/or health-care decisions for a specified person.

(If you are an agent under someone's power of attorney, then you might be required to show your document for any transaction you sign for the grantor. Always keep the original. Give those who request the document a copy. Sign any document on behalf of the grantor by clearly indicating that you are acting as *attorney-in-fact* for the grantor.)

Some states permit the agent of a durable power of attorney to make medical decisions for the grantor (you'll see some mention of that in the sample document here). However, it is probably better to execute a separate health care power of attorney (also known as a healthy care *proxy* or health care representative form) for health-related issues.

A Living Will and a Health-Care Power of Attorney

State laws recognize the right of competent adults to consent to, or refuse to consent to, medical treatment. Likewise, the law permits a competent adult to delegate his or her medical decisions to another person.

The *living will* is a legal form directing that the declarant's life not be artificially prolonged if he or she is in a terminal condition or persistent vegetative state.

The *health-care power of attorney* (or proxy) provides that an agent named by the grantor is authorized to make medical decisions when the grantor is not capable of doing so.

If you have no close relatives, then it's especially important for you to designate someone to make medical decisions for you. Doctors might have limited options, and indeed may have to go to court if a proposed medical procedure is risky.

Tip

A lawyer can probably draw up a durable power of attorney, living will, and health-care power of attorney for you at a "package rate" for all of those documents.

You can decide to have a living will, or such a will plus a health-care power of attorney. If you want artificial life support measures terminated if you find yourself in that situation at some point in your life, then make sure that your health care power of attorney acknowledges your wish. (First, of course, you must inform your agent fully about all your options, and your wishes, in this area.)

Discuss all of these issues with your family, of course. They need to know how you feel about the subject. And you just might find that opening such a conversation leads to an interesting and informative talk about one another's wishes.

There's just one note here: As valuable as a living will can be, it is sometimes ignored by hospitals, nursing homes, rehabilitation facilities, etc. This is because some personnel are reluctant to take such drastic wishes into account. It's far better to have a health-care power of attorney to go along with the living will (or instead of it)—it's harder to ignore.

In any event, the following pages show samples of a living will and a health-care power of attorney.

Again, there might be slight regional differences in these forms, so be certain you use one applicable to where you are. You can see a lawyer, or ask around at community and regional hospitals, many of which keep these forms on file for use by patients and others.

 Watch Out _____

If you have executed a living will or health-care power of attorney in a state where you have previously lived, the form may not be valid in your new state. Check local law on this subject.

LIVING WILL DECLARATION

Declaration made this _____ day of _____, 20__. I, _____, being at least eighteen (18) years of age and of sound mind, willfully and voluntarily make known my desires that my dying shall not be artificially prolonged under the circumstances set forth below, and I declare:

If at any time my attending physician certifies in writing that: (1) I have an incurable injury, disease, or illness; (2) my death will occur within a short time; and (3) the use of life prolonging procedures would serve only to artificially prolong the dying process, I direct that such procedures be withheld or withdrawn, and that I be permitted to die naturally with only the performance or provision of any medical procedure or medication necessary to provide me with comfort care or to alleviate pain, and, if I have so indicated below, the provision of artificially supplied nutrition and hydration. (Indicate your choice by initialing or making your mark before signing this declaration):

continues

(continued)

I wish to receive artificially supplied nutrition and hydration, even if the effort to sustain life is futile or excessively burdensome to me.

I do not wish to receive artificially supplied nutrition and hydration, if the effort to sustain life is futile or excessively burdensome to me.

I intentionally make no decision concerning artificially supplied nutrition and hydration, leaving the decision to my health-care representative appointed under [state statute cite] or my attorney in fact with health-care powers under [state statute cite].

In the absence of my ability to give directions regarding the use of life prolonging procedures, it is my intention that this declaration be honored by my family and physician as the final expression of my legal right to refuse medical or surgical treatment and accept the consequences of the refusal.

I understand the full import of this declaration.

_____ signed _____

City, County, State of residence printed _____

The declarant has been personally known to me, and I believe him/her to be of sound mind. I did not sign the declarant's signature above for or at the direction of the declarant. I am not a parent, spouse, or child of the declarant. I am not entitled to any part of the declarant's estate or directly financially responsible for the declarant's medical care. I am competent and at least eighteen (18) years of age.

Witness _____ Date: _____

Witness _____ Date: _____

APPOINTMENT OF HEALTH-CARE REPRESENTATIVE

I, _____, name _____,
as my representative to act for me in matters affecting my health, in particular to:

(1) Consent to or refuse health care for me.

(2) Employ or contract with servants, companions, or health-care providers for me.

(3) Admit or release me from a hospital or health-care facility.

(4) Have access to records, including medical records, concerning my condition.

(5) Make anatomical gifts on my behalf.

(6) Request an autopsy.

(7) Make plans for the disposition of my body.

I authorize my representative to make decisions in my best interest concerning the withdrawal or withholding of health care. If at any time, based on my previously expressed preferences and diagnosis and prognosis, my representative is satisfied that certain health care is not or would not be beneficial, or that such health care is or would be excessively burdensome, then the representative may express my will that such health care be withheld or withdrawn and may consent on my behalf that any or all health care be discontinued or not instituted even if death is the result.

My representative must try to discuss this decision with me. However, if I am unable to communicate, my representative may make such a decision for me, after consultation with my physician or physicians and other relevant health care providers. To the extent appropriate, my representative may also discuss this decision with my family and others, to the extent they are available.

Date: _____   signed _____

                                 printed _____

_____ has been personally known to me, and I believe him/her to be of legal age and capable of making decisions regarding his/her health care.

I am competent and at least 18 years of age.

Date: _____   Witness _____

Date: _____   Witness _____

By the way—a not unimportant point—your witnesses to these documents should never be members of your family, or anyone who has a financial obligation for your support or who would inherit from you. That makes sense, of course. Execute a single copy, and then make photocopies as necessary.

Where should you keep your original? Ask your attorney. Often providing your physician with a copy for your medical records file will ensure that your wishes will be followed.

I have a health-care power of attorney, as does my wife, naming each other as the agent, and then naming our oldest child as the alternate agent. If I am in a coma, or otherwise incompetent, I want to know that people I trust will make the right decision. Usually the medical authorities will ask next-of-kin for consent anyway, but this makes my wishes quite clear.

My wife and I also have living wills because we personally believe that there is no quality of life when it is sustained by artificial means. This is an important and very personal decision for each of us. Of course, your decision might be quite different.

You can change your mind after you have executed either document; simply destroy the original document and retrieve any photocopies.

> **Watch Out**
>
> Don't forget: If you are a seriously committed unmarried couple, it's especially important to execute the documents I've mentioned in this chapter. Without them your partner has no right to make legal and health-related decisions for you if you want him or her to be your spokesperson.

> **Tip**
>
> A durable power of attorney, living will, and health-care representative form (or health-care power of attorney), taken together are *advance directives*. You'll see that expression often in reading about elder health issues.

Becoming an Organ Donor

Anatomical gifts is not an easy subject to write about. Frankly, I have long resisted the idea of giving up any of my body parts. But I don't any longer. If I can give another person life, or a better quality of life, then that extends the purpose of my own life.

An *anatomical gift* is a donation of a body part, which may include organs, tissue, eyes, bones, arteries, blood, and other portions of the human body.

State laws permit the donor to make an anatomical gift in a number of ways, including mention in a will. However, because time is usually vital, most gifts are made through a donor card or other document the donor always carries with him or her. Many states provide for an anatomical gift on the driver's license.

The donation document requires at least one witness.

In addition, the law may allow the next of kin to make an anatomical donation from the deceased's body even if that individual does not carry an organ donor card. You might not want to count on that, though. In times of grief your relatives may not be comfortable with such a decision, or might not want to go ahead with the donation, feeling as strongly in their anti-organ donation views as you do in your pro-donation stance.

Make things easier for everyone: tell your family about your decision, and carry an organ donor card with you at all times, probably in your wallet.

A sample organ donation form follows. You can fill it out and use it, but you might find it easier to call your local hospitals, many of which supply small organ donor cards that easily fit into a wallet.

ORGAN DONOR DECLARATION

This is to inform you that I want to be an organ and tissue donor if the occasion ever arises. Please see that my wishes are carried out by informing the attending medical personnel that I am a donor. My desires are indicated below:

In the hopes that I may help others, I hereby make this gift for the purpose of transplant, medical study, or education, to take effect upon my death. I donate:

(　　) Any needed organs/tissues

(　　) Only the following organs/tissues

_____

Specify the organ(s)/tissue(s):

_____

_____

Limitations or special wishes, if any:

_____

_____

continues

(*continued*)

This is a legal document under the Uniform Anatomical Gift Act or similar laws, signed by the donor and the following two witnesses in the presence of each other.

_____

Donor's signature

_____   _____

Donor's date of birth   City and State

_____   _____

Witness   Witness

_____   _____

Next of Kin   Telephone

Last Words, Last Rites, and Other Finalities

Throughout this book I've discussed estate planning techniques and documents, but have said very little about organizing them (although I did suggest you keep them in a safe place, and the ones that will be needed right away—like a will—*not* in a bank safe deposit box). Now is the time to talk about organization.

Your will, revocable living trust, and life insurance policies should be stored in a safe, central location. Tell your executor where they are. You should have photocopies made and placed elsewhere.

Important legal papers should be kept together in a safe location. That would be deeds to real estate or certificates of title to cars, a marriage license, military discharge papers, and other documents important for your executor or next-of-kin.

You might want to make a master list of all vital documents and indicate where they are located and who has copies of them. Give your spouse, child(ren), and/or executor a copy of that list. Too often assets you know about are overlooked, so keep a current Estate Planning Information Sheet (see Chapter 2) with important documents.

Burial Wishes

If you have any strong feelings in this area, talk them over with your family. In fact, you might want to make a few plans now. For example, do you have a cemetery plot? Or mausoleum space, if that's what you prefer? If you do not, and have a spouse, and perhaps even children, this might be the time to bite the bullet and look into purchasing a final resting place for you and some or all of your family.

> **Quote, Unquote**
>
> The future is like heaven—everyone exalts in it but no one wants to go there now.
>
> —James Baldwin, "A Fly in the Buttermilk," *Nobody Knows My Name* (1961)

If cremation interests you more, express that wish clearly to your loved ones. You may want to put it in writing and, because this is not as widely understood a concept as in-ground burial, attach some information about a local service you have called, or any other material your family is likely to find helpful when the time comes. You can put your wishes in your will but, as I've often said, perhaps no one will consult that document until it is too late.

Plan but Don't Prepay Your Funeral

What a concept: Pay now, die later! According to a survey by the AARP, some 32 percent of Americans have prepaid their own funerals and burials. They've paid some $25 billion, making this advanced payment plan, so to speak, the funeral industry's fastest-growing business.

Clever for funeral homes and cemeteries, but not so good for you, caution financial planners and those involved in eldercare issues. Why not? Well, for one thing, why spend $5,000 to $7,500, or more of your money when you could invest it and have it bring you a nice return? Why instead let the cemetery or funeral home invest it, making *them* richer?

There's a lot more involved here, including sometimes high-pressure sales tactics by some funeral home and cemetery personnel to buy the best (and naturally most expensive) of everything. Such pre-need sales are *not* regulated by federal law, so let the buyer beware.

> ## Quote, Unquote
>
> Life does not cease to be funny when people die any more than it ceases to be serious when people laugh.
>
> —George Bernard Shaw, *The Doctor's Dilemma* (1913)

And one more thing: you might move, and if you aren't allowed to transfer your prepayment you could end up being buried far from your family.

A far better method here is to write down your funeral wishes and make sure your next-of-kin know them. You might want to investigate casket and coffin styles and prices, and maybe even write your funeral service, selecting the music as well. All of that will direct your nearest and dearest toward the funeral you want without your having to spend money beforehand.

For more information on this topic, visit the AARP website (www.aarp.org), the Funeral Consumers Alliance website (www.funerals.org), and the Federal Trade Commission website (www.ftc.gov).

Your death will be traumatic enough for your family without their having to search not only for funeral wishes, but also other estate planning documents. Make sure everything is easy for them to find, and clearly understandable once they have done so.

The Least You Need to Know

- A durable power of attorney is one way to avoid a guardianship and have the person you yourself designate make decisions for you when you can no longer do so.

- A living will may be used to terminate artificial life support.

- A health-care power of attorney designates someone to make medical decisions for you when you cannot, and can sometimes be enforced more easily than a living will.

- It's important to organize all your estate planning documents, including your funeral wishes, and tell someone where they can be found.

Chapter 24

Life's Big and Little Surprises

In This Chapter

◆ Helping your folks manage

◆ Getting married?

◆ Getting divorced?

◆ Updating your assets list

The title of this chapter says it all. It seems there's no such thing as sitting back and taking it easy. Just when we do—bingo—Dad becomes ill and it looks as if he's not going to be able to live on his own anymore. Or bingo—but good news this time—it looks as if we're getting married, or getting married again. Or divorced. There are any number of things going on in our lives to cause a flurry of happiness or concern.

All of those major happenings can affect your estate plan, of course. Still, you *can* keep on track, no matter what's going on in your life now, and no matter what changes lie ahead.

Looking Out for Aging Parents

Of course *you're* aging, too—and so am I—but you know what I mean here. If you are 27 and your parents are in their 50s, this next section probably won't concern you, unless one of your folks has serious health concerns. But if your parents are in their 60s, 70s, or beyond, then by all means continue reading. You might have some grave problems and worries, not only about their health, but also about their, and perhaps your, finances.

We often have difficulty admitting our parents are getting older—no, getting *old*—and a role reversal may be at hand. Many of us are living longer and enjoying life's bounty in our senior years, but there may come a time when aging brings a certain dependency. We must prepare for that contingency.

Here are some suggestions for handling specific issues with elderly, perhaps ailing, parents or other relatives you are close to and for whom you feel some responsibility. I'll use as an example in the next few pages, Mom, although you can, of course, substitute your father or Aunt Mary if you wish.

Briefs
No matter what our age, we must beware of stereotyping the 65-plus crowd and consigning them to a rocker. In the spring of 1997 a team of Los Angeles doctors announced that five months earlier a 63-year-old woman in their care had delivered a healthy baby girl, the oldest woman in the world to give birth. While the event brought a news and feature article flurry, one fact was buried in most of the stories: The woman was staying at home to take care of the baby—and was being helped by her mother, who was in her 80s!

Before I go any further, let me state the obvious: If your mother is competent, then of course she should be allowed to make her own decisions, even if they do not agree with yours. The suggestions that follow apply if she needs some help with those decisions, with learning what options she has, or if she cannot make decisions at all.

Managing Property

You may want to consider a revocable living trust for your mother if she has significant assets but cannot manage them. You've read about trusts in previous chapters, particularly Chapter 9. In addition to managing her property, the trustee can pay her bills, a task that a child, who is often hundreds of miles away, cannot easily perform.

As I explained in Chapter 23, avoiding guardianship should be one of your goals because of its expense and complications. Another option in that area besides the trust: a durable power of attorney (see Chapter 23), which continues even if your mother is no longer competent to manage her affairs.

Living Arrangements

There are several choices your parent can make (or you can help make with or for her), some of which may not have occurred to you:

♦ **Adapting her present residence.** She might continue in a present living arrangement. If that's a house, it could be made more adaptable and safer for an elderly resident. Maybe you or she can find a housemate to share the rooms and expenses. A local senior citizen agency might be able to help with making a match.

♦ **Senior citizen housing.** If she needs smaller quarters and is on a limited income, look into government-sponsored senior citizen housing, which exists in almost any community of any size. There are income ceilings, of course, and the nicer buildings and complexes have quite a lengthy waiting list. You might enter Mom's name soon—you can always withdraw it if things change.

♦ **Reverse mortgage.** You may want to look into a reverse mortgage, to provide Mom with some monthly income. If she owns her home and is 62 or older, she might be able to draw on the equity in that place in the form of a monthly pay-check, or a line of credit that's ready and waiting if she needs it. The lender adds interest, closing costs and any other charges at the end of the loan, so Mom won't have to pay those fees at the beginning. These loans, including all charges, are payable when the homeowner moves or dies.

Tip

Check out the American Association of Homes and Services for the Aging website, www.aahsa.org.

For more information, visit the website of the U.S. Department of Housing and Urban Development (HUD), www.hud.gov or the AARP website, www.aarp.org.

- **Assisted living.** A housing option that is growing furiously these days is the assisted-living facility (ALF), which will offer Mom some help with day-to-day living—meals, for example—but no serious medical supervision. An elder services agency in your area can direct you toward ALFs near you.

- **Continuing care communities.** CCRC is another set of initials you'll come across if you're looking for a specific type of care. It stands for continuing care retirement communities. These are high-rise buildings or sprawling complexes that buyers usually move through in phases. The first is independent living, where you buy a patio home, condominium, or cottage, or you might rent an apartment.

Stage two is assisted living, where there is some help with meals and other services. Stage three is a nursing home, which provides skilled nursing care.

For more information about CCRCs, contact the Continuing Care Accreditation Commission (CCAC), which is run by the American Association of Homes and Services for the Aging. They look closely at the quality of those residences, including their financial stability.

Medical Care

High medical expenses can devastate an estate (your Mom's—or yours, as you help her). Medicare can help, but it's likely to be reduced in coming years, so supplements like the ones I mentioned in Chapter 22 are important. For example, you might want to look into long-term care insurance. Medicaid, which generally requires a significant reduction of the parent's property, can be a last resort.

Watch Out

Unless you are an only child, your parents should not use your attorney. If a disproportionate distribution of your folks' assets is being considered, your siblings might later claim that you unduly influenced Mom and Dad through your lawyer.

Life Insurance

At this stage of your mother's life you'll want to review her life insurance policy to determine if coverage is necessary. If a parent is terminally ill, many insurance companies will permit a partial pre-death distribution of the proceeds. I've also written about a viatical settlement (in Chapter 4), where companies buy an ailing person's policy for a percentage of its value. Either of those steps might be helpful in paying for Mom's medical expenses.

Estate Planning

Your mom's estate plan—investments, will, etc.—may need revising. Remember, though, it is *her* plan. If she is competent, by all means talk with her about a living will and durable power of attorney. If she is not able to make decisions for herself, talk with her attorney.

How a Community Can Help

Don't forget to contact the local office on aging in your mother's community. There are many senior services that can help her, at little or no cost. For example, Meals on Wheels can deliver a nutritious meal to her home five days a week, either free or at a cost of a couple of dollars per meal. Senior offices can help elders fill out medical forms for insurance purposes at no cost. They often get those folks money back, too!

These agencies can also refer you to civic, educational, and religious groups that do various volunteer chores for the elderly, such as driving them to doctors' appointments and visiting with them in their homes for an hour or two when there is a special need. Adult day care may cost money, but some religious institutions and social service agencies do it for free. Ask!

As you can probably see by now, there is all sorts of assistance out there for a child looking after an aging parent—and incidentally, there is more than one "kid" in his 60s caring for a parent in his or her 90s! On the following page is a worksheet that can help you get a handle on where help can be found for your relative, and whether he, she, you, or a local or federal agency is likely to pick up the tab.

Long-Distance Caregiving

It's one thing if you can pop in on Mom every few days, or even every couple of weeks. But what can you do when you're too far away for frequent visits? If you can, arrange for someone in your mother's community to be a *secondary* caregiver, someone who will check on her periodically, in person and by phone, look over the mail, see that Mom has food in the refrigerator, and so forth. Yes, you will probably have to pay for the

> **Tip**
>
> You might want to contact an attorney specializing in elder law, such as Social Security, health care issues, elder abuse, and the like. This is a relatively new specialty that, while growing quickly, is still not available everywhere. To see if there is an eldercare lawyer near you, visit the AARP list on its website (www.aarp.org).

service, but your peace of mind will be worth the money that goes with having him or her keep in touch with Mom, and then you.

Home Care Assistance Worksheet

This worksheet is designed to help identify needs and ways to pay for them for both the caregiver and the care receiver. A senior often is able to remain independent in his or her own home with a little help from friends, neighbors, family, and outside resources. And a caregiver, whether living close by or far away, can often arrange services for loved ones and themselves.

Service	Program	Cost	Payment Source
Examples:			
Caregiver respite	Adult Day Care	$ a day	Aunt Jane once a month
Meals			
Daily	Neighbor Jones (Dinner nightly)	$ a week	Mom's income
Weekly	Meals on Wheels (Lunch Mon-Fri)	Free	Local agency
Special occasion	Sunday dinner	$	Me
Caregiver respite			
Daily			
Weekly			
Vacations			
Care receiver			
Socialization			
Home health care			
Transportation			
Doctor visits			
Shopping			
Pharmacy			
Yardwork/Maintenance			
Housework, light			
Housework, heavy			

Service	Program	Cost	Payment Source
Meals Daily Weekly Special occasion			
Bill paying			
Telephone reassurance			
Home safety			
Home security			
Other			

Source: Florida Care Giver, PO Box 380108, Jacksonville, FL 32205

When There's Marriage or Divorce

I'm talking about you now, not your parent (although, of course, he or she could remarry or divorce, too).

Obviously, a marriage or divorce will require some changes in what you thought was a firm, unalterable estate plan.

Tying the Knot

With the nuptial tie come the new spouse's rights in your estate. A husband or wife can elect against a deceased spouse's will, and may take from one third to one half of the probate estate (and other property, such as a trust). Some states may limit the amount the electing spouse can receive, depending on whether the couple had children together.

Prenuptial agreements can limit a spouse's right to elect against the estate, as well as what he or she may receive if there is a divorce.

Quote, Unquote

Grow old along with me! The best is yet to be, The last of life, for which the first was made: Our times are in His hand Who saith "A whole I planned, Youth shows but half; Trust God; see all nor be afraid!"

—Robert Browning (1864)

A prenup should be considered when people remarry after the deaths of their spouses and want to keep in each of their separate families after death what they bring to the new marriage.

Community property states give the new spouses certain vested property rights in assets obtained after marriage. In addition, many couples create joint ownership with right of survivorship. Proper estate planning must consider these spousal co-ownership rights.

If there's marriage on your horizon, you'd be wise to review the sections of this book that deal with issues relating to a new marriage—from styles of property ownership, to a will or trust, to the prenuptial agreement (which can also be drawn up *after* the wedding)—in Chapter 3.

Splitting Up

Frankly, the best estate planning suggestion I can give you if you're going to divorce is to hire a good divorce lawyer. Not a nasty one, just a good one who will ensure that you will be treated fairly. Although both of you may go into the divorce with all intentions of splitting marital assets equally, the reality might be quite different.

> **Watch Out**
>
> If you are about to enter into marriage or divorce at this time, take a good look at all your estate-planning documents, not just your will (divorce usually invalidates any provision in the will for an ex-spouse), such as an insurance policy, pension plan, and the like. Sometimes we never seem to get around to that paperwork.

First, there's the property division, with significant tax consequences. Then alimony, which is income to one and a deduction to the other parent. Child support may mean a tax exemption to the parent who's paying it.

Pension plans could be divided, and that would affect the income expectations of both ex-spouses when they retire.

Marital debts might not be divided equally, providing an estate burden for one ex-spouse. If there is an equitable division, the debts are still considered by the creditors as joint. If one person doesn't pay, even in violation of a divorce order, the creditors will go after the other.

If You Become Disabled

Few of us are prepared to be seriously put out of commission. Disabilities due to illness or accident can range from temporary to permanent, from partial to full.

A disability may have a substantial financial impact on you and your family by reducing income and assets by requiring additional expenses for the disabled person. If the disability is severe, he or she may not be capable of managing affairs or assets.

If a disability does occur, you or your family should …

◆ Assemble all estate planning documents and consult an attorney about their effect, and any changes that are necessary.

◆ Contact your employer or disability insurance carrier to file a claim.

◆ File for any benefits with Social Security or the Veterans Administration.

◆ Review any business agreements, such as a partnership agreement, that may have disability provisions.

◆ Consult an attorney about employment rights under the Americans With Disabilities Act.

> **Watch Out**
>
> Think ahead—think insurance. If you're on someone else's payroll, your employer may have a disability insurance policy for you, but if you're self-employed, you don't have such coverage and you may want to consider purchasing it. You're likely to find Social Security disability payments insufficient to maintain your family the way you would like.

> **Quote, Unquote**
>
> Life is simply one damned thing after another.
> —Ascribed to Elbert Hubbard (1856–1915)

Tick-Tock: Checking Your Estate Plan

When I was in the Army, I had a retired military officer come in for a new will. I asked when he executed the last one. Just before he was shipped overseas, he responded—in 1944. Since then he had married and had several children; he had retired from the service and then from another job.

That's 30 years (it was 1974)—more than a bit too long between wills!

Tip

You might make it a practice to revise your assets list when you do your income taxes. (You can use the Estate Planning Information Sheet in Chapter 2.) Much of the information that you need is readily at hand then.

Tip

If you are going to make substantial changes to your will, such as revising beneficiaries, it's better to execute a new will rather than add a codicil to the present one. That may reduce the possibility of a beneficiary whose devise is reduced or eliminated from one day contesting the will.

We need to remind ourselves that our will and estate plan are not cast in stone. They need to be regularly reviewed, and revised when necessary.

Most experts suggest that we should review an estate plan at least every three years and more than that when there are significant changes in finances or family.

You ought to pull out your estate documents when any of the following occurs:

- You move to another state

- Your assets or liabilities change substantially

- Laws change

- Your family changes (remarriage, divorce, children become self-supporting adults, grandchildren are born, etc.)

- You desire to change beneficiaries in your will, life insurance policy, trust, and/or retirement plan

The Least You Need to Know

- If an elderly parent requires your assistance, there are lots of private and public sources of assistance.

- Marriage immediately gives a spouse certain rights to your estate.

- Disability insurance paid for by your employer, or by you, should be part of your estate plan.

- Review your will and overall estate plan at least every three years.

Chapter 25

Stage by Stage: Estate Planning Throughout Your Life

In This Chapter

- Looking ahead if single
- Single parent strategies
- Planning with minor children
- Retired, and still planning

Now, with 24 chapters of information and advice under your belt, you should have a good idea of what you've got in the way of assets, how they are likely to grow, and how you want your estate plan to proceed.

To sum up and review things in this final chapter what I'm going to do is ... well, I hate to say put you in a category—we're all different, after all—but put you in a Census Bureau–like category of people: married/ single, with children/without, that type of thing. Such simple categorization should help you find yourself quickly and see what you need to do to ensure an estate that's in fine order now, and likely to remain so in the future, thanks to your continued diligence.

Broadly Speaking

There are some points I've made in past chapters that apply to all of us, and some that do not. For example, we all need a will, but not everyone needs a trust. A durable power of attorney is more appropriate for some than others. Life insurance is an excellent idea for those with a young family, but a close-to-retirement policyholder might want to rethink some coverage.

Quote, Unquote

The great business of life is to be, to do, to do without, and to depart.

—John Morley, *Address on Aphorisms*, Edinburgh (1887)

Take a look at the worksheet on the following page to see what still needs to be done to complete *your* estate plan which will, of course, differ from those of Harry down the street and your co-worker Linda.

Now let's get on with some tips for what you might be doing planning-wise at various stages of your life, based on how things are with you right now.

Single, with No Kids

Many assume that the life of a single person is free of responsibilities. If you are single, you know that that is frequently not the case. You may have an elderly parent to care for or other family responsibilities. You might put in long hours at work. Perhaps you are the driving force behind a successful, but demanding, local volunteer effort.

Quote, Unquote

As wise women and men in every culture tell us: The art of living is not controlling what happens to us, but *using* what happens to us.

—Gloria Steinem, *Revolution from Within* (1992)

Your estate planning needs are clearly different in many respects from those folks who have children.

At a minimum you should have a will. The state intestate law provides that your heirs will be your siblings and your parents, if any of them survive you. If you have no immediate family, your nieces, nephews, and cousins may inherit. Probably not all of them are deserving of your estate, so a will allows you to specify whom you want the inheritors to be.

If you are entering retirement years, I would also suggest a revocable living trust and a durable power of attorney. You may need someone to manage your affairs when you no longer can and have no children to rely on. Also, put as much money into your retirement plans as possible because living on just Social Security may mean some significant changes in your lifestyle at retirement.

Estate Document Checklist

You've read, you've pondered. But have you taken any action yet on the suggestions in this book? Here is a checklist of what you might need to do to complete your own estate plan. Not every item will apply to you, of course. Or at least not just now. (The most important paper is, of course, a will.)

In the third column, under "Comments," you can jot down what you need to complete a particular course of action. For example, under "Will" your comment may be "reviewed on (date) and revised." Under "Trust," it might be "N/A" for "not applicable."

	Accomplished		
Estate Plan Ingredient	Yes	No	Comments
1) Estate Planning Information Sheet			
2) Will			
3) Trust			
4) Life insurance policy(ies)			
5) Company pension plan			
6) IRA, 401(k)			
7) Prenuptial agreement			
8) Guardianship for minor children			
9) Trust for children			
10) Durable power of attorney			
11) Living will			
12) Health care representative			
13) Organ donor card			

A Few Words for the Single Parent

Single parents have to do double duty during the child-rearing years; not an easy task in the best of times. Often they must be father and mother and … no, make that *triple* duty. There's also work, and perhaps more than one job at that.

Hectic days and nights might not give you time to think much about estate planning, after all, you've got more pressing demands, right? Wrong. You may be the only source of support for those growing children, and your untimely death would leave a significant emotional and financial void. You can ensure that at least the financial void will be minimized with good planning. Here are my suggestions:

♦ Get as much term life insurance coverage as possible; this is an inexpensive means of leaving a substantial estate for the children.

Tip

After a divorce make sure that your life insurance policies and retirement plans are changed; more than one person has benefited from his or her ex's procrastination.

♦ Put as much as you can into your 401(k) plan at work, so you won't have to depend only on Social Security when you retire.

♦ Make a will, and provide for a trust and a guardianship for minor children. If you are divorced, your ex-spouse may be entitled to custody of the children if you die; if you do not think that that is appropriate, contact an attorney to determine what you can do to avoid it.

♦ Execute a durable power of attorney and make your agent someone you trust implicitly; you want to make it effective only if and when you become incapacitated.

♦ Finally, if you are divorced and your ex-spouse is behind in child support, see an attorney about enforcing your children's rights in that regard.

If you are a single mother and your child's father is not in the picture (you are widowed, the child has been adopted by you as a single person, etc.), then of course there is no possibility of child support. You must pay particular attention to your estate plan, especially guardianship for your child.

If you are a single parent with a significant other, then you should have a will, and consider whether it is appropriate to provide for the other person in the will, as well as name the other person guardian for your children, particularly if both of you have assumed parenting responsibilities.

Married with No Children

Wills for each spouse are important here. If children are likely in the future, there should be a clause in each spouse's will making any afterborn or adopted children the secondary beneficiaries of that will. The will should also have a third beneficiary to receive the probate estate if both spouses die simultaneously and there are no children. Although the law doesn't require the same provisions in both husband and wife wills, each spouse should at least discuss with the other any differences, particularly as to differences regarding children's inheritances.

Tip

With no children, your life insurance needs will be modest if your spouse is working and can support himself. However, if children are planned, then purchase a policy that allows higher coverage when the kids begin arriving.

Mature spouses need to establish a revocable trust to manage their affairs when they don't want to or cannot do so. They also need the "powers" that can help: durable power of attorney, health care power of attorney, and a living will.

Deciding who benefits after both spouses' deaths may be difficult. If this applies to you, then no doubt you are close to some relatives and particular friends. You might want them to inherit. Or you might prefer that part of your estate go to charity. A charitable remainder trust (where you receive income during your lives, and then the charity is entitled to the balance after death) could be a viable choice for part of your estate (see Chapter 18).

Married with Children

Children are with us at all ages, which makes your estate planning needs vary from one age, or stage, to another. The family with youngsters has different concerns than the family with adult children. Here is a checklist for both.

First, here's what both husband and wife with kids of any age will need:

♦ Wills

♦ Durable powers of attorney

◆ Substantial life insurance coverage

◆ Individual retirement plans

> **Quote, Unquote**
>
> Children are a great comfort in your old age, and they help you reach it faster, too.
>
> —Lionel Kauffman

Both young and mature couples should discuss executing:

◆ Living wills

◆ Health care powers of attorney

Obviously families are not all alike, but these documents are essential to any estate planning.

When There Are Minors

Let's look in more detail at the family with minor children—those under 18. If that's you, then I suggest a testamentary or revocable living trust for those children.

If you have minor children who are going to inherit at least $100,000, you especially should have a trust that manages their property beyond age 18 to a more mature age when they are less likely to waste that inheritance.

In addition, young parents must consider the selection of a guardian to rear those children, and to manage their funds if there is no trust.

When the Children Are Adults

How about mature parents of adult children?

You may want to help your kids save for your grandchildren's college fund by establishing a custodial account and making periodic gifts to it in amounts that would be exempt from the gift tax ($11,000 per donee each year, $22,000 if both parents join in the gift; see Chapter 17).

Most parents, in their desire to be fair to their children, simply divide their estate equally. That is your call. But "fair" and "equal" are not necessarily the same. For example, the child with a serious disability that will limit his or her earning potential is likely to require more from you. If you do distribute your assets unequally, be sure to explain your reasoning in your will, or in a personal note to those involved.

If you're contemplating an unequal distribution of your estate, consider, as an alternative, buying a term life insurance on your life to provide for the more needy child.

If you've remarried you may have children from a prior marriage. Often prenuptial agreements will specify that each spouse's will distributes his or her probate estate to his or her children from a prior marriage. You don't want one family to resent the other for taking what they consider to be their share of their parent's estate.

Watch Out _____

Even a prenuptial agreement will not be effective if you and your spouse have all your assets in joint ownership. The surviving spouse will take the property no matter what the prenup says.

Retired but Not Retiring

Retired folks are living longer and seem to be enjoying their retirement years more these days. Part of this is because of the considerable planning they did when they were younger—planning that's paid off in a comfortable lifestyle now.

If you are approaching retirement, you ought to sit down with your financial advisor to determine just how much money you are going to have for those years. *Exactly* how much. Obviously the big unknown could be the cost of health care. Because Medicare isn't sufficient, you might want to consider a Medigap policy, and/or long-term care insurance.

Besides a will, you should certainly have a durable power of attorney, a revocable living trust, a living will, and a health care power of attorney. You truly do need these papers.

In addition, I would suggest the following:

◆ Sign a certificate of competency. Consider the fact that we all, naturally, like to think we can recognize our own weaknesses. In that respect, if you think there could be any question as to your mental capacity to execute a will or other legal document, avoid a later contest by obtaining a physician's certificate showing that you are indeed competent.

◆ Examine your life insurance policy to determine if you can draw upon the death benefits during your life—to pay medical expenses, for example.

◆ If you have more than one residence, resolve any conflicts about which is your legal residence (domicile).

◆ Examine your estate's liquidity to pay death taxes.

◆ Review the contents of your safe deposit box and remove anything that you may want to give away. You might make those gifts now instead of promising the recipients the items will be left in your will.

◆ Examine your entire set-up if you own or co-own a business; you may need to let go of control, but not at a significant sacrifice to your financial well-being.

Watch Out

Remember when selling your home and looking toward that tax exclusion for the first $250,000 ($500,000 if married) of profit, you are only allowed that if you owned/occupied it for two of the last five years.

◆ Consider whether making gifts to the family now makes financial and tax sense; death tax reduction might be at the sacrifice of income tax savings to your heirs.

◆ Arrange your finances to minimize the death tax impact on both your estate and that of your spouse.

◆ Make a mental note to review your estate planning at least annually. Your financial picture may change and certainly tax and other laws change often.

Briefs

An extremely old John Quincy Adams was feebly walking down a Boston street when an old friend stopped him. Shaking Adams's trembling hand, the friend asked "And how is John Quincy Adams today?"

"Thank you," said the ex-President. "John Quincy Adams is well, quite well. But the house in which he lives at present is becoming quite dilapidated. It is tottering upon its foundations. Time and the seasons have nearly destroyed it. Its roof is pretty well worn out. Its walls are much shattered, and it trembles with every wind. The old tenement is becoming almost uninhabitable, and I think John Quincy Adams will have to move out of it soon. But he himself is quite well, quite well."

How Far You've Come Since Chapter 1!

You may recall back in that first introductory chapter I asked you to fill out an estate planning checklist, which includes a number of questions you should be answering while reading this book, from how you can reduce income taxes now to gauging your expected retirement income. I suggested you might turn down the corner of that page and refer to it again later. This would be a good time to take a look at it. The questions probably sound quite familiar now that you've read about all those topics. You might even have moved a long way past some of them by now.

See how much you have learned?

Quote, Unquote

We do not live an equal life, but one of contrasts and patchwork; now a little joy, then a sorrow, now a sin, then a generous or brave action.

—Emerson, "Journals" (1845)

And in Conclusion ...

If you haven't yet completed your estate plan you're certainly quite prepared to do it now. And when you do, you'll have documents that will serve you well for the years ahead. Think of the peace of mind you'll have, just knowing that you've put things in order and have done what you can to look after your family and others close to you through a will or trust.

Don't forget to refer to your plan often through the years, always fine-tuning the decisions you have made and projects you have undertaken. And stay in touch with your estate planning team as new family and lifestyle situations and financial possibilities crop up in your life. These professionals can really help.

Much luck and good fortune to you in the years ahead. May all the new elements that arise in your life having to do with your estate plan be beneficial, perhaps even profitable, ones, bringing you satisfaction and contentment.

The Least You Need to Know

◆ Everyone needs a will, and some need a trust, and should frequently review both.

◆ A single person should have a durable power of attorney, which becomes effective only if he or she becomes incapacitated.

- A trust might be the answer for minor children.

- If you are nearing retirement, execute a revocable living trust to manage your assets when you cannot.

Glossary

Words for the Wise—Key Terms You'll Want to Remember

401(k) plan   A qualified retirement plan, usually involving contributions made by both employer and employee.

actuarial value   Value of a property interest, or a right that you own, based on life expectancy tables; for example, a life estate is valued based on the life expectancy of that person.

administrator   Person appointed by a court to represent an estate when no will was provided or the will does not name an executor. May also be called a personal representative.

alternate valuation date   A date no more than six months after a person's death that may be used for evaluating assets in an estate for federal estate taxes.

annuity   Investment that pays a fixed amount for a specified number of years or for life.

annuity trust   One form of charitable remainder trust that pays a fixed amount regularly according to the value of a gift at the time it is set up, age of donor, and interest rates.

appreciated or appreciating asset   An asset whose value has increased or continues to increase in value due to a variety of factors, including inflation.

beneficiary   A person designated to receive income or assets in a will or trust.

buy-sell agreement   Contract between partners or co-owners of a business that determines the conditions and price for a buyout by one or more of the owners at the death or retirement of one.

cafeteria plan   Employee fringe benefit plan permitting the employee to select among a variety of tax-free and taxed benefits.

cash surrender value insurance   Life insurance that contains a savings account along with coverage for the life of the insured.

charitable lead trust   Gift made in trust to a recognized charity that includes income payable to the charity for a set time, with the remainder returned to the donor or another non-charity.

charitable remainder trust   Gift made in trust to a recognized charity that includes income payable to the donor during that person's lifetime. At the death of the donor, the remaining value of the gift belongs to the charity.

codicil   A written and properly witnessed legal change or amendment to a will.

community property   Assets and property acquired after marriage and owned equally by marriage partners (such property is recognized in nine states).

community property agreement   A document that legally transfers title of property owned by both the marriage partners to one of the surviving spouses.

condominium   Several persons owning their own apartments in a building or complex, with an undivided interest in the common areas.

cooperative   Housing style where buyers purchase shares in the corporation that owns the building. Tenant shareholders hold a proprietary lease that gives them the right to their units.

Coverdell Education Savings Account   A savings account established to pay for qualified educational expenses; maximum annual contribution is currently $2,000.

custodian   A person who is trustee of any Uniform Gift to Minors Act accounts or property set up for minors.

devise   A gift by will.

domicile   A person's fixed place of residence that he or she considers the permanent address.

donee   Person who receives a gift.

donor   Person who gives a gift.

durable power of attorney   A power of attorney is a legal document that gives another person full legal authority to act on that person's behalf, including signing checks and similar means of handling money. A durable power of attorney continues to be in effect when the person giving the power is incapacitated or disabled.

estate planning   Orderly arrangement of assets and a plan for conveying them to heirs and others in a manner calculated to minimize taxes, expenses, and delays.

estate tax   Federal and state tax that taxes the transfer of wealth upon death.

executor   Person or institution named in a will to carry out its provisions and instructions. The female term is executrix.

fair market value   A price agreed to by a willing buyer and a willing seller in a free negotiation.

fiduciary   A person acting primarily for another's benefit in confidence, good faith, prudence, and fair dealing, such as a trustee or executor.

future interest   A property interest that gives right to future possession or use; a remainder interest in a trust is a future interest.

grantor   The person who establishes or creates a trust. Also called a settlor.

gross estate   Total dollar value of all one's property for estate tax purposes.

group life insurance   Term life insurance provided at group rates, usually by an employer.

guardian   A person who is legally responsible for managing the affairs and the care of a minor or incompetent person. A guardian is appointed by the court.

health-care power of attorney   A document that gives another person the authority to make medical decisions for the person executing it.

heir   A person legally entitled to receive another person's property through inheritance.

imputed interest Rate of interest assigned by Internal Revenue Service to a less-than-market rate loan or a no-interest-rate loan. Lender must pay taxes on imputed interest even if no money is actually received from borrower, who usually is a family member.

incidents of ownership Usually associated with insurance. Includes any control, such as being able to change a beneficiary, encumber a cash balance for loan collateral, or cancel a policy.

individual retirement account (IRA) A retirement account established by an individual and not an employer, where the contributions may be tax deductible.

inheritance tax A tax levied in some states on inherited property. Tax rates typically depend on the relationship of the heir to the deceased.

intestate Dying without a will.

irrevocable When applied to a trust indicates, it cannot be changed or canceled.

joint tenancy Owning property jointly in some form, with the right of survivorship.

kiddie tax Slang for federal income tax on minors up to age 14.

life estate An interest, such as income from a trust, that continues for the life of the person holding that interest. Can also refer to real estate, where ownership is divided in half: one half is the length of the homeowner's life, the remainder willed to the heir and becoming his or hers when the property owner dies.

living trust A revocable or irrevocable written agreement into which a person (called settlor or grantor) transfers assets and property along with instructions to the trustee for the management and future distribution of assets.

marital deduction A federal estate tax deduction for property received by the deceased's spouse.

Medicaid A state-run program, with federal government contributions, to pay for the health care of needy persons, particularly the elderly.

Medicare A federal government program to assist elders in the payment of medical expenses.

pay-on-death An account or bond where a person is named to receive property upon the death of the owner.

personal property   Movable property (tangible), such as furniture and motor vehicles, and property that represents an interest in other property (intangible), such as stock certificates and bank accounts.

personal representative   Another name for a person who is charged with managing an estate; same as executor or administrator.

pick-up tax   An estate tax levied by some states equivalent to the federal state death tax credit.

pooled income trust   Charitable remainder trust where cash or readily marketable securities are combined with similar contributions from others and managed like a mutual fund.

pour-over will   A will designed to cover property that has not been transferred to a living trust. Assets are "poured over" into the trust for management.

prenuptial agreement   A contract agreed to by a couple prior to marriage that defines rights upon death or divorce.

probate court   A specialized court in each state set up to handle the management of wills, estates of persons dying without a will, and other functions, such as guardianships.

probate estate   Property and assets of the deceased, distributed under direction of the probate court.

QTIP trust   A marital trust that permits the estate to receive a marital deduction even though the surviving spouse has only an income interest in the trust.

qualified retirement plan   A plan that is entitled to special tax treatment upon contributions to that plan and income earned during its existence. Defined benefit, defined contribution, and 401(k) plans are examples.

remainder interest   Property usually left in trust to another after the death of one or more who have an income interest.

Roth IRA   Individual retirement account with nondeductible contributions and earnings that are tax-free.

separate property   Property owned only by one marriage partner that is kept segregated from the couple's community property.

settlor   Another term for the person who establishes and funds a trust. Also called grantor.

spendthrift trust   Trust established for a beneficiary who lacks money management skills to prevent the beneficiary from spending a legacy unwisely.

supervised procedure   Formal probate court procedure where every action of the estate is subject to court supervision. Contrasted with unsupervised or limited supervision probate.

tax basis   Taxpayer's tax investment in property, usually the cost *plus* improvements *less* depreciation.

taxable estate   Gross estate less deductions such as marital and charitable deductions, debts, and administrative expenses.

tenancy in common   Co-ownership in property without right of survival: each owner can leave his or her share to whomever they choose.

tenancy in the entirety   Joint ownership limited to married couples that includes right of survival.

term life insurance   Pure insurance coverage only, with no savings component.

testamentary trust   A trust in the deceased's will.

trust   A written and formal agreement that enables a person or institution to hold property and manage it for the benefit of identified beneficiaries in accordance with instructions in the trust agreement.

trust agreement   Document setting out instructions for managing property left in a living trust, including who is to receive each portion of the trust assets.

trustee   Person or institution empowered to manage trust property according to the instructions contained in the trust agreement.

unitrust   Form of charitable trust whereby donor receives at least a minimum annual return based on an annual valuation of assets.

viatical settlement   Insurance payout for those with terminal, or even chronic, illnesses. Essentially, this is an advance draw on insurance proceeds that would ordinarily be paid at death.

will   Basic document for transferring property to successors through probate court.

Index

B

D

E

F

G

J–K

L

Q

T

U

V

Check Out These
Best-Selling
COMPLETE IDIOT'S GUIDES®

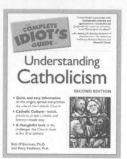

Understanding Catholicism
SECOND EDITION

1-59257-085-2
$18.95

Learning Spanish
THIRD EDITION

0-02-864451-4
$18.95

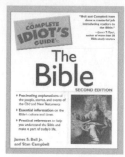

The Bible
SECOND EDITION

0-02-864382-8
$18.95

Being a Groom
SECOND EDITION

0-02-864456-5
$9.95

Grammar and Style
SECOND EDITION

1-59257-115-8
$16.95

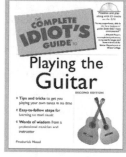

Playing the Guitar
SECOND EDITION

0-02-864244-9
$21.95 w/CD

Personal Finance in Your 20s & 30s
SECOND EDITION

0-02-864374-7
$19.95

Knitting and Crocheting
SECOND EDITION
Illustrated

1-59257-089-5
$16.95

The Perfect Resume
THIRD EDITION

0-02-864440-9
$14.95

Buying and Selling a Home
FOURTH EDITION

1-59257-120-4
$18.95

Low-Carb Meals

1-59257-180-8
$18.95

Calculus

0-02-864365-8
$18.95

More than *450 titles* in *30 different categories*
Available at booksellers everywhere

ALPHA